CONSTRUCTING

MANCHESTER
1824
Manchester University Press

# Manchester Medieval Studies

SERIES EDITOR  Professor S. H. Rigby

The study of medieval Europe is being transformed as old orthodoxies are challenged, new methods embraced and fresh fields of enquiry opened up. The adoption of interdisciplinary perspectives and the challenge of economic, social and cultural theory are forcing medievalists to ask new questions and to see familiar topics in a fresh light.

The aim of this series is to combine the scholarship traditionally associated with medieval studies with an awareness of more recent issues and approaches in a form accessible to the non-specialist reader.

ALREADY PUBLISHED IN THE SERIES

*Peacemaking in the middle ages: principles and practice*
Jenny Benham

*Money in the medieval English economy: 973-1489*
James Bolton

*Reform and the papacy in the eleventh century*
Kathleen G. Cushing

*Picturing women in late medieval and Renaissance art*
Christa Grössinger

*The Vikings in England*
D. M. Hadley

*A sacred city: consecrating churches and reforming society in eleventh-century Italy*
Louis I. Hamilton

*The politics of carnival*
Christopher Humphrey

*Holy motherhood*
Elizabeth L'Estrange

*Music, scholasticism and reform: Salian Germany 1024–1125*
T. J. H. McCarthy

*Medieval law in context*
Anthony Musson

*The expansion of Europe, 1250–1500*
Michael North

*Medieval maidens*
Kim M. Phillips

*Gentry culture in late medieval England*
Raluca Radulescu and Alison Truelove (eds)

*Chaucer in context*
S. H. Rigby

*The life cycle in Western Europe, c.1300–c.1500*
Deborah Youngs

MANCHESTER MEDIEVAL STUDIES

# CONSTRUCTING KINGSHIP
## THE CAPETIAN MONARCHS OF FRANCE AND THE EARLY CRUSADES

James Naus

Manchester University Press

Copyright © James Naus 2016

The right of James Naus to be identified as the author of this work has been asserted by him in accordance with the Copyright, Designs, and Patents Act 1988.

Published by Manchester University Press
Altrincham Street, Manchester M1 7JA
www.manchesteruniversitypress.co.uk

British Library Cataloguing-in-Publication Data
A catalogue record for this book is available from the British Library

ISBN 978 0 7190 9097 4 hardback
ISBN 978 1 5261 2725 9 paperback

First published by Manchester University Press in hardback 2016
This edition first published 2018

The publisher has no responsibility for the persistence or accuracy of URLs for any external or third-party internet websites referred to in this book, and does not guarantee that any content on such websites is, or will remain, accurate or appropriate.

Typeset by Out of House Publishing
Printed by Lightning Source

To Gaby and Charlotte

# CONTENTS

Acknowledgements ix
List of abbreviations xii

Introduction 1

## Part I Crisis

1 Framing the Capetian miracle 15
2 The First Crusade and the new economy of status, 1095–1110 28

## Part II Response

3 Suger of Saint-Denis and the ideology of crusade 59
4 Louis VII and the failure of crusade 85
5 Philip Augustus, political circumstance, and crusade 112

Bibliography 141
Index 157

# ACKNOWLEDGEMENTS

I have accumulated many debts over the course of researching and writing this book, far too many to mention here. I am eternally grateful for all the support I have received, and it gives me great happiness that the final task that remains for me is that of acknowledging all those who have helped me along the way. Thomas Madden has guided and supported my research since I started graduate school at Saint Louis University in 2004. Though I finished in 2011, he has remained a mentor and supporter of my work, for which I am grateful. Marcus Bull also has been a supporter of this project from the beginning. He read a complete draft of the manuscript, tirelessly offering his comments. The final piece is vastly richer as a result of this process, and I am happy for the chance to have learned from such an erudite and kind scholar. I met Damien Kempf in 2010 while he was undertaking research in the Vatican Film Library at Saint Louis University. When it soon became clear that we were working on congruous projects, he generously shared his expertise, helping me with material related to Robert the Monk and also teaching me to navigate the sometimes tricky Parisian archives. I thank him for his support. I feel particularly fortunate to be writing at a time of rapid and exciting growth in medieval French studies and crusades studies. Many scholars who work in those fields have influenced and inspired me, and my debt to them is ongoing and immense. My graduate school colleagues, particularly Vince Ryan, Walker Cosgrove, and David Parnell, remain close friends, and for this I am grateful, but all of them have also read and commented on various sections of this project over the years, going far beyond any normal expectation of friendship. I have been fortunate to have had many excellent teachers over the years. In particular, Zachary Vlahos first inspired a fascination with European history, and Louis Haas fostered my interest in the Middle Ages. Thanks to them both.

 A University Research Committee Faculty Summer Fellowship from Oakland University allowed me to complete the final research for this book in the summer of 2014. Individual support from Kevin Corcoran, Dean of the College of Arts and Sciences, and Dorothy Nelson, Vice Provost for Research, allowed me to spend time in Paris and London working on

Chapters 4 and 5. While I was still at Saint Louis University, a Brennan Summer Fellowship allowed me to spend considerable time in Paris, where I began the early stages of this book. During all these trips abroad, the librarians and archivists were very kind to me. I especially thank the staff at the Bibliothèque nationale de France and the Bibliothèque Mazarine in Paris, as well as the Archives départmentales Marne, annex de Reims. The librarians at the Pius Library at Saint Louis University and the Kresge Library at Oakland University have tracked down many obscure sources for me, and always in a timely fashion. It is not hyperbole to say that such a book would not be possible without such excellent research resources. Much of this book has been presented in various forms at conferences, and I am grateful for all the helpful feedback I have received along the way. In particular, a portion of the third chapter was presented to the Crusades Seminar at the Institute for Historical Research in London in the autumn of 2013, and the comments I received were helpful in shaping the final version. The same is true for portions of Chapter 4, which were presented at the International Medieval Congress in Leeds, UK, in the summer of 2014. Portions of Chapters 2 and 3 are taken from the articles 'The French Royal Court and the Memory of the First Crusade', *Nottingham Medieval Studies* 55 (2011), 49-78; and 'Crusading as Legitimacy: Suger of Saint-Denis and the Narrative of Kingship', *French Historical Studies* 36/4 (Autumn 2013), 525-41; and from the chapter 'The *Historia Iherosolimitana* of Robert the Monk and the Coronation of Louis VI', in *Writing the Crusades: Text, Transmission and Memory*, ed. Damien Kempf and Marcus Bull (Woodbridge, 2014), pp. 105-15. I thank the editors of those publications for permission to reprint, and also the anonymous reviewers for those journals, who provided excellent feedback.

In August 2013 I began working at Oakland University in Rochester, Michigan. I am fortunate to have landed at a supportive institution. My colleagues have encouraged me from the day I arrived. In particular, Derek Hastings, Sara Chapman Williams, Craig Martin, Liz Shesko, and Dan Clark have all provided sound advice that has saved me from more embarrassing mistakes than I care to admit. I have learned much from them, and am all the more lucky to count them as friends. Janet and Johanna in the Department of History at Oakland University have helped me navigate the administrative red tape that has allowed me the freedom to travel to archives and libraries to undertake my research and to conferences to present it.

It is commonly said that academic publishing is a difficult business. I have not found it to be so, and this is largely the result of Emma

Brennan at Manchester University Press. I thank her for her continued work in support of this book. By shepherding it through the various phases of publication she has made an intimidating scholarly landmark a pleasant process. Steve Rigby, the editor for the series in which this volume appears, has been a great asset. Having received his extensive comments on an early chapter, I learned quickly to trust his editorial hand, which he exercises with a stern but gentle fashion. If the book is readable, then Steve deserves much of the credit. I have learned to be a better writer as a result of the editing process. I also thank the Press's anonymous reviewers for their close reading of the manuscript and thoughtful comments. It goes without saying that any mistakes that remain are my own.

Most successful academics have supportive families to thank, and I am no different. Mine has always encouraged my interests in every possible way. I have never lacked a cheering section in whatever I have tried, no matter whether I have succeeded or failed. In my estimation this places me among the luckiest people around. I am particularly thankful that, from an early age, my parents taught me to love reading. In many ways, this book is the consequence of that. Being the spouse of an academic is no easy task, particularly of one whose research interests drag him away to far-off places at (oftentimes) inconvenient times of the year. My wife, Gaby, has endured extended absences demanded by foreign research and conference travel, what must have seemed like my absence when working at home, and even a cross-country move to the bitterly cold north! She handled it without complaint, and it is simply the truest fact that none of this would be possible without her. Very soon before submitting the initial manuscript of this book, we welcomed our first child, Charlotte. There could not possibly be a better reward for completing this task, and it is my greatest joy to dedicate the completed book to them both.

# ABBREVIATIONS

| | |
|---|---|
| *Actes* | M. Jean Dufour, *Recueil des actes de Louis VI, roi de France (1108–1137)*, 4 vols (Paris, 1992–94) |
| BB | Baldric of Bourgueil, *The Historia Ierosolimitana of Baldric of Bourgueil*, ed. Steven Biddlecombe (Woodbridge, 2014) |
| *CCCM* | *Corpus Christianorum, continuatio medievalis* |
| *EHR* | *English Historical Review* |
| *GF* | *Gesta Francorum et aliorum Hierosolimitanorum*, ed. and trans. Rosalind Hill (Oxford, 1962) |
| GN | Guibert of Nogent, *Dei gesta per Francos*, ed. R. B. C. Huygens, *CCCM* 127A (Turnhout, 1996) |
| *JMH* | *Journal of Medieval History* |
| *MGH SS* | *Monumenta Germaniae Historica, Scriptores*, ed. G. H. Pertz *et al.*, 32 vols (Hanover, 1926–34). |
| *NMS* | *Nottingham Medieval Studies* |
| OD | Odo of Deuil, *De profectione Ludovici VII in orientem: The Journey of Louis VII to the East*, ed. and trans. Virginia G. Berry (New York, 1947) |
| *Oeuvres* | Suger, *Oeuvres*, ed. and trans. Françoise Gasparri, 2 vols (Paris, 1996–2008) |
| OV | Orderic Vitalis, *Historia ecclesiastica*, ed. and trans. Marjorie Chibnall, 6 vols (Oxford, 1969–80) |
| *PL* | *Patrologiae cursus completus, series latina*, ed. J.-P. Migne, 221 vols (Paris, 1844–64) |
| *RHC Oc.* | *Recueil des historiens des croisades: Historiens occidentaux*, 5 vols (Paris, 1844–95) |
| *RHGF* | *Recueil des historiens des Gaules et de la France*, ed. Martin Bouquet, rev. by Léopold Delisle, 24 vols (Paris, 1869–1904) |
| RM | Robert the Monk, *The 'Historia Iherosolimitana' of Robert the Monk*, ed. Damien Kempf and Marcus Bull (Woodbridge, 2013). |

## LIST OF ABBREVIATIONS

RS  [Rolls Series] *Rerum Britannicarum medii aevi scriptores: Chronicles and Memorials of Great Britain and Ireland*, ed. William Stubbs *et al.*, 99 vols (London, 1858–96)

*VLG*  Suger, *Vie de Louis VI le Gros*, ed. and trans. Henri Waquet (Paris, 1964).

# Introduction

Louis IX – the future St Louis – swore his first crusade vow in late 1244.[1] Sources close to the royal court paint a sombre picture of the occasion, noting that a majority of French nobles and high-ranking clerics were sceptical of the King's decision to lead a crusade to the East.[2] For these men and women, there had been too many failed attempts to rescue Jerusalem in recent memory to justify another costly expedition to the East, particularly one they believed stood little chance of success.[3] Louis's own mother, Blanche of Castile, was particularly vocal in her objections, believing that Louis's extended absence from France (and potential death in the East) would have dire consequences for the health of the monarchy, which had only recently entered a period of relative stability. Thus, she convinced Pope Innocent IV to release her son from his vow on the grounds that he had undertaken it during a bout of delirium brought on by a recent illness.[4] Louis's crusading ambition was not fleeting, however, and he soon took the vow again, this time with proof that he possessed all his mental faculties. Crusading soon became one of Louis's principal means of expressing his piety. At the end of the thirteenth century, his participation in two crusades (in 1244 and 1270) played an important role in securing his canonization, an honour ultimately granted by Pope Boniface VIII in 1297.[5] Over the course of the succeeding centuries, astonishing stories of Louis's crusading adventures fuelled the spread of his legend and, in the words of Collette Beaune, 'encircled the image of Louis with the miraculous aura of the crusades'.[6] From this point onward, French kings would be fundamentally linked to the crusading movement. As late as the nineteenth century it was taken for granted by the public and scholars alike that French kings and crusading went hand in hand.[7] Few scholars have ever asked why.

## INTRODUCTION

Set against the widespread opposition to Louis's plan, we ought to wonder what inspired the King to take the crusading vow on two occasions in the first place. Scholars have long agreed that Louis possessed a heightened sense of piety and that he used the link between crusading and royal authority to promote bureaucratic, institutional growth in France. One might ask, though, why his personal piety seemed to demand a particular devotion to crusading, as opposed to other expressions of piety. What was it about the crusading movement that inspired the King to promote royal authority in *that* way? After all, there were other suitable outlets that presented much less risk to the King. For example, French kings had long demonstrated their sacrality by founding new religious houses and supporting existing ones. Both themes were commonly deployed in early medieval texts that sought to promote the sacred status of French kings.

Moreover, Louis IX had less need for such external bulwarks to royal power than had previous kings. In 1244, when Louis took his first vow, he was in a comparatively strong political position in France.[8] He controlled a larger and more centralized kingdom than had his predecessors, and venturing off to the East was a dangerous and expensive business. His own father, Louis VIII, had died in 1226 while returning from the Albigensian Crusade, forcing a hasty coronation of a twelve-year-old Prince Louis and a tumultuous regency under a domineering mother. The King's first son (Louis) was not born until February 1244, which means that the risk of another regency government was high. More poignantly, the spectacular failure of the Fifth Crusade at Damietta in 1221 would have been fresh in the King's memory, and he would not have wanted his name to be attached to another expedition like that one. And yet, he never seemed to have thought twice about committing to his vow because he understood his participation in the crusades to be a necessary function of being the French King.[9] When and how did such an idea emerge? It is true that Louis's three immediate predecessors had all taken part in crusades, but none had demonstrated his unwavering commitment to the movement or confronted the same level of noble disapproval. Importantly, all three ruled over much weaker kingdoms and thus had less to lose from a potential failure in the East. All three, it should be noted, were also generally unsuccessful in their military endeavours.[10] Faced with this background, we must search for the origins of Louis's crusading piety in deeper convictions than a simple desire to be a good Christian or to follow family precedent. The King's relentless support of the crusade bespeaks a broader and deeper connection between kingship and crusade. It is the principal objective of this book to consider the origin and development of this idea in France.

# INTRODUCTION

This book is about the relationship between the crusading movement and the twelfth-century French kings. It is not, however, a history about what the French kings did in the East, though several such episodes will be considered. It is rather an examination of the various ways in which crusading intersected with Capetian self-fashioning and understandings of rulership among those closest to the royal court. Crusading had a greater significance for French royal history than the frequently disappointing deeds of the kings would suggest. In fact, the unimpressive crusading careers of the French kings may help explain why such a topic has not been treated in detail before. Historians of the institutional components of the crusades have preferred to focus on explaining success rather than dwelling on failure, a fact that obscures the ways in which crusading informed the cultural and political ethos of medieval rulers. Thus, at its core this is a book about the place of the crusading movement in the cultural and political development of France. Crusading kings, French or otherwise, tend to exert a unique hold on the historical imagination, and it is easy to forget, therefore, that European rulers were not in the beginning enthusiastic participants in the movement. The First Crusade was launched in 1095, yet the first monarch did not join the movement in a meaningful way until 1146, when the French King Louis VII took the cross to lead the Second Crusade.[11] What impact did fifty years of non-participation in one of the most significant movements of the Middle Ages have on the image and practice of European kingship and the discursive parameters of cultural development? This book considers this question by examining the challenge to political authority that confronted the French kings and their family members in the first half of the twelfth century as the result of their failure to join the early crusades – what can be appropriately termed the 'crisis of crusading'. A further objective is to consider the various ways in which subsequent kings and other members of the royal court deployed crusading propaganda and imagery in support of their claims to rule. It helps explain, in other words, why Louis IX felt such a strong compulsion to take a crusading vow.

A central argument of this book is that over the course of the twelfth century, as various actors near to the Capetian court came to fuse emerging crusade ideas with ancient ideas of sacred kingship, a new royal identity emerged that was fundamentally connected to and shaped by the crusading movement. By the late twelfth and early thirteenth centuries, the constructed image of the French royal crusader had become an essential element in the French kings' collective claim to be the 'most Christian rulers', a term first used in the Carolingian era but which, since the early

3

twelfth century, had developed an association with the crusades.[12] In 1970 Joseph Strayer argued that medieval French political legitimacy depended not only on administrative and institutional centralization and efficiency, but also on the ability of the French kings to shape and promote the proper image of kingship.[13] The French kings, Strayer argued, needed to convince their subjects that they were actually the 'the most Christian'. The crusades had become an important means of demonstrating divine favour, and thus, they came to form a key element in the French kings' claim. The process of promoting a French royal crusading narrative built on a longstanding attempt to imbue French kings with a sacred aura by linking them to important events or people, such as the Old Testament kings. The royal link to crusading is thus crucial to understanding the larger transformation of the French kingdom.

The ideology of the French royal crusading tradition was shaped, preserved, and protected by various religious houses with ancient connections to the royal court, most notably Saint-Denis. The French royal ethos was imbued deeply enough with the ideology of crusade that when Louis IX was faced with the opportunity to lead an expedition to the East, his response was, in part, preconditioned by nearly a century's worth of image-making. The implication of this argument has significance well beyond the specific subject of the crusading movement. From a political perspective, this period of French history was a difficult one for its kings. The late eleventh and much of the twelfth century were characterized by constant political and cultural change and were often punctuated by acute crises, many of which threatened the very foundation of the monarchy.[14] From this uncertain crucible emerged sometime in the last quarter of the twelfth century the idea of France as a centralized kingdom ruled over by a strong and powerful king. Scholars have long sought to understand the intricacies of this development; in fact, it has been a dominant trend in the historiography of medieval France since the late nineteenth century. And yet, the exact way in which the French King transformed himself from personal ruler to impersonal bureaucratic ruler has yet to be fully explained, though not for lack of trying. In part this has been the result of a focus on administrative and institutional approaches to understanding French kingship. More recently, though, as cultural and anthropological methodologies are applied, new ways of interpreting the transformation of kingship have emerged, and it is one aim of this book to contribute to this growing literature.

Historians have long looked to the institutional developments of the central Middle Ages to explain the rise of the modern French State.[15] Even before the Middle Ages had ended, monks close to the French court were arguing in the *Grandes Chroniques de France* that French identity was part and parcel to the dynastic integrity of the kings.[16] The Bourbon kings would later seize on this in support of their own claims of legitimacy.[17] Deeply rooted in these traditions, and drawing on their fundamental assumptions concerning the nature of the birth and gestation of the State, modern French historiography has often blended a positivist methodology with a nationalist search for the beginning of the institutional elements of the modern French State. Implicit in many French histories produced in the late nineteenth and early twentieth centuries is a belief that irrespective of whether they recognized it at the time, France had existed as a sovereign nation throughout the Middle Ages, at least since the Capetian accession in 987. Robert Fawtier would summarize this position elegantly in the introduction to his 1942 book *Les Capétiens et la France*, which sought to understand 'the part played by the Capetian dynasty in the creation of the French nation'.[18] A major consequence of this has been a strong focus on administrative and institutional history by scholars interested in medieval France. The individual points of emphasis have differed, of course, but many historians have sought to pinpoint the specific point at which France became a bureaucratically impersonal and centralized kingdom.[19]

The historiography of medieval France was driven in the latter decades of the twentieth century by a focus on social, economic, and cultural history, the works of scholars such as Marc Bloch and George Duby leading the shift away from political and institutional questions. And yet, as Marcus Bull has pointed out, when the '*annaliste* ice age' began to thaw in the 1990s, it became clear that the more traditional historiographical interests had not disappeared, but were being approached in new and creative ways by scholars applying the methods of cultural anthropology and social history to questions of politics and institutional development.[20] Administrative sources were not ignored, but rather set against descriptions of ritual and ceremony and art and architecture to paint a fuller picture of medieval French kingship.[21] This development should be considered alongside a thriving study of the relationship between the administrative requirements of the crusade and the centralizing policies of the French kings of the thirteenth century. In 1979, William Chester Jordan demonstrated that Louis IX's crusading ambition was fundamentally connected to the royal image and, thus, to the King's authority.[22] John Baldwin has studied the administrative changes undertaken by Philip Augustus as part of his preparation for the Third Crusade, arguing that they ultimately begot a more centralized and administratively less personal kingdom.[23] Many others have

INTRODUCTION

studied the various ways in which crusading had an impact on the kings of France over the course of the thirteenth century.[24] Far less attention has been paid to the French kings and the crusades before the reign of Philip Augustus, perhaps because the kings failed in their endeavours (Louis VII) or else did not participate (Philip I and Louis VI).

There is good reason to consider the relationship between the French kings and the crusading movement during this transitional period (and to reconsider it during the reign of Philip Augustus). Crusading had more than an administrative impact on the West; it shaped and defined the ideas of power that were central to the French monarchs' claims of legitimacy. Over the past several years, the need for a study of the role of the crusades in shaping western political culture has been recognized, and the methodological tools more suited to such a task developed. Thomas Bisson highlighted the effectiveness of understanding the operation of power in contributing to the broad and complex conversation about the relationship among government, rulership, and authority in this period that has continued to shape the historiography of medieval France.[25] Crusade studies have also begun moving away from narrative and logistical history to recognize the importance of family history, crusader identity, and historical memory, to note only a few of the promising topics that have been studied.[26] Study of the crusades has moved to focus on the culture and society of the crusaders themselves and their families, as well as the broader place of the crusading movement in European history. It is a principal goal of the present book to draw together the hitherto independent traditions of crusade studies and socio-political history and to examine the role played by the crusades in the development of the French monarchy.

Since the aim of the present work is to build on recent trends in both crusading and French history, some justification of the geographic and thematic focus of this project is in order. If it is true that the First Crusade had an impact on the traditional power system of the non-participating elite, then it is likely that this phenomenon was not limited to northern France. In the same way, while prestige was a crucial element in the operation of power at this time, participation in the crusades obviously was not the only way to accrue it. This book focuses on France for several reasons. Around 1100 royal power was very tenuous, and as such, we might expect any anxiety to be more amplified and appear more clearly in the French sources, which are both diffuse – scattered across annals, chronicles, royal acts, architecture, and artwork – and legion. It was also around this time that the monks at Saint-Denis, under the guidance of Abbot Suger, began producing royalist texts at an unmatched rate. Germany and England lack this consistent source base for royal ideology, and thus, while there may well be similar patterns developing elsewhere, the most consistent and best evidence is for France. In the same vein, the Capetian dynasty was remarkably long-lived and concerned with its own dynastic integrity and heritage. Thus, the images and ideas created at Saint-Denis and enshrined in the sources produced there were passed down in a remarkably consistent fashion, the end result being a connection between crusading and kingship that bespoke a strong historical tradition.

My choice to focus on the crusades as a central influencing factor of royal ideology in this period is born out of the monumental and transformative impact that the early crusading movement had on western society. Indeed, the First Crusade captured the medieval imagination on an unprecedented scale, helping to usher in many of the crucial developments of the twelfth century.[27] One metric by which to assess its impact on medieval society is the level of textual production that followed the event. In addition to several letters composed by participants while still on the expedition, at least four eyewitness narrative accounts were circulating throughout western Europe by 1110. These, in turn, inspired the production of a host of other sources, and it is, as a consequence, difficult to think of another event in the Middle Ages that piqued this level of interest.[28] Indeed, the editors of one First Crusade chronicle looked all the way back to the histories produced in the 330s and 320s BCE to celebrate the conquests of Alexander the Great to find an appropriate literary parallel.[29] As further evidence for the expedition's place in the western mindset, a text begun in 1096, and continued over the course of the First Crusade, provides an excellent gauge of the suddenness with which the First Crusade impacted western culture.[30] In that year, Count Fulk of Anjou had set out to compose a family history for the purpose of shoring up his claims of political legitimacy. Fulk was still working on his text in 1098, when he felt compelled to abandon the dynastic project to devote his attention to recording the scattered bits of news trickling in from the crusading host in Syria. And thus, interspersed in what was otherwise a secular, family history, is extensive material relating to the progress of the First Crusade. Even before the expedition had reached Jerusalem and fulfilled its prophetic mission, it seems that stories of crusading heroism were commanding the attention of western audiences.

It is also worth emphasizing that many of those who undertook the monumental task of writing about the First Crusade had a difficult time finding adequate language to frame the expedition, and virtually all of them resorted to Old Testament examples – such as the Maccabees or Gideon – to interpret its success. Robert the Monk, a Benedictine writing around 1110, noted that the capture of Jerusalem 'was not the work of humans, but that of God'.[31] Robert's contemporary and fellow chronicler of the First Crusade, Guibert of Nogent, filtered the success of the First Crusade through the memory of the Old Testament wars of the Israelites:

> We said not once but as it happens many times, nor is it displeasing to repeat, such that never happened since the era of pagans. If the sons of Israel are mentioned to me, and the miracles performed for them by God, I will provide them a sea parted and filled with gentiles ... to them [the crusaders]. Christ, himself a model of strength and uprightness, provided inspiration; he strengthened them when they had no hope, with the food of the word of God.[32]

The title selected by Guibert for his chronicle synthesizes prevailing twelfth-century opinion in an elegant expression of meaning: *Gesta Dei per Francos* (Deeds of God done through the Franks). Although a predominant number of the crusading texts were produced by monks, the awesome nature of the First Crusade meant that it also functioned as a widespread cultural referent, a common point of orientation for medieval men and women. Set against this background, it is not a hollow claim that crusading prestige had the potential to be a significant shaper of political destiny over the course of the twelfth century. Since crusading is the dominant theme of this book, it has also dictated the chronological limits of 1095–1229. The year 1095 is when Urban II called the First Crusade, and 1229 is when the Treaty of Paris was signed, ending the Albigensian Crusade and ushering in the Age of St Louis, a period of French History for which many excellent treatments exist.

The book is divided into two sections, each with a distinct focus. The first section (Chapters 1 and 2) examines the political, religious, and cultural context in which the 'crisis of crusading' appeared, covering a period (roughly) from 1090 to 1110. Chapter 1 establishes the narrative and conceptual framework necessary to interpret this crucial period of crusading. In particular, it examines the state of Capetian France on the eve of the First Crusade. While many historians have considered this period, few have done so from a non-administrative perspective. That is to say, the prevailing narrative explains the rise of Capetian power in the early twelfth century in terms of fiscal centralization and land acquisitions that began at the end of the eleventh. This is not incorrect, but neither is it the full picture. Thus, the chapter argues that this period cannot be fully understood without considering the role of prestige in the transformative process. In this way, the pre-crusading history of France is an essential component in understanding the eventual impact of the crusades on the image and practice of kingship.

Given the importance of prestige in the practice of rulership, Chapter 2 argues that the First Crusade had a polarizing impact on French society. The unlikely success of the expedition opened a new route to power for ambitious mid-ranking nobles and castellans, who suddenly were presented with the opportunity to transform heroic deeds done in the East into political status and capital at home. A good number of these men and women amassed political and economic benefits on the basis of their crusading reputations, a point that has (rightly) led many to argue that the First Crusade had a generally positive impact on European society. And yet, the expedition's success also occasioned a serious challenge for Europe's non-crusading elite – in particular, the kings of France, who had very quickly to adapt their ruling methods to compete in the new 'economy of status'. Through a close examination of Capetian marriage patterns and royal involvement with the production of crusade-related texts, this chapter builds up a picture of cultural frames, scripts, and schemata that in the early years of the twelfth century combined and resulted in what can appropriately be termed a 'crisis of crusading' for the French royal court.

With the framework of crisis set out in the first section of the book, the remaining chapters consider the royal reaction to the lack of crusading prestige and its impact on the cultural practice and discursive elements of power. Chapter 3 focuses on Abbot Suger of Saint-Denis's close relationship with the French royal court and his hitherto neglected concern for a lack of crusading prestige. Virtually none of the vast literature on the Abbot has considered his attitude toward the early crusading movement, which, this chapter argues, is long overdue. In particular, this chapter focuses on Suger's well-known biography of Louis VI, the *Gesta Ludovici Grossi*, a text that combined Carolingian notions of kingship with the newer crusade ideology to fashion a highly selective narrative of Louis's reign that, at once, casts doubts on the value of many crusaders and their exploits while also asserting that the French King possessed such virtues. The text, in short, is rife with inconsistency, which has been a difficult point for scholars to reconcile. By setting the text within the context of the crusades, however, the contradictions begin to make more sense. Far from supporting an image of Suger as the quintessential ideologist and progenitor of French royalist propaganda, his attitude toward the crusade instead demonstrates the traditional and flexible way he worked to create a smooth, positive account of the Capetian dynasty as a time of major political and cultural transformation. This was crucial in the evolution of the Capetian image and power structure, and reinforces the important connection that existed between French kings and the crusading movement, even in the years before they took the cross themselves. Chapter 4 examines the impact of Louis VII's decision to join the Second Crusade in 1146 on the practice of kingship. Louis was the first French king to take the cross, and despite the disastrous failure of that campaign, it nevertheless had a profound impact on his vision of rulership. The image that Suger had created for Louis VI carried on during the reign of Louis VII so that he was already beginning to understand the institution of crusading to be fundamentally linked with French kingship, despite his own negative experience in the East. Chapter 5 builds on this last point to consider the various ways in which Philip II Augustus was remembered as a great crusader, despite failing to participate in most of the expeditions launched during his reign. By this point in the late twelfth century, as we will see, the crusading image had already been firmly attached to French ideals of rulership so that a king's actual participation on the crusade was less important than the constructed heritage of French royal crusading. When Louis IX took the cross in 1244, therefore, he believed he was following the destiny of great French kings, regardless of their actual experiences in the East.

## Notes

1 William Chester Jordan, *Louis IX and the Challenge of the Crusade: A Study in Rulership* (Princeton, 1979), p. 3.
2 Matthew of Paris, *Chronica majora*, ed. Henry Luard, 7 vols (London, 1872), Vol. V, pp. 3–4.
3 For a survey of crusading in the first half of the thirteenth century see Christopher Tyerman, *God's War: A New History of the Crusades* (Cambridge, MA, 2006), pp. 477–769. Also useful is Richard W. Southern, *The Making of the Middle Ages* (New Haven, 1953), pp. 55–6.
4 Matthew of Paris, *Chronica majora*, Vol. V, pp. 312 and 354.
5 M. Cecilia Gaposchkin, *The Making of Saint Louis: Kingship, Sanctity, and Crusade in the Later Middle Ages* (Ithaca, NY, 2008), pp. 30–3 and 48–66.
6 Collette Beaune, *The Birth of an Ideology: Myths and Symbols of Nation in Late-Medieval France*, trans. Susan R. Huston, ed. Fredric L. Cheyette (Berkeley, 1991), pp. 97–9, quote on 99.
7 Joseph Françoise Michaud's six-volume *Histoire des croisades*, published between 1812 and 1822, celebrated the royally directed crusades as expressions of French national greatness. A similar idea penetrated the popular imagination through public memorials to French royal crusading history, such as those found in the *Salles des croisades* at Versailles.
8 Elizabeth M. Hallam and Judith Everard, *Capetian France, 987–1328*, 2nd edn (Harlow, 2001), pp. 263–346.

## INTRODUCTION

9 See Jean Richard, 'La politique orientale de saint Louis: La croisade de 1248', in *Septième centenaire de la mort de saint Louis: Actes de colloques de Royaumont et de Paris (21–27 mai 1970)* (Paris, 1976), pp. 197–207.

10 Louis VII participated in the Second Crusade. Philip II Augustus participated in the Third Crusade. Louis VIII went three times to southern France to take part in the Albigensian Crusade.

11 Earlier kings had indeed taken part in the Spanish expeditions; however, I am thinking here particularly of those crusades to the East. See Marcus Bull, 'The Capetian Monarchy and the Early Crusade Movement: Hugh of Vermandois and Louis VII', *NMS* 40 (1996), 25–46.

12 Beaune, *The Birth of an Ideology*, pp. 173–5.

13 Joseph R. Strayer, *On The Medieval Origins of the Modern State* (Princeton, 1970).

14 Useful surveys of this period can be found in Hallam and Everard, *Capetian France*, esp. pp. 83–256; Jean Dunbabin, *France in the Making, 843–1180*, 2nd edn (Oxford, 1985).

15 Much of what is discussed below is helpfully reviewed in Sean L. Field and M. Cecilia Gaposchkin, 'Questioning the Capetians, 1180–1328', *History Compass* 12/7 (2014), 567–85; 'Introduction', in Marcus Bull, ed., *France in the Central Middle Ages* (Oxford, 2002), pp. 1–4.

16 Gabriele M. Spiegel, *The Chronicle Tradition of Saint-Denis: A Survey* (Brookline, MA, 1978), pp. 72–91; Bernard Guenée, 'Les grandes chroniques de France, le "Roman aux roys" (1274–1518)', in *Les lieux de mémoire*, ed. Pierre Nora, 2 vols (Paris, 1986), Vol. II, pp. 189–214.

17 Field and Gaposchkin, 'Questioning the Capetians', p. 567.

18 *Ibid*. Such an approach, it might be noted, also had an impact on histories of the crusading movement written by French scholars. See René Grousset, *Histoire des croisades et du royaume franc de Jérusalem* (Paris, 1934–36).

19 Several recent examples are cited and discussed by Field and Gaposchkin, 'Questioning the Capetians', pp. 567–8. Yves Sassier, *Louis VII* (Paris, 1991); John Baldwin, *The Government of Philip Augustus: Foundations of French Royal Power in the Middle Ages* (Berkeley, 1986); Jordan, *Louis IX and the Challenge of the Crusade*; Jacques Le Goff, *Saint Louis*, trans. Gareth E. Gollrad (South Bend, IN, 2009).

20 Bull, 'Introduction', in *France in the Central Middle Ages*, p. 3.

21 Some have called this 'New Institutional History'. Particularly good examples are Oliver Canteaut, 'Quantifier l'entourage politique des derniers Capétiens', in *Les entourages princiers à la fin du Moyen Âge: Une approche quantitative*, ed. Alexandra Beauchamp (Madrid, 2013), pp. 77–92; Xavier Hélary, *L'armée du roi de France: La guerre de Saint Louis à Philippe le Bel* (Paris, 2012).

22 Jordan, *Louis IX and the Challenge of the Crusade*.

23 Baldwin, *The Government of Philip Augustus*.

24 Peter Thorau, 'Der Kreuzzug Ludwigs des Heiligen: Planung – Organisation – Durchführung', in *Stauferzeit: Zeit der Kreuzzüge*, ed. Karl-Heinz Ruess (Göppingen, 2011), pp. 124–43; M. Cecilia Gaposhkin, 'Role of the Crusades in the Sanctification of Louis IX', in *Crusades: Medieval Worlds in Conflict*, ed. Thomas

Madden, James Naus, and Vince Ryan (Aldershot, 2010), pp. 195–209; M. Cecilia Gaposhkin, 'Louis IX, Crusade and the Promise of Joshua', *JMH* 33 (2008), 245–74; Michael Lower, 'Conversion and Saint Louis's Last Crusade', *Journal of Ecclesiastical History* 58 (2007), 211–31.

25 Thomas N. Bisson, *The Crisis of the Twelfth Century: Power, Lordship, and the Origins of European Government* (Princeton, 2009), esp. pp. 229–43. Also see Dominique Barthélemy, *La mutation de l'an mil a-t-elle eu lieu? Servage et chevalerie dans la France des Xe et XIe siècles* (Paris, 1997).

26 Representative examples would include Nicholas L. Paul, *To Follow in Their Footsteps: The Crusades and Family Memory in the High Middle Ages* (Ithaca, NY, 2012); M. Cecilia Gaposchkin, *The Making of Saint Louis*.

27 Bisson, *The Crisis of the Twelfth Century*.

28 Jay Rubenstein, 'What Is the *Gesta Francorum*, and Who Is Peter Tudebode?', *Revue Mabillon* 16 (2005), 179–204; John France, 'The Anonymous *Gesta Francorum* and the *Historia Francorum qui ceperunt Iherusalem* of Raymond of Aguilers and the *Historia de Hierosolymitano itinere* of Peter Tudebode: An Analysis of the Textual Relationship between the Primary Sources for the First Crusade', in *The Crusades and Their Sources: Essays Presented to Bernard Hamilton*, ed. John France and William Zazaj (Aldershot, 1998), pp. 39–70; Elizabeth Lapina, '"Nec signis nec testibus creditor": The Problem of Eyewitnesses in the Chronicles of the First Crusade', *Viator* 38 (2007), 117–39; Yuval Noah Harari, 'Eyewitnessing in Accounts of the First Crusade: The *Gesta Francorum* and Other Contemporary Narratives', *Crusades* 3 (2004), 77–99.

29 RM, p. ix.

30 Paul, *To Follow in Their Footsteps*, pp. 21–7; Nicholas L. Paul, 'The Chronicle of Fulk Réchin: A Reassessment', *Haskins Society Journal* 18 (2007), 19–35.

31 RM, p. 4.

32 GN, p. 308.

# Part I

Crisis

1

# Framing the Capetian miracle

The last Carolingian king, Louis V, died in the spring of 987 from injuries sustained from a fall from a horse. Since Louis left behind no legitimate heirs, his uncle, Duke Charles of Lorraine, claimed the throne for himself. The monk who chronicled this transformational moment in the history of the French monarchy alleged that Charles declared that 'everyone knows that by hereditary right I should succeed my brother and my nephew'.[1] As it happened, though, not everybody agreed with this claim. Archbishop Adalbero of Reims led the opposition against Charles, delivering an impassioned speech on behalf of Hugh Capet, who, as duke of the Franks, made his claim to the throne on the basis of his descent from the Robertians. Adalbero argued that Charles, while perhaps a viable candidate from a hereditary perspective, did not possess the necessary wisdom to govern France effectively. The Archbishop thus presented the crowd with a clear choice: 'If you wish misfortune on France, then elect Charles to the throne, but if you prefer that [France] is blessed, then crown as king the distinguished Duke Hugh'.[2] Hugh's subsequent election and elevation to the throne in the summer of 987 was a monumental event in the history of France; the dynasty he founded would produce fourteen successive kings who would rule France uninterrupted for more than three and a half centuries.[3] By the time the last Capetian, Charles IV, died in 1328, the French King was among the most powerful rulers in Europe, reigning over a strong and bureaucratically centralized State. This was a far cry from the kingdom that Hugh inherited; his power extended only to the limits of the Ile-de-France, and even there it was routinely challenged.

The seemingly miraculous survival (and slow but steady growth) of French royal institutions during Capetian rule has long captivated the interest of historians, who have sought in various ways to understand the mechanisms of transformation in this crucial period.[4] It is precisely because of the contested nature of early French kingship that it is worth revisiting this issue. In the particular context of the crusades, the tenuous nature of early French kingship required a close relationship with a number of religious houses, which ultimately played a key role in shaping the crusading image of the French kings in the central Middle Ages.

The stock narrative of French royal institutional growth almost always celebrates the reign of Philip II Augustus in the late twelfth century as the key period of transition. After this period, French kingship looks more like it would during the reign of Charles IV in the fourteenth century, slowly pushing onto the pinnacle of royal power in the seventeenth century. It is important, however, not to read the climactic period back onto an early age. During most of the period covered by this book, French kingship was not so strong. In fact, it was quite weak. For much of the early Middle Ages the main element that separated the French kings from their (often more powerful) nobles was a claim to divine selection, what was commonly considered to be a sacred claim to rule. Indeed, it was this claim to a sacred status that allowed the Capetians to enjoy the status as 'first among Franks', when, according to one author, they were in reality mere 'servant[s] in the order of kings'.[5] In the late eleventh century, on the eve of the First Crusade, the sacred foundation on which French kingship depended only tenuously survived the increasing challenges from lower-ranking nobles. This is a crucial point, because up to the period of the First Crusade, castellans and other low-ranking nobles had not had the ability to challenge the sacral status of the French kings, or, more to the point, were not able to claim such a prominence for themselves. They were able to enjoy the ability to exercise real power, particularly as the knightly class began being recognized as part of the nobility, thus recasting the value of fighting and power. And yet, no matter how strong a castellan or knight would become, none other than kings could claim a consecrated status. The First Crusade changed that, and this is a point that lies at the core of this book's argument. To understand the gravity of the challenge to Capetian power that came from the successful capture of Jerusalem in 1099 by French nobles, it is important first to understand the stakes. Why did the failure of the Capetians to participate in the First Crusade present such a unique challenge to their power and prestige?

It is an issue worthy of revisiting, since any consideration of the Capetian status in the century before the First Crusade must confront a broader historiographical debate concerning the nature of social and political transformation taking place at this juncture. Many historians in the early twentieth century argued that the collapse of the Carolingian principalities in the tenth century was the precursor to a period of anarchy in which quotidian violence was the dominant theme in the sources.[6] Although such a position has been challenged and often revised over the past several decades, nevertheless, scholars must recognize that during the course of the eleventh century the public power of the Carolingians had, in effect, disintegrated into territory locally dominated by a single family who controlled the castle. These men and women – called castellans – proved one of the main challengers to Capetian supremacy. It is significant that this group also contributed a good portion of the first crusaders. The purpose of this chapter is to consider the various ways by which the Capetians held off the challenges of these low-ranking nobles and castellans in the period leading up to the First Crusade. As we will see, a claimed sacred status, forged and preserved at a number of religious houses, provided enough counterweight against the rise of the castellans to keep them at bay. However, should the latter group acquire a claim to a sacred nature, the stakes for the Capetians could be very high indeed. Such is what happened on the First Crusade.

## The basis of sacred kingship

The claim by generations of Capetian kings to be God's anointed was based on a tradition that stretched back to the early Middle Ages. By the time Hugh Capet ascended the throne in 987, he was the inheritor to a late Carolingian vision of monarchy that held up claims of sacral status and legitimacy as the main components of kingship.[7] These ideas were Carolingian in origin, and gained a special importance in the context of the fragmentation of the empire that followed the death of Charlemagne in 814. The inability of the later Carolingians to revive the centralized political structure of Charlemagne's reign put them at risk of deposition by ambitious and treacherous nobles, and, thus, the claims of legitimacy and sacrality afforded them a claim to rule, seemingly in spite of their inability to do so.

Through the Treaty of Verdun (843), Charles the Bald inherited the Western Frankish Kingdom, his two surviving brothers gaining the remainder of the Carolingian territory. The early years of his reign were reasonably peaceful, but in 859, following the death of the third brother, Louis the German invaded Western Francia and attempted to overthrow Charles. He did so with the tacit approval of several disaffected nobles, who hoped that Louis would prove more generous in his gifts of land. So weak and unpopular was Charles that he could not muster an army, and was forced instead to flee to neighbouring Burgundy. When the recalcitrant nobles attempted to have Charles deposed in favour of his brother (whom they wanted to crown), the only thing that saved him and his office was the refusal by the Frankish bishops to crown a man they saw as a usurper king. It was not out of love of Charles that they did this, however, but rather from a firm belief that secular society did not have the right to depose an anointed king. In the ninth century, the anointing and coronation of a king recalled the Old Testament coronations of David and Saul, and perhaps the more recent imperial coronation of Charlemagne in 800. In all these cases, the anointing ceremony transferred to the new King a sacred status that could not be undone by a layman. Thus, at a time when kingship was weak by any practical standard, the legitimacy conferred by royal coronation functioned as a key mechanism by which the early French kings held onto their power and transferred it to their heirs. As late as 1108, Abbot Suger of Saint-Denis would describe the coronation of Louis VI in terms of his assumption of a sacred responsibility. 'With the approval of the clergy and the crowd', Suger recalled how 'in addition to the other royal insignia, he [the Archbishop] solemnly handed him [Louis] the sceptre and the rod that symbolize the defence of the church and the poor'. From this point onward, Louis was referred to as 'King of the French by the grace of God'.[8] Indeed, legitimacy through coronation would be a key marker of early Capetian kingship. It is significant that the first king to feel strong enough not to have his son crowned as co-ruler during his own lifetime was Philip Augustus, who is often seen to have marked the transformation of French kingship to a strong and centralized monarchy.

The early medieval French kings were in need of the sacral claims to legitimacy since they were very often much weaker than the nobles around them. During the reigns of the first Capetians, in fact, their weakness was openly acknowledged. Based on the annals of Vendôme, the ineffectiveness of the first three members of that dynasty almost reached a comical level. The text describes Duke Hugh as 'the son of Robert the pseudo-king, father of that other whom we saw ruling like a dead man. His son, Henry, the present kinglet, had departed not a whit from his father's laziness.'[9] As the effective power of the French kings continued to decline in the late tenth and early eleventh centuries, the kings and those close to them began looking for new sources of royal propaganda. They found them in a small circle of religious houses that had historical connections to the French kings and thus a vested interested in promoting the image of legitimacy and sanctity. This is a crucial point because it was from these sites (and particularly from Saint-Denis) that the image of the 'crusading king' was shaped and transmitted to a broader audience.

### Spiritual centres and the royal image

> The kingdom [of France] is not gained by hereditary right; no one should be raised to it unless he is distinguished not only by nobility of birth, but also by the wisdom of his soul and unless he is strengthened by faith and greatness of spirit … In conclusion, set the duke [Hugh] over yourselves, a man famed for his deeds, his nobility, and his wealth.[10]

So argued Archbishop Adalbero in his speech in favour of Hugh Capet's election. The force and intent of the passage is clear, if a break with tradition. Hugh's coronation was not a dynastic rupture since he was legitimized by his deeds. Indeed, the real break in dynastic continuity occurred a few months later, when Hugh had Adalbero crown his young son Robert as co-ruler.[11] It was then that the hereditary foundation of the French crown was reasserted, and it was then that the question of royal legitimacy became a central concern for the Capetian family. While hereditary succession may have been achieved early on, according to Marc Bloch, this was not necessarily accepted as proof of dynastic legitimacy, which remained an issue with which the Capetians struggled for more than a century and a half.[12]

Scholars have hitherto been correct to point out the remarkable smoothness with which the Capetians ascended the French throne. Gabrielle Spiegel, for example, has pointed to the lack of invective directed against the royal family and the speed with which Capetian rule was accepted.[13] This does not mean, however, that key actors were not still concerned with the new royal family's image and claims of legitimacy. In fact, the concern for the royal image helps explain why a number of religious houses deliberately began crafting a positive view of Capetians in the century leading up to the First Crusade. Saint-Denis was one such house. The extensive efforts of the Dionysian monks to control to the royal image have been well studied, perhaps better than those of any other French religious house. As a consequence, the mid-twelfth-century dominance of Saint-Denis is often cast backwards onto an earlier period as if the success was a pre-destined event. It was most certainly not, a point that helps us appreciate both the stakes involved in the lack of a Capetian crusading image and also the motivation of Abbot Suger and the other Dionysian monks to create one. Thus, it will be useful to have a broad understanding of the eleventh-century competition among various religious centres for the royal court's attention.

Saint-Benôit-sur-Loire (known generally as Fleury) forged a strong connection with the Capetian court from an early point.[14] In addition to the immense prestige that came from possessing relics of Benedict of Nursia, which the abbey had acquired from the temporarily abandoned monastery of Monte Cassino, Fleury profited from its location in the Loire valley, midway between the cities of Senlis and Orléans.[15] This made it a particularly attractive prospect for royal patronage, especially during the reign of Hugh Capet, when the real power of the French King was quite limited. Fleury's location in the middle of royally controlled territory meant that it was one of a handful of centres with both means and opportunity to forge an early connection to the new dynasty. The relationship was nurtured in a variety of ways, and began under the abbacy of Abbo (r. 988–1004). Abbo had a close relationship with Hugh Capet and his son Robert. During this period, the abbey received a number of grants of protection and immunity from the royal court, and it stands to reason, therefore, that the force of such acts was dependent on the relative strength of the Capetian court that granted them.[16] Thus, Abbot Abbo charged one of his monks, Aimo, with composing a history of France and the French kings.[17] The resulting text, known as the *Historia Francorum*, set out for the first time the early origins of the Capetians and, according to Guenée, 'managed to give the French people … a continuous account that could serve as the collective memory of its entire past'.[18] In other words, Fleury had a vested interest in supporting (creating?) an image of a strong and legitimate king because the house relied for its political standing on royal grants; the King, in turn, benefited from a willing abbey promoting the image of royal power.

At Fleury, the vision of Christian kingship that the Capetians relied upon for their claims of sacral legitimacy was most clearly shaped and promoted by Helgaud, who in the first decade of the eleventh century composed a hagiographical biography of King Robert II (Robert the Pious, r. 996–1031).[19] Helgaud's *Life of Robert the Pious* is an interesting text and has been well discussed by historians, many of whom have commented that the sobriquet 'the Pious' does not quite match up to historical reality.[20] Perhaps this is the case, but perhaps that was not the point of the text. Jean Dunbabin has argued that the innovative part of Robert's text was not his fusion of Old Testament kingly qualities with a modern example, but rather 'making David [the second King of Israel] a saint of the church'.[21] Through the text, Helgaud describes Robert as a miracle worker. In one case, water that had been used to wash the King's hands cured the blindness of the poor man.[22] In another instance, Robert was able to heal the sick by performing the sign of the cross with his hands.[23] Scholarly consensus is that the first French king to be believed to cure scrofula with the famed 'royal touch' was probably Philip I, in the late eleventh century. In portraying Robert II as a miracle worker in his own time, therefore, Helgaud was setting the framework for the later claims of French kings to possess spiritual powers of healing.

While Fleury may have enjoyed a close relationship with the early Capetian court, it was not the only religious house making a bid for royal attention. The spiritual establishment at Reims had a much different connection to the court, though it was also concerned with promoting a dynastically strong monarchy. The special relationship between Reims and the French King was old, beginning in the final years of the fifth century, when St Remigius, Bishop of Reims, baptized Clovis, thus converting the King and (by extension) all of France to Roman Christianity.[24] According to popular legend, as Remigius and Clovis waited at the church to celebrate the latter's baptism the cleric carrying the holy chrism was blocked by the massive crowd from reaching the Bishop. Remigius intervened with impassioned prayer, and suddenly a white dove appeared carrying in its beak a phial filled with holy chrism.[25] The baptism thus proceeded, and in the long term the French monarch was forever attached to the city of Reims and its patron. Of course, Reims's eventual status as a sacred city was based on more than the legend of Clovis's baptism.[26] It took the work of Hincmar, archbishop of Reims from 845 until 882, to realize fully the city's exceptional role in French king-making. Through a carefully orchestrated translation of St Remigius's relics to a new home in the church of Saint-Remi and the production of a widely read life of the saint, Hincmar introduced his patron to a national audience. Most crucially for our purposes is that part of this effort involved the reinforcement of the Clovis legend by means of a coronation ritual. Specifically, while crowning Charles the Bald king of Lotharingia in Metz in 869, Hincmar for the first time highlighted his patron's role in Clovis's baptism and his church's role in establishing a continuous line of legitimate French kings.[27] In so doing, Hincmar effectively associated the legitimacy of French kingship with the performing of the coronation ceremony, thus helping to imbue subsequent French kings with the sacral ethos discussed above. Part of this process, however, involved a claim to act as the dispenser of the holy chrism, which was housed in Saint-Remi and miraculously replenished before the coronation of each new monarch.

The city's status as the giver of royal sacrality was thus based on the twin acts of coronation and unction.

The relationship was strengthened further over the course of the eleventh century, as the Archbishop of Reims enjoyed an unprecedented monopoly over performing the coronation ritual of the Capetian kings. In June 1017 at Compiègne Archbishop Arnulf crowned Robert's son, Hugh, as associate king. Following Hugh's death, in 1027 Ebles of Roucy celebrated the coronation of the future Henry I. And then, on 23 May 1059, Archbishop Gervais celebrated the coronation of Philip I. The last of these neatly demonstrated Reims's growing status as an ecclesiastical-royal city by weaving together several elements discussed above into a single display. The Archbishop presided over a group of bishops and abbots gathered to witness the young King's coronation. Henry I signalled his assent to the election of his son, and the crowd agreed. Gervais then placed the staff of St Remigius in Philip's hand, anointed him with the holy oil, and proclaimed him king.[28]

Philip's reign marked a crucial step forward in the relationship between Reims and the Capetians. In December 1089, Pope Urban II officially recognized the rights of the archbishops 'to consecrate, anoint and ordain' both the King and Queen, thus lending papal endorsement to the legend of Clovis's baptism and the modern coronation ceremony.[29] For his part, Philip demonstrated a clear affection for Reims, and particularly Saint-Remi.[30] In one 1090 act, the King remarked upon St Remigius's status as an apostle of the French and his decision to support his patron's house. The act records that 'although we must defend the holy Church as a whole, we more especially decided to grant our protection to St Remigius ... because he was chosen by God as apostle of the Franks, and because he exerts his patronage on our crown and kingship through apostolic authority'.[31] Against this background, it is clear that religious institutions in Reims would expect a continued close relationship to the French kings, and that they would be particularly troubled by any potential threat to the status of French kingship. Like the monks at Fleury, those in Reims depended on the health of the monarchy for the continued prosperity of their own institutions.

The Dionysian monks had much at stake in assuring the strength of the French kings. From at least the sixth century, the abbey had enjoyed close ties to the royal court, so much so that by the twelfth century, Saint-Denis's position was indivisibly linked to the health of the monarchy.[32] In 570, Queen Arnegonde – wife of the Merovingian King Clothar I – became the first member of the royal court to be buried in the abbey, thus beginning a tradition.[33] By the end of the Carolingian period there were more French kings buried at Saint-Denis than any other location. Among the early Capetians, only

Philip I chose to be buried elsewhere (at Fleury).[34] In addition to its early position as the royal necropolis, Saint-Denis was the beneficiary of several forms of Merovingian patronage. Sometime in the sixth or seventh century, kings began depositing copies of royal documents in the abbey's archives, many of which would later serve as the base texts for Suger's ambitious historiographical programme.[35] Also in the seventh century, King Dagobert I accorded a sweeping series of economic privileges to the abbey, including rights to *tonlieux* and rents; exemption from custom duties; independence from the Bishop of Paris; and, most importantly, the profits from the Fair of Saint-Denis, held each October on the saint's feast day.[36]

On these foundations, the link between abbey and court grew strong in the succeeding centuries, when the abbots began playing a more visible role in royal politics. Abbot Fulrad (abbot from 749 to 784) was one of two prelates sent to Rome to convince Pope Zachary to withdraw his support for the Merovingian kings in favour of the Carolingian usurper. Fulrad then played a crucial rule in elevating Pippin to the throne as the first Carolingian king. As one might expect, Pippin was remarkably generous over the course of his reign to his patron. Among other things, he appointed Fulrad the *maître de la chapelle*, an advisory role that ensured the Dionysian abbot's continued role in politics. The relationship was also important because it prefigured the close association between Dionysian abbots and French kings in the succeeding centuries. Hilduin (abbot from 814 to 840) had particularly close connections to the royal court. Louis the Pious made him archchaplain by 822, and in this position, he accompanied one of Louis's sons to Rome in 824.[37] As a gauge of how powerful the Dionysian–Frankish connection was, in 834, following his son's failure to unseat him, Louis the Pious made the unusual selection of Saint-Denis as the site for his ceremonial re-crowning.[38] What began under the Merovingians and Carolingians continued under the first three Capetians. Hugh Capet, Robert II 'the Pious', and Henry I all made substantial gifts to Saint-Denis and were all buried at the abbey as well.[39] And yet, there is evidence that the relationship between abbey and royal court had deteriorated during this period as well. Robert the Pious (r. 996–1031) issued a charter in the early eleventh century that sought to restore the *ordo monasticus* to the abbey, which it admitted had been neglected since the time of Charles the Bald. Gabrielle Spiegel has discussed this charter, and pointed out that the tone of the document suggests a reverse suffered by the abbey over the course of the tenth century.[40] More to the point, Philip I's decision not to be buried at Saint-Denis suggested a waning relationship between the monastery and the Capetians.

The deterioration of the relationship between a religious centre and the royal court could have real and serious consequences. Although it is difficult to measure precisely the impact of such connections, it is not long after that reports of the deteriorating state of Saint-Denis began to appear. Later in his life, Suger recalled the poor state of Dionysian holdings early in his career at Saint-Denis.[41] Particularly lamentable for Suger was the lax spiritual life of the monks and the amount of land owned by the monastery that had passed out of cultivation in the late eleventh century. For his part, Abelard took great satisfaction in chiding Abbot Adam (1099–1122) for the level of corruption and spiritual degradation that existed at Saint-Denis under his watch.[42] Abelard's comments no doubt reflect the bias and hostility of the author, but should not be disregarded completely. They are, to some extent, supported by Bernard, who in a letter to Suger once described Saint-Denis under his predecessor as a place where 'without any deception or delay it rendered to Caesar his dues, but not with equal enthusiasm what was due to God'.[43]

This chapter has demonstrated two crucial points for the subject at hand. First of all, it has set out the foundation on which the Capetians based their sacral claims, which, until the First Crusade, provided a bulwark against the growing power of the castellans and knightly class. It has also described the competition for the attention and support of the King that occurred in the late eleventh and early twelfth centuries as it was manifested in various attempts by spiritual centres to reinforce claims of the dynastic legitimacy and integrity of the Capetian house. These spiritual centres, we have seen, gained a tremendous amount of their own power and legitimacy from supporting a strong monarchy, and thus, as we turn to discuss the challenge to the political legitimacy occasioned by the First Crusade, it should not be much of a surprise that the earliest responses would come from these places – especially Saint-Denis, which in the early twelfth century came to eclipse Reims and Fleury as the royal monastery par excellence. Thus, with the background now in place it is to that story that we now turn our attention.

### Notes

1 Richer of Saint-Rémi, *Histories*, ed. and trans. Justin Lake, 2 vols (Cambridge, MA, 2011), Vol. II, p. 214.
2 *Ibid.*, Vol. II, p. 221.
3 Yves Sassier, '*Rex Francorum, dux Francorum*: Le gouvernement royal au dernier demi-siècle carolingien', in *Le monde carolingien: Bilan, perspectives, champs de*

*recherches. Actes du colloque international de Poitiers, Centre d'Etudes Supérieures de Civilisation médiévale, 18-20 novembre 2004*, ed. Wojciech Falkowski and Yves Sassier (Turnhout, 2010), pp. 357-75; Jean-François Lemarignier, 'Autour de la date du sacre d'Hugues Capet (1er juin ou 3 juillet 987?)', in *Miscellanea mediaevalia in memoriam Jan Frederik Niermeyer*, ed. Dirk Peter Blok (Gronigen, 1967), pp. 125-35.

4 See the opening comments in Field and Gaposchkin, 'Questioning the Capetians', esp. p. 567.

5 Adalbero of Laon, *Poème au roi Robert*, ed. Claude Carozzi (Paris, 1979), p. 30.

6 Cf. Marc Bloch, *Feudal Society*, trans. L. A. Manyon, 2 vols (Chicago, 1961); George Duby, 'The Evolution of Judicial Institutions', in *The Chivalrous Society*, trans. Cynthia Postan (Berkeley, 1977), pp. 15-88; Jean-Pierre Poly and Eric Bournazel, *The Feudal Transformation: 900-1200*, trans. Caroline Higgitt (New York, 1991); Barthélemy, *La mutation de l'an mil a-t-elle eu lieu?*; Thomas N. Bisson, 'The "Feudal Revolution"', *Past and Present* 142 (1994), 6-42; Barthélemy, *The Crisis of the Twelfth Century*.

7 Much of what follows is drawn from Bernd Schneidmüller, 'Constructing Identities of Medieval France', in *France in the Central Middle Ages*, ed. Marcus Bull (Oxford, 2002), pp. 15-42.

8 *VLG*, p. 86.

9 Cited and translated in Dunbabin, *France in the Making*, p. 133.

10 Richer of Saint-Rémi, *Histories*, Vol. II, pp. 218-20.

11 *Ibid.*, pp. 224-6; Karl-Ferdinand Werner, 'Die Legitimität der Kapetinger und die Entstehung des *Reditus regni Francorum ad stirpem Karoli*', *Die Welt als Geschichte* 12 (1952), 203-25 (p. 214); Andrew W. Lewis, 'Dynastic Structures and Capetian Throne Right: The View of Giles of Paris', *Traditio* 33 (1977), 225-52.

12 Bloch, *Feudal Society*, Vol. II, pp. 383-9, esp. p. 388.

13 Gabrielle M. Spiegel, 'The *Reditus regni ad stirpem Karoli Magni*: A New Look', in *The Past as Text: The Theory and Practice of Medieval Historiography* (Baltimore, 1997), pp. 117-18.

14 Bernard Guenée, 'Chanceries and Monasteries', in *Rethinking France: Les lieux de mémoire*, ed. Pierre Nora, trans. Deke Dusinberre, 4 vols (Chicago, 2014), Vol. IV: *Histories and Memories*, pp. 1-26. See also Barbara H. Rosenwein, Thomas Head, and Sharon Farmer, 'Monks and Their Enemies: A Comparative Approach', *Speculum* 66 (1991), 764-96 (pp. 779-80).

15 Thomas Head, *Hagiography and the Cult of Saints: The Diocese of Orléans, 800-1200* (Cambridge, 1990), pp. 23-4.

16 See *Recueil des chartes de Saint-Benoît-sur-Loire*, ed. Maurice Prou and Alexandre Vidier (Paris, 1900), pp. 182-5 n. 70. See also Rosenwein, Head, and Farmer, 'Monks and Their Enemies', pp. 782-3; Jean-François Lemarignier, 'Le monachisme et l'encadrement religieux des campagnes du royaume de France situées au nord de la Loire, de la fin du X à la fin du XIe siècle', in *Le istituzioni ecclesiastiche della 'Societas Christiana' dei secoli XI-XII: Diocesi, pievi e parrocchie* (Milan, 1977), pp. 363-75.

17 Robert-Henri Bautier, 'La place de l'abbaye de Fleury-sur-Loire dans l'historiographie française du IXe au XIIe siècle', in *Etudes ligériennes d'histoire*

*et d'archéologie médiévales*, ed. René Louis (Auxerre, 1975), pp. 23-33; Frederick S. Paxton, '*Abbas* and *rex*: Power and authority in the literature of Fleury, 987-1044', in *The Experience of Power in Medieval Europe, 950-1350*, ed. Robert F. Berkhoffer, Alan Cooper, and Adam J. Kosto (Aldershot, 2005), pp. 197-212.

18 Bernard Guenée, 'Les généalogies entre l'histoire et la politique: La fierté d'être Capétien, en France, au Moyen Âge', *Annales* 33 (1978), 450-77 (pp. 450-2).

19 For an overview of biography at Fleury see Head, *Hagiography and the Cult of Saints*, pp. 270-5.

20 See Sarah Hamilton, 'A New Model for Royal Penance? Helgaud of Fleury's Life of Robert the Pious', *Early Medieval Europe* 6 (1997), 189-200; Claude Carozzi, 'La vie du roi Robert par Helgaud de Fleury: Historiographie et hagiographie', *Annales de Bretagne et des pays de l'Ouest* 37 (1980), 219-35.

21 Dunbabin, *France in the Making*, p. 135.

22 Helgaud of Fleury, *Vie de Robert le Pieux*, ed. Robert Henri Bautier and Gillette Labory (Paris, 1965), p. 77. Cited in Dunbabin, *France in the Making*, p. 135.

23 Helgaud, *Vie de Robert le Pieux*, p. 128; Dubabin, *France in the Making*, p. 135.

24 James Naus, 'The *Historia Iherosolimitana* of Robert the Monk and the Coronation of Louis VI', in *Writing the Early Crusades: Text, Transmission, and Memory*, ed. Damien Kempf and Marcus Bull (Woodbridge, 2014), pp. 105-15. On the baptism of Clovis see Claude Carozzi, 'Du baptême au sacre Clovis selon les traditions rémoises', in *Clovis: Histoire et mémoire, le baptême de Clovis, son echo à travers l'histoire*, ed. Michele Rouche, 2 vols (Paris, 1997), Vol. II, pp. 29-44; Philippe Depreux, 'Saint Remi et la royauté carolingienne', *Revue historique* 578 (1991), 235-60.

25 Jacques Le Goff, 'Reims, City of Coronation', in *Realms of Memory: The Construction of the French Past*, ed. Pierre Nora and Lawrence D. Kritzman, trans. Arthur Goldhammer, 3 vols (New York, 1966), Vol. III, pp. 193-251 (196-8); Marie-Céline Isaïa, *Remi de Reims: Mémoire d'un saint, histoire d'une église* (Paris, 2010), pp. 87-113.

26 Michele Bur, 'Reims, ville des sacres', in *Le sacre des rois: Actes du colloque international d'histoire sur les sacres et couronnements royaux* (Reims, 1985), pp. 39-48; Robert-Henri Bautier, 'Sacres et couronnements sous les Carolingiens et les premiers Capétiens', in *Recherches sur l'histoire de la France medieval: Des Mérovingiens aux premiers Capétiens* (London, 1991), pp. 7-56.

27 Isaïa, *Remi de Reims*, pp. 575-91; J. M. Wallace-Hadrill, 'History of the Mind of Archbishop Hincmar', in *The Writing of History in the Middle Ages: Essays Presented to R. W. Southern*, ed. R. H. C. Davis and J. M. Wallace-Hadrill (Oxford, 1981), pp. 43-79.

28 *Ordines coronationis Franciae: Texts and Ordines for the Coronation of Frankish and French Kings and Queens in the Middle Ages*, ed. Richard A. Jackson (Philadelphia, 1995), pp. 217-32, esp. pp. 230-2.

29 Patrick Demouy, *Genèse d'une cathédrale: Les archevêques de Reims et leur église aux IXe et XIIe siècles* (Langres, 2005), pp. 564-74.

30 Spiegel, *The Chronicle Tradition of Saint-Denis*, p. 28.

31 *Recueil des actes de Philippe Ier, roi de France (1059–1108)*, ed. Maurice Prou (Paris, 1908), pp. 305–6 n. 120.

32 For general comments on the relationship between the earlier Frankish kings and Saint-Denis see Geoffrey Koziol, 'Charles the Simple, Robert of Neustria and the *Vexilla* of Saint-Denis', *Early Medieval Europe* 14 (2006): 371–90; Geoffrey Koziol, 'Is Robert I in Hell? The Diploma for Saint-Denis and the Mind of a Usurper, January 25, 923', *Early Medieval Europe* 14 (2006): 233–67.

33 Edouard Salin, *Les tombes gallo-romaines et mérovingiennes de la basilique de Saint-Denis (fouilles de janvier-février, 1957)* (Paris, 1958), p. 192; Sumner McKnight Crosby, *The Royal Abbey of Saint-Denis from Its Beginning to the Death of Suger, 475–1151*, ed. Pamela Blum (New Haven, 1987), pp. 9–12.

34 *VLG*, pp. 80–4. For discussion see Rolf Grosse, *Saint-Denis zwischen Adel und König: Die Zeit vor Suger (1053–1122)* (Stuttgart, 2002), pp. 131–6.

35 Crosby, *The Royal Abbey of Saint-Denis*, p. 9. Much of what follows relies on the excellent survey in Spiegel, *The Chronicle Tradition of Saint-Denis*, pp. 11–34.

36 'Gesta Dagobert I regis Francorum', ed. Bruno Krusch, *MGH SS rerum Merovingicarum* 2, pp. 306–425 (pp. 406–7); Spiegel, *The Chronicle Tradition of Saint-Denis*, pp. 18–19.

37 Crosby, *The Royal Abbey of Saint-Denis*, p. 86.

38 *Ibid.*

39 Alain Erlande-Brandenburg, *Le roi est mort: Etude sur les funérailles, les sépultures et les tombeaux des rois de France jusqu'à la fin du XIIIe siècle* (Geneva, 1975), pp. 73–5.

40 Spiegel, *The Chronicle Tradition of Saint-Denis*, pp. 27–8.

41 *Oeuvres*, Vol. I, pp. 54–5.

42 Abelard, *Historia calamitatum*, ed. Jacques Monfrin (Paris, 1959), p. 82.

43 Bernard of Clairvaux, 'Letter 78', in *Sancti Bernardi opera*, ed. Jean Leclercq and Henri Rochais, 8 vols (Rome, 1955–77), Vol. VII, p. 203.

2

# The First Crusade and the new economy of status, 1095–1110

In the spring of 1106, a sizeable crowd gathered at Chartres Cathedral to witness the marriage of the Norman crusader Bohemond of Antioch to Constance, the eldest daughter of King Philip I of France.[1] Few could have predicted a royal bride for the Norman warlord, the son of a cattle poacher turned duke who only a decade before had faced the prospect of a landless existence after losing his inheritance to a half-brother.[2] When he took the cross for the First Crusade in 1096, Bohemond was little more than an itinerant noble in southern Italy helping his uncle besiege the city of Amalfi with the hope of carving out a small territory of his own. Yet, when he began his search for a suitable marriage partner in 1103, following closely on the heels of a spectacular performance on the First Crusade, his prospects had improved markedly. By the time that Bohemond travelled to the West in 1105, he not only enjoyed the substantial material rewards that accrued from ruling the principality of Antioch, but also considerable celebrity from his crusading reputation. He was famous enough that a monk from Angers used the occasion of his visit to date a transaction.[3] Henry I discouraged him from visiting England on the grounds that his personal magnetism might tempt away the best English knights to join him in the East.[4] In France, so many nobles asked Bohemond to stand as godfather to their children that Orderic Vitalis observed 'henceforth his name was popularized in Gaul, though previously it had been virtually unknown to most people in the West'.[5]

Long before his 1105 trip to France, Bohemond had been staging elaborate ceremonies with the goal of promoting his crusading heritage. After the seemingly miraculous defeat of the Turkish Atabeg Kerboga in 1098 before the walls of Antioch, Bohemond sent the Muslim leader's tent to the major pilgrimage centre at the Church of St Nicholas in Bari, ensuring that it would be seen by the large crowds of pilgrims who visited the shrine each year.[6] Nicholas Paul has shown how crusading memorabilia could function as memorial pegs for recalling the heroic deeds of the individual responsible for an object's translation, and interpreted in this way, Bohemond's decision to deposit Kerboga's tent may well have been an attempt to ensure that future generations would remember his crusading deeds.[7] In much the same fashion, Bohemond used to his advantage his imprisonment by the Turkish leader Ghumushtgin from 1100 until 1103. Early in the Norman's return to Europe in 1105 he made a pilgrimage to the shrine of Saint-Léonard-de-Noblat, the patron of prisoners, where he gave thanks for his deliverance from Muslim captivity.[8] Stories of his daring escape soon appeared in St Leonard's *miracula*, and quickly began circulating throughout the great courts of France and Germany, further inflating his reputation and making him arguably the most famous crusading hero in the decade following the capture of Jerusalem.[9] The longer his journey lasted, the more people flocked to see him and the more enamoured with him they became.[10]

The 1106 wedding celebration at Chartres was designed to be the culmination of these efforts. The circumstances were certainly ideal for such a crowning display of theatrics. Since Constance was a French princess, the ceremony was a major affair of state, and an appropriately esteemed crowd was on hand to witness the nuptials. Alongside Philip and Prince Louis (the future Louis VI) stood the most influential prelates and magnates in France.[11] Although we might wonder if his new bride was enthusiastic about her wedding being used to promote her husband's upcoming expedition against the Greek Emperor Alexius I, Bohemond had no such qualms. By all accounts he put on a fantastic show, impressing the crowd with stories of his heroics at Antioch, a clever political move meant to connect the revered First Crusade with his upcoming expedition to Byzantium, thus lending the latter a degree of respectability.[12] As Orderic Vitalis described the scene at Chartres, having mounted the pulpit Bohemond 'urged all those who bore arms to attack the Emperor with him, promising them wealthy towns and castles in return'.[13] Several weeks later he followed up with an appearance at the Council of Poitiers, where again he broadcast a call to arms, undoubtedly interspersed with an account of his own deeds.

Bohemond knew how to inspire nobles and knights who had come of age in the new era of crusading. These men were accustomed to measuring their conduct against what David Crouch has described as constructed archetypes of nobility, a mixed group of real-life heroes as well as many others drawn from the *chansons de geste*.[14] The *Song of Roland* had appeared in the decades leading up to the First Crusade, and served as a particularly effective yardstick for a noble hoping to measure his heroics. After 1099, of course, crusaders such as Bohemond and Godfrey of Bouillon were added to the mix, taking their places alongside men such as Ganelon and Roland. In this way, it would seem that the stars had aligned for the nobles to whom Bohemond now pitched his message, since they had the rare opportunity not only to follow in the footsteps of a great hero, but actually to retrace the steps of the first crusaders alongside a living veteran of the well-known expedition. It is worth noting that many of those who witnessed these performances had been on the First Crusade themselves or came from a crusading family. Therefore, they would have been familiar with Bohemond's reputation, and his promises of earthly rewards would have found purchase among a sympathetic audience. It is perhaps also significant that a majority of those who participated in the Norman's 1107 expedition came from the region between Poitiers and Chartres, an area that produced a high concentration of first crusaders and one in which Bohemond focused the majority of his recruitment efforts.[15]

## Realignments of power

Bohemond's meteoric rise in the West, and his successful parlaying of Eastern deeds into western political currency in the immediate years following the First Crusade afford us an excellent point of entry into the watershed nature of the expedition in the medieval imagination. Indeed, as noted in the introduction, scholars have long pointed to the astonishing ways in which the First Crusade transformed the West, and, in particular, have repeatedly stressed the point that few other episodes from the Middle Ages sparked the same level of literary output.[16] For this reason, we are on solid ground to believe that the memory of the expedition penetrated deeply into the western imagination, shaping the actions and behaviour of the noble class that contributed a majority of the participants. This is both a blessing and a challenge to modern historians. So extraordinary were the nature of the expedition and the well-known stories of its leaders, that the amount of evidence produced has apparently satisfied the appetites of medieval historians, who on most topics must piece together bits of information from fragmentary sources.

The overwhelming focus on successful crusaders has obscured the serious problems faced by non-participants and those who abandoned the expedition: they lacked the crusading prestige necessary to compete in the developing economy of status. From their perspective, the more legendary the First Crusade became, the more pronounced their problem, since additional attention would be drawn to their failure. Chief among those who felt such concern over their crusading heritage were the French monarchs, because when it came to crusading, they were both latecomers and failures. As a result, anything that drew attention to this point was a potential threat to the royal prestige. This was no minor concern. As we saw in the previous chapter, at the time of the First Crusade French royal power was fragile. It was also, to a large extent, based on the daily acceptance of regnal authority by the political elites – nobles, churchmen, and later, urban leaders.[17] Indeed, French royal power in the Middle Ages depended more on negotiated compromise than coercive force; it was closer to a vision of power as guidance than to the common view that power equated to the ability to exercise force.[18] Without the elites' acquiescence, the system would have come apart at the seams, and thus kings feared anything that threatened to upset the perception that they were God's rulers on earth.

When it came to lofty crusading reputations, the Capetians had more to lose than other nobles. This is because they had much at stake in the legacy of Charlemagne. They portrayed themselves – and generally were understood by others – to be the continuators of Charlemagne's Frankish Kingdom: God's chosen representatives on earth.[19] At the end of the eleventh century, this was an image that the French kings worked hard to foster. King Philip selected a Carolingian-inspired name for his eldest son (Louis), and also demonstrated a marked bias toward Compiègne, a favoured Carolingian church that contained several royal tombs.[20] By the early twelfth century, Charlemagne was close to becoming the gold standard by which other European rulers were measured. The First Crusade accelerated this process, since it occurred around the same period that Charlemagne's deeds in the East gained in notoriety, in part through the popularity and widespread dissemination of texts such as the *Song of Roland*.[21]

Indeed, at the time of the First Crusade, the various Charlemagne legends provided a common memorial corpus that allowed a diverse set of participants a shared set of cultural referents, explaining, among other things, the common appearance of descriptors such as *Franci* to describe the various armies of the crusade. In calling together a diverse group of knights from across Europe, Pope Urban II was understood by contemporaries to have transformed these men from Norman, Breton, German back into Franks. This is certainly how twelfth-century writers saw things. Robert the Monk recalled Urban's insistence that the potential first crusaders remember their Carolingian lineage: 'Oh most valiant soldiers and descendants of victorious ancestors, do not fall short of, but be inspired by, the courage of your forefathers.'[22] Guibert of Nogent was equally pointed when he recorded how:

> although the call from the Apostolic See was directed only to the Franks, as though it were specific, what nation under Christian law did not send forth hordes to that place? In the belief that they owed the same allegiance to God as did the Franks, the crowds strove to the full extent of their power, to share the danger with the Franks.[23]

We might reasonably imagine that if Charlemagne had been present at Clermont in 1095, he would have been among the first to take up the cross. It is worth asking, therefore, what did it mean, if anything, that his Capetian successors did not do so.

The Capetians had a sorry record when it came to the First Crusade. King Philip had not participated because he had been excommunicated. Even if he had wanted to go, it would have been difficult. Royal power was still personal in 1095, and the court probably could not have survived the prolonged absence of the King. Philip's brother Hugh of Vermandois did go, though he abandoned the host in 1098 after the siege of Antioch, which was potentially more problematic for the Capetian image.[24] Fulcher of Chartres noted that those who abandoned the crusading host were 'vile before God and men', while the papal legate, Bishop Adhémar of Le Puy, called upon western bishops to pronounce anathema on returning crusaders who had not fulfilled their vows.[25] Hence, the Capetians had much to lose. Although Hugh would ultimately return to the East to discharge his vow as part of the crusade of 1101, nobody in 1098 could have known the lasting impact of his initial flight. The long-term effect of shame was a real problem, and could be easily dredged up for use by one's political enemies, sometimes many years after the fact. The case of Stephen of Blois – the most famous deserter of the First Crusade – is instructive on this point. While most authors ultimately came to forgive Stephen for his actions, at least one surviving variant of the crusade chronicle of Baldric of Bourgueil went to some length to chastise Stephen for his cowardice. Nicholas Paul has studied the corresponding manuscript and has argued that it demonstrated that it was produced on the instructions of political enemies of Stephen's, belabouring the story of his flight with the goal of undercutting his political standing in the West.[26] With the same goal in mind, in the mid-twelfth century Abbot Suger linked the ongoing treachery of Hugh of Le Puiset with the ignoble crusading career of his father, Everard III, a well-known crusader in his own right, to cast a long shadow over the entire family.[27] Hugh of Vermandois's high profile would have made him an attractive target for castellans hoping to undercut Capetian power in the region around Paris. Within this context, it must have been discomforting for Philip and Prince Louis, less than five years later, to watch Bohemond use the occasion of a royal wedding to recount his crusading achievements and try to convince the flower of French knighthood to follow him to Byzantium. After all, the crusader was an interloper if judged by aristocratic rank, but the prime attraction if judged by attention. To be sure, the original purpose of the marriage may have been to appropriate some of Bohemond's crusading prestige for the royal family, but not at the cost of overshadowing their own reputation. Many of those who followed the Norman were, after all, vassals of the French King.

The wedding celebration at Chartres thus captures one of the basic – if hitherto underappreciated – legacies of the First Crusade: the complexity of the challenge to Capetian power and authority. This was not simply a consequence of Hugh's departure from Antioch and Philip's non-participation; it was related to a host of issues connected to French royal power. At its core, though, the threat posed to the Capetian court by the First Crusade was manifest in, and to a degree a product of, the rise of what we might appropriately term the 'crusading castellans'. The success of the expedition challenged the prevailing European system of power by redirecting the martial energy of the mid-ranking nobility toward an ecclesiastically sanctioned cause, redefining the terms by which social status and rulership came to be valued, with greater emphasis now on military success and heroic crusading, both elements imbued with a distinctly Christian ethic.[28] In practical terms, the First Crusade opened up a fresh, and perhaps unprecedentedly fruitful, source for acquiring prestige, valour, and heroism: all crucial ingredients for an ambitious castellan or mid-ranking noble hoping to climb the socio-political ladder in early-twelfth-century France.[29] As we saw in the previous chapter, this was the same group that had been challenging royal authority for years, attempting to aggrandize power at the King's expense. The First Crusade gave them the necessary traction to do so in a much more effective way. If, as Thomas Bisson has argued, scholars must be more alive to the increasing role of charisma and prestige in attaining power in the early twelfth century, then it is a point in need of consideration in the particular context of the Capetian experience.[30] From 1099 onward, there was little in Christendom more heroic than being a crusader, and as veterans returned from the East with their new-found prestige in hand, the circumstance was primed for new systemic tensions to be introduced into the long-term social competition between the King and his nobles.

How transformative could the crusade be for one's reputation? We have already seen the extent to which Bohemond gained standing on the basis of his eastern deeds. Abbot Suger of Saint-Denis wrote that Constance 'was not seeking another marriage with somebody unworthy of her', and so Philip selected Bohemond.[31] The implication in this sentence, of course, is that Bohemond *was* worthy of a royal bride. But what made him so? A few sentences before, Suger suggested that his bravery at the 1098 siege of Antioch had much to do with it.

> About that time Bohemond, the famous prince of Antioch, came down to France. As the great siege of the city ended, the garrison there admired his valor and chose to surrender only to him. He had won fame and celebrity among the people of the East, and the Saracens themselves praised his noble deeds, which could never have been done without the help of God.[32]

The French kings took marriage decisions very seriously; indeed, much of the Capetian accrual of power over the tenth and eleventh centuries was the result of well-chosen partners, a point borne out by the various marriages of King Henry I (r. 1031–60).[33] Constance's first marriage was to Hugh of Troyes, the Count of Champagne, and thus a noble with an ancient and esteemed pedigree. Though the union was not long-lasting – it was annulled for consanguinity in 1104 – Hugh's status is deserving of closer attention.[34] The counts of Champagne were among the most powerful magnates in France, a point that fits well with what we know about Capetian marriage patterns in general. In 1033, King Henry was engaged to the daughter of the German Emperor Conrad II, and within a year of her death he had married another German princess, Matilda.[35] After she died in 1044, the French King married Anna, daughter of the Grand Duke of Kiev, Yaroslav I.[36]

The pattern was clear. Kings and their children married other royalty and their children. Constance's own marriage experiences, however, identify a crucial transformation that took place in the French political structure. The next successful suitor after Hugh of Troyes was a Norman parvenu with little other than a heroic reputation to recommend him, and King Philip surely would not have accepted the proposal if he had not believed the union would add value to the Capetian dynastic cause. Considering the prominence given to Bohemond's crusading experience in the surviving sources, it is reasonable to conclude that Philip wanted

Bohemond linked to his family because he hoped to benefit from his reputation.[37] At least one French chronicler tried to do just this. Writing around 1108, Guibert of Nogent assigned Bohemond a quasi-French status 'since his family was from Normandy, a part of France, and since he had obtained the hand of the daughter of the French King'.[38] Although there are no known similar accounts produced after this date, this may be the combined result of Bohemond's failed 1107 attack on the Byzantine empire (which undercut his reputation in the West) and the fact that he proved to be a cruel husband to Constance. Philip, of course, could not have known this when he made the initial decision, and it is therefore significant that at the same time that he accepted Bohemond's proposition, Philip also agreed to marry another of his daughters, Cecile, to Tancred, a Norman crusade veteran (and Bohemond's cousin) who remained in the Latin East.[39] The King's attempts to link his family to established crusading heroes bespeaks a change in the complexion of the twelfth-century power structure. Crusaders with prestige could, quite suddenly, command the attention of kings and marry their children.

Other examples demonstrate this transition. For instance, Guy the Red, the Count of Rochefort, organized a remarkable reception for himself in 1102 upon his return to his lordship southwest of Paris. Guy's is one case in which the failure of the 1101 crusade – which he joined to redeem himself for deserting the First Crusade in 1098 – did not seem to undercut his celebrity.[40] As he approached the abbey of Morigny, he was 'met with a procession' and was 'welcomed with the highest honours'.[41] The next morning, the Abbot escorted Guy on the twenty-mile journey to Saint-Arnoult-en-Yvelines, where he was met again by a monastic procession as well as a large crowd of local notables who had gathered to catch a glimpse of the returning hero. By 1104, Guy had regained the post of royal seneschal and arranged the engagement of his daughter Lucienne to King Philip's oldest son, the future Louis VI.[42] Suger hinted that Guy's crusading experience was a key factor in Philip's willingness to agree to the nuptials by describing Guy as 'a man of experience and a veteran knight who had returned from the expedition to Jerusalem renowned and rich'.[43] Of course, Louis's marriage to a member of the Montlhéry family might also be explained in terms of Capetian weakness – as evidence of Philip's desperation to forge an alliance with the most troublesome of his nobles. Yet, this does not reveal the full picture. Had Philip simply wanted a political alliance with Guy's family, this marriage could have easily been arranged before the crusade. Guy was, after all, the royal seneschal at this time. The fact is that something about Guy's position had changed after his return from the East, and Suger's comments are strong evidence for the Count's enhanced status as the result of the First Crusade. It is worth noting that Guy's family, the Montlhérys, also benefited from his reputation, converting it into a spectacular rise to prominence in France and the Latin East.[44]

Robert of Flanders also parlayed crusader credentials into power, first by orchestrating an impressive ceremony to mark his return to the West. Before departing for home, he sent ahead to the abbey of Anchin a relic of St George that he had acquired. The translation narrative produced at the abbey to mark the occasion indicates that Robert sent the relic in advance specifically so that it would generate positive publicity. When he did finally return to Flanders, the narrative records how Robert was welcomed as a triumphant hero and how he entertained the monks with stories of his crusading adventures.[45] He continued to work hard to realize the positive benefits of his heroism. Over the succeeding decade, Robert never missed an opportunity to highlight his eastern deeds, and eventually he won for himself the title of 'son of Saint George' in the monastic chronicles and *chanson de geste* of the twelfth century.[46]

Likewise Robert of Normandy and Rotrou of Mortagne both returned home to the 'well-deserved praises of their close friends and relatives'.[47] Members of the Le Puiset family, one of the most celebrated crusading dynasties in northern France, they emphasized their eastern deeds in support of rising political ambitions at home.[48] Despite blistering criticisms by chroniclers for his actions before and after the First Crusade (not to mention those directed at his abhorrent conduct toward Jews in the early stages of that campaign), Thomas of Marle still received praise for his heroism at the battle of Dorylaeum. He was even feted by one author as a 'valiant' crusader with a 'loyal heart'.[49] Gauging the practical impact of such sentiment is difficult, but it is certainly instructive that Thomas's nefarious character had been mostly forgotten by later twelfth-century authors, having been replaced by the memory of his crusading heroics as preserved in sources such as the *Chanson de Jérusalem*.[50] Indeed, in 1219 the monks of Nogent-sous-Coucy were ordered by one of Thomas's descendants to 'honourably translate' the body of the infamous crusader to a more prominent position in the church choir, ostensibly so that he was more visible to visiting pilgrims.[51] Based on this, it would seem that crusading prowess had an enduring power to shape the long-term memory of one's reputation. Indeed, in some cases it was the defining element.

The transformative impact of crusading prestige introduced a serious potential challenge to the prevailing conceptions of kingship by significantly broadening the field of those who could participate at the highest levels in what had been a rigidly structured and closed power system.[52] The twelfth century was marked by profound social and political transformation. This was particularly evident in views on kingship, which, as we saw in the previous chapter, underwent fundamental changes in this period. Crusading intersected with this phenomenon as it was received, memorialized, and interpreted in the West. In some cases, crusading provided ambitious nobles with their first opportunity to compete directly with more prestigious rulers. Ritual celebrations (i.e. *adventus* and *triumphus* celebrations) on the scale of and of the sort engineered by Guy the Red and Bohemond had previously belonged to kings, emperors, and a select few of the most powerful aristocrats. Since Roman times such displays had been the privilege of the *vicarius Christi* and were taken as demonstrative evidence of his sacral nature.[53] The celebration of military triumph, in particular, was a tool that secular rulers since Constantine had used to articulate a hierarchical view of society at whose summit they stood as Christ's representatives on earth.[54] Indeed, they modelled their ceremonial on Christ's entry into Jerusalem on Palm Sunday, with the clear intention of stressing their roles as *christomimetes* – imitators of Christ. This was a lofty promise for an earthly ruler to be sure, but this was the conception of sacral kingship that framed the early Middle Ages. It was also a tenacious idea, even outlasting the ecclesiastical reform movement of the eleventh century. The Norman Anonymous, writing around 1100, could still note without hesitation that the 'power of the King is the power of God ... whatever he does, he does not simply as a man, but as one who has become God and Christ through grace'.[55]

Imperial entry celebrations were designed to evoke an image of Christ-centred kingship, and crusading veterans were attempting to participate in and gain status from the same ritual performance. In such a context, Guy's reception by the monks and nobles at Saint-Arnolt was more than a hastily organized welcome-home ceremony. Rather, it was an act designed to elevate him to the level of sacral ruler and to accrue the accompanying political and social benefits. The links and threats to kingship implicit in such instances were not far-fetched. To command military forces and lead nobles in battle were long recognized as crucial functions of early medieval rulers. Charlemagne was well known for personally commanding his army.[56] Indeed, the contemporary histories of his life, as well as the various legends that appeared long after his death, were largely based on his military prowess.[57] He was also known to ensure loyalty by distributing the conquered territory as payment to his supporters. In 793 he famously lavished rich rewards on his leading counts simply because they had not joined the rebellion of his son Pippin.[58] Things had changed for the French kings by the twelfth century. Philip and the soon-to-be Louis VI did not have the political, military, or ecclesiastical resources to make such gifts or promises, but neither did anyone else. The First Crusade changed this, in part because it narrowed the gap between noble and king, creating, effectively, a new class of noble warriors that embodied elements traditionally associated with kingship. Bohemond promised 'wealthy towns and castles' to those nobles at his wedding ceremony who chose to follow him to the East.[59] Everywhere he went in France, the Norman distributed relics along with 'gold, silver, gems, and silk' while recounting sensational stories of his crusading adventures.[60] To members of the audience, who were mostly familiar with Carolingian legends, he would have looked like Charlemagne reborn, bestowing wealth and power on those who supported him. The impressive number of leading nobles from northern France who followed him to the East lends force to this point. Could Bohemond now challenge Philip's position, completing the transformation from Italian marauder to French powerbroker? One must not underestimate the effect of the scene that played out at Chartres; like Guy the Red, the Norman warlord was appropriating a traditional royal function for himself.

Nobles, of course, had been imitating rulers and vying for a participatory stake in royal privilege for quite some time. In addition, the reforming papacy was growing increasingly uncomfortable with the sacral elements that had been attached to kingship since the early Church. Yet, these were mostly abstract concerns and neither of these points had much impact on how rulership was *actually* practised at the turn of the twelfth century.[61] Kings continued to set themselves apart from those they ruled with ritual demonstrations of their divine selection. They were acclaimed with *laudes*, anointed, and ceremonially recrowned on high feast days.[62] Geoffrey Koziol has argued that the great eleventh-century princes consciously used the *adventus* ceremony, in particular, as a means by which to separate themselves from the rising power of the castellan class, which included men like Guy and Bohemond.[63] Yet, this was also a crucial period of transition. It is worthwhile following Bisson in setting the First Crusade alongside other transformative events such as the 1066 invasion of England and the Investiture Contest that began what he has described accurately as the 'crisis of the twelfth century'.[64] In so doing, it bears asking what it meant for contemporary views of kingship, power, and dynasticism that no rulers had taken part in the First Crusade, an event so important to the medieval imagination that one contemporary chronicler considered it to rank alongside the 'creation of man' and 'the mystery of redemption on the cross'.[65]

Robert the Monk, who probably witnessed Urban's speech at Clermont, recalled how the Pope instructed potential crusaders to mimic the 'worth and greatness of Charlemagne, his son Louis and other kings who destroyed the pagan kingdoms and brought them into Christendom'.[66] Such a passage had troubling implications for Europe's current rulers, since according to Urban they were not living in the image of Charlemagne. Had kings lost their divinely sanctioned status? And if so, how did this affect a ruler's ability to govern as the representative of Christ? After all, the crusaders had been victorious without them, and no less, they were victorious in Jerusalem, the city of Christ. Indeed, Guibert of Nogent wrote of the virtues that came from the non-participation of kings, 'lest the visible royalty seem to seize divine operations for itself'.[67] The sacred status enjoyed by European monarchs had always depended on the ruler's ability occasionally to demonstrate it, and thus the failure of kings to participate in the First Crusade introduced the potential to challenge such long-held assumptions. Hugh of Fleury, writing in the first decade of the twelfth century, produced a text called the *Liber qui modernorum regum Francorum continent actus*, which he dedicated and presented to Louis VI. Recalling Hugh Capet's rise, Hugh remarks, 'and thus passed away the second line of Frankish kings, with royal power transferring to a third, selected by the judgement of God, whom he wishes to elevate, and whom he humbles'.[68] The Capetians, Hugh argues, remained divinely selected.

The problem was not that the French kings necessarily lost their sacred image; the problem was that the returning crusaders were now claiming a piece of that for themselves, and in this case sacredness was a zero-sum game. As a consequence, the prestige from participating in this most momentous event was very suddenly diffused among a wide base of people – a majority of crusading families in northern France – with the result being a dramatic shift in the complexion of power. Many mid-ranking nobles now had the traction necessary to vie for privileges that had previously belonged to the *vicarius Christi*, to kings, emperors, and a select group of aristocrats. It is therefore easy to see how a lack of crusading prestige could be considered a liability by members of the ruling elite whose claim to divine approval and the authority that depended on it was the most vulnerable. The First Crusade established a new economy of status in which heroics and prestige were the needed currency, and those who were prestige-poor were at a marked competitive disadvantage.

## Crisis and response

This phenomenon obliged rulers to confront long-term systemic social tensions within the European power system, and it was by no means a purely French experience. Such whispers appear in sources from across Western Europe. The desire to tap into crusading prestige may help explain why in January 1103 Emperor Henry IV wrote a letter to his godfather, Abbot Hugh of Cluny, outlining his plan to lead an armed expedition to the Holy Land as a means of shoring up his political position against recalcitrant nobles and, most especially, his son.[69] In the Anglo-Norman world, Robert Curthose's reputation profited from his crusading experiences, with stories and objects related to his time in the East circulating long before Robert's own arrival from Jerusalem in the late summer of 1100 when, according to Orderic Vitalis, he may have celebrated an *adventus* ceremony at Rouen.[70] Robert of Torigni noted in the late 1130s that Robert Curthose's crusading reputation had afforded him (relatively) comfortable imprisonment at the hands of his younger brother, King Henry I of England, who chose to treat him 'not as an enemy captive but rather as a noble pilgrim'.[71] William of Malmesbury wrote that Robert's bravery was the result of 'many feats ... such that neither Christian nor pagan could throw him from his horse'.[72] Whereas William described how the Lotharingian leader Godfrey of Bouillon had cut several Turks in two, more significant is his claim that Robert killed the Muslim leader Kerboga at Antioch.[73] This story, of course, is not true, and an author as well informed as William of Malmesbury would have known as much. Henry of Huntingdon also went to great lengths to explain Robert's post-1099 failings in explicit crusading terms, asserting that his loss of Normandy in 1106 was the result of his refusal to accept the crown of Jerusalem in 1099.[74] This claim was also fabricated. In fact, Robert was never offered the crown. But as Henry tells it, Robert chose to return home rather than to 'toil for the Lord of kings', and as a result 'God condemned him to everlasting inactivity'.[75] That Henry felt the need to link the loss of Normandy with Robert's crusading career is notable because it means that a writer who was in tune with aristocratic opinion felt that Robert's lack of post-1099 success needed explaining, presumably because it was the opposite of what would have been expected. It is unfortunate that Henry says little else, but this example nevertheless provides enough evidence to show that a real concern was present – lurking below the surface. In France, however, royal power was extremely fragile and was threatened not only by King Philip's non-participation, but also by the premature departure of his brother, Hugh of Vermandois. Therefore, one might expect any anxiety to be more intensified.

In 1072, as a way to secure an alliance with Robert the Frisian, who had just defeated him in battle, King Philip married Robert's daughter, Bertha.[76] The union was never a happy one, perhaps because Bertha struggled with infertility for nearly a decade before giving Philip a male heir (the future Louis VI) in 1081. Two more children (both girls) eventually followed, but soon it became clear that the Queen was now barren. In 1092, the King left her for Bertrade of Montfort, the wife of Fulk of Anjou, whom Philip met while touring the region. Not only was Bertrade still reasonably young and therefore likely fertile, she also was descended from a family that wielded tremendous power in the Capetian heartland.[77] From both a dynastic and political perspective, therefore, she was an ideal match for the King. Thus, with the blessing and assistance of an obliging bishop, the King married Bertrade before an audience of leading French bishops.[78] However, while Philip was ultimately reconciled with Fulk, the King's refusal to take back Bertha was unacceptable to Pope Urban II. Philip and Bertrade were excommunicated on three separate occasions: by the papal legate Hugh of Die in 1094, by Urban in 1095, and then again by the papal legate John in 1099.[79] It is the first two of these that concern the present discussion, since they rendered Philip canonically ineligible to join the First Crusade. Scholars have used this point to form a stock narrative about the French King's failure to participate and Urban's decision to avoid carefully the royal principality on his preaching tour of France between November 1095 and July 1096.[80] Their argument is that the rift between King and Pope was yet another manifestation of the larger battle between the papacy and secular powers. It is true that Philip did not want to take the cross in the first place, and was probably more than happy to be rid of troublesome nobles for an extended period and to reap the political benefits that came from providing departing crusaders with cash in exchange for territory.[81] Indeed, no European rulers joined the First Crusade, probably believing, as Jay Rubenstein put it, that the entire 'plan was insane'.[82]

But absence from the expedition does not prove disinterest in the crusade and we must be careful to keep the two points distinct.[83] The biggest flaw with this line of reasoning is that it fails to recognize that for very different reasons neither Philip nor Urban could afford to give the other any room to manoeuvre. From the King's point of view, there were major political complications that prevented him from repudiating Bertrade and returning to Bertha as the Pope wished. In addition to the Queen's aforementioned inability to conceive, Philip may genuinely have preferred Bertrade. Magnifying this point was the fact that these events were playing out at precisely the time when Philip was engaged in a war against William Rufus who, as Suger reminds us, aspired to the French throne.[84] Thus, Philip needed to make sure that he could produce more sons (in case Louis died) and he also needed to ensure that his children with Bertrade were legitimate. For this reason Philip and the French bishops worked hard to ensure that Bertrade was recognized as the French Queen (by his subjects if not the Pope) and not merely as a concubine.[85] For his part, Urban could not allow any leeway for the king either. To be sure, had the Pope wished to annul Philip's union with Bertha, there was clear precedent for doing so. After all, medieval popes were not strangers to annulling the marriages of Europe's nobility, and Bertha and Philip were related within the prohibited degrees, as were Fulk and Bertrade.[86] What made the circumstance different in 1095 was that the crusade was on the horizon, which, in the words of Marcus Bull, 'was the brainchild of an assertive reformist papacy' that was still recovering from doing battle with the German Emperor.[87] Thus, kings or emperors, while probably not interested in participating anyway, were nonetheless most unwelcome from the perspective of the Pope.

Although political circumstances and his excommunication obliged Philip's direct exclusion from participating in the expedition, there is reason to believe that he directed events from the background, playing a key role in coordinating the northern French response to Urban's appeal. According to Guibert of Nogent, writing around 1108, Philip and his brother Hugh of Vermandois jointly hosted a meeting of leading French magnates at Paris in early February 1096 – just three months after Urban's Clermont sermon – to discuss their participation in the upcoming expedition.[88] Guibert is vague in identifying who was present at this meeting, but three of Philip's household officers – Guy the Red, Wallo II of Chamont-en-Vexin, and Gilbert Payen of Garlande – were likely on hand, since they ultimately joined the French host. Bull has speculated further, on the basis of the routes taken to the East by other leading French nobles, that Stephen of Blois, Robert of Normandy, and Robert of Flanders were either participants in this meeting or at least aware of it, which strengthens the case for Philip's oversight in coordinating the northern French crusaders.[89] It also means that Philip had influence over the early plans of some of the most important crusaders from Northern Europe. While the king could not go himself for reasons stated above, he did lobby hard for his brother to serve as his representative in the East. In 1096, Philip announced Hugh's acceptance of the crusading vow to Urban at the Council of Nîmes.[90] According to the Byzantine chronicler Anna Comnena, Hugh carried with him a papal banner, almost certainly a *vexillum beati Petri* given to him by the Pope.[91] Guibert of Nogent notes that Hugh was sent to Constantinople ahead of the main force to negotiate with the Greek Emperor, the assumption being that his royal birth made him a de facto leader of the crusade. Anna also records a letter that Hugh allegedly sent to the Byzantine Emperor demanding a 'magnificent reception' upon his arrival in Constantinople because of his royal status.[92] No western source mentions such a letter, and we must doubt whether it ever existed. However, what is important is that Anna's reference makes plain that Hugh's royal identity was well known, presumably because he was trading on his brother's political capital.

Philip obviously had a clear interest in the details and progression of the First Crusade and ensured that a close family member would be a leader of the expedition. In a sense, therefore, Philip was hedging his bets in case Urban's gamble paid off and the crusaders were successful. They were, of course, but Philip's wager did not pay off, because Hugh was hardly an ideal crusader. While Hugh's name appears in the major crusade narrative chronicles, this is more because of his royal status than for any specific accomplishments. The eyewitness *Gesta Francorum*, for example, names Hugh seven times, almost always in a list of crusaders, suggesting that the royal brother was important because of his status but played a secondary role among the expedition's leaders.[93] One event that draws significant attention is Hugh's departure from the Christian army in July 1098, following the siege of Antioch. Along with Count Baldwin of Hainault, Hugh was sent to Constantinople as an envoy to meet with Alexius. The sources are not clear on the purpose of the trip – the two men were either chiding Alexius for his failure to support the crusaders or urging him finally to join the army – but this is of secondary importance.[94] At some point during their journey, Turkish or Turkopole marauders attacked them. Baldwin disappeared (presumably killed), and Hugh ultimately arrived safely in Constantinople. This harrowing experience (on top of the dire nature of the situation at Antioch) apparently frayed his nerves and he decided to return home to France rather than rejoin his fellow crusaders at Antioch. The sources are not in agreement on the details of Hugh's departure, though there is some reason to believe that he was seen as bearing the stain of cowardice. Moreover, Hugh's eagerness to join the ill-fated crusade of 1101 suggests that he was concerned about the stigma of failure. Hugh's wife, Adela, made a donation to the abbey of Saint-Arnoul in Crépy in 1118, and the fact that she highlighted Hugh's participation in the 1101 expedition without any mention of the more famous 1096–99 crusade underscores this point.[95]

Considering Hugh's public desertion of the crusading host and his close relationship to the King in the years leading up to the First Crusade, it is possible that Philip was a factor in Hugh's decision to head back to the East in 1101, as a way of staving off negative publicity for the royal court. Indeed, we have already seen how, at the turn of the twelfth century, heroic deeds were one of the main factors in establishing one's prestige and authority. The converse also held true, of course, and when Hugh returned to France after deserting the crusading army, he did so under a cloud of shame, which, by extension, hung over the royal house. Hugh was, after all, Philip's closest crusader relative, and had played a key role in governing France before his departure in 1096.[96] It may be helpful here to compare Hugh's case to that of Stephen of Blois, the well-known deserter whom Orderic Vitalis described as an 'object of contempt' for his abandonment of his fellow crusaders at Antioch.[97] So badly was Stephen treated that he ultimately returned to the East in 1101 at the insistence of his wife, Adela of Blois, lest he bring dishonour to his family.[98] Although the parallel is not exact, the basic narrative is instructive: as the story of the miraculous capture of Jerusalem began spreading across Europe in the autumn of 1099, there is reason to suspect that Philip and those who functioned in his immediate orbit were troubled over the juxtaposition of the crusade's success and the failure of the royal contingent. Given this, the important questions to ask are: what was the response, where did it originate, and who initiated it? The answer is that early efforts to sanitize the Capetian crusading experience came in various forms and from a number of places, both inside and outside the royal court.

Internally, Philip made a concerted effort to link his relatives by marriage with well-known crusaders and their families. As previously discussed, Philip married off two of his daughters to the Norman crusading heroes Bohemond and Tancred. In 1104, after Guy the Red returned from 'the expedition to Jerusalem renowned and rich ... [Philip] soon persuaded [Louis] to take the daughter [Lucienne] of the count in solemn marriage'.[99] Suger wrote that this marriage resulted from the growing friendship between Philip and Guy that blossomed after the former's return from the East, hinting that Guy's crusading experience was the key factor in Philip's willingness to agree to the proposed nuptials.[100] Guy Trousseau, who participated in both the 1099 and 1101 expeditions, convinced the King to agree to a union between his daughter, Elisabeth, and Count Philip of Mantes, second in line to the French throne after Prince Louis.[101] Between 1104 and 1106 four of the King's five surviving children married either First Crusade veterans or their daughters. These were significant departures from the typical French royal marriage pattern, bespeaking deliberate attempts on the part of the royal court to link the Capetians with crusading prestige.

While members of the royal court were arranging marriage alliances with crusaders, various crusade chroniclers also sought to mitigate the stigma of Hugh's desertion and Philip's failure to participate, though for different reasons.[102] Of particular relevance to a consideration of the French royal court are those texts composed within the *loci* of Capetian power. Between about 1106 and 1110 several Benedictine monks from northern France – Robert the Monk, Baldric of Bourgueil, and Guibert of Nogent – revised and adapted the *Gesta Francorum*, a Norman text that was the most popular eyewitness narrative of the First Crusade, to fit better into a western European intellectual framework.[103] The author of the *Gesta* did not have the luxury of time to polish his text into a piece of exegetical writing. But monks had nothing if not an abundance of time, as well as the necessary scriptural knowledge. Because of their territorial and temporal proximity and shared common source, these 'second-generation' accounts are often considered part of a common genre of early-twelfth-century monastic crusading chronicles – what Jonathan Riley-Smith referred to as the 'theologically refined' version of the expedition. Scholars have long sought to work out the particular relationships among the texts, but in so doing have tended to flatten the individual characteristics of each.[104] Indeed, the fact that all three texts were copied from a common source allows for a rare glimpse into the minds of these monks by considering the additions and deletions made in each text, an approach that raises new questions about authorial motivation, textual composition, and, as we will see, monastic competition. In terms of the French court and the crusade, a close review of these texts reveals a keen interest in protecting the royal image.

Of the three chronicles, Robert the Monk's *Historia Iherosolimitana* is an excellent case study, having the distinction of being far and away the most popular in the Middle Ages, surviving in over eighty manuscripts scattered across France, Flanders, and Germany.[105] It is also the most useful for questions involving the royal court because Robert was a monk at 'a certain monastery of Saint-Remi' that had explicit connections to the Capetian family.[106] Until recently there has been general consensus that Robert completed his history no later than 1108, the terminus date assigned because of parallels between Robert's chronicle and a German text of that year, the *Magdeburger Aufruf*.[107] If the strong relationship between the texts is correct, then 1108 must indeed be so, but recent work by Marcus Bull and Damien Kempf has called this claim into question, citing the thinness of the argument for thematic and lexical borrowings from the *Historia Iherosolimitana*. As a consequence, it now seems likely that Robert's work was composed between about 1108 and 1110.[108] This is a crucial point because the relationship between the Capetian court and Saint-Remi changed dramatically in 1108, when Louis VI was crowned in Orléans, instead of the usual site at Reims, perhaps explaining Robert's motives for composing a text with a clear Capetian bias.

After learning of Philip's death, Louis and his advisors had to work fast to secure his position because, as Suger notes, 'a conspiracy of wicked and evil men would have excluded him from it had it been possible'. As a result, at the strong urging of Ivo of Chartres, Louis did not make the trip to Reims, but rather was crowned at Orléans. The Archbishop of Reims was not pleased, and sent several letters of objection to the Pope asserting the illegitimacy of the coronation and reasserting Hincmar's claim that Reims was the only legitimate site of the ceremony. Indeed, the matter was ultimately settled only by the careful diplomatic assuaging of Ivo of Chartres, who recognized Reims's claims, but argued for the legitimacy of the 1108 ceremony on the grounds that it was performed 'for the common good'.[109] Nevertheless, this instance is important because it bears witness to the seriousness with which the religious officials at Reims took their connection to the royal family and the reluctance with which they accepted even the appearance of challenges to that relationship. It is worth considering Robert the Monk's chronicle in the context of the strained complexion of the relationship between the Capetians and Saint-Remi in 1108.

The fact that Robert's text is fundamentally based on the *Gesta Francorum* makes it especially valuable, since it is possible to consider in great detail what changes he made to the eyewitness account, either by deletion or addition. Although the author of the *Gesta Francorum* remains unknown, the text has a clear Norman bias, the overall impact being to enhance and celebrate Bohemond's role on the expedition. Thus, the author's interest in crusaders from the Ile-de-France is limited to those of some renown. Nevertheless, when describing the difficult days at Antioch, the *Gesta* does include a list of several French crusaders who fled the host: 'William of Grandmesnil, his brother Aubré, Guy Trousseau, and Lambert the Poor'.[110] Given the context, the list of names is not essential to advance the narrative, and thus, the most likely reason for the author's decision to include it was to highlight the terrible conditions, making Bohemond's role stand out as a shining example of bravery and heroism. It is worth noting that three of the four are absent from Robert's chronicle, a deliberate omission without question. When the *Gesta* began circulating around northern France in the early twelfth century, passages that negatively portrayed crusaders from that region – such as Guy Trousseau, who at this very time was arranging to marry his daughter to the King's son – were most unwelcome. Therefore, Robert attempted to mitigate the negative reputation of the deserting crusaders by deleting their names. This is a small example, to be sure, but it is an excellent point of entry into the textual changes that Robert made to the base narrative of the *Gesta Francorum* in his endeavour to sanitize the Capetian image.

While Robert could simply delete the list of French knights who fled from Antioch because most people would not notice the absence of four seemingly unimportant knights, he faced a more difficult challenge with the desertion of Hugh of Vermandois.[111] By virtue of his royal status, Hugh was too prominent a figure to leave out of the chronicle, and his shameful return to the East in 1101 was well known among a French audience.[112] Faced with such a prospect, Robert effectively reworked the narrative of the crusade to cast Hugh as a genuine hero, one on a par with Godfrey of Bouillon and even Bohemond. Specifically, where the *Gesta* glossed over Hugh's royal status, Robert is careful to place Hugh into just such a context. In his description of Bohemond receiving news of the crusade Robert wrote that Bohemond 'was told by his sources about the princes: Hugh the Great, brother of King Philip of France'.[113] Of course, this does not equate to writing a royal version of the First Crusade, and one must allow for the fact that Robert was writing in northern France and would have been more likely to go into detail about local crusaders. But the fact that Hugh's royal status is inserted into Robert's text on four separate occasions, and that the corresponding passages in the *Gesta* make no such reference, is a clear indication of the author's desire to bolster Hugh's leadership role on the crusade in every way possible.

More telling is the way in which Robert reworked a story from the *Gesta Francorum* that described a prophecy made by the mother of Kerboga, the Turkish governor of Mosul. She told her son, who at the moment was planning an attack on the Christians at Antioch, that if he fought against the crusaders he would be defeated. In an effort to understand his situation more fully, Kerboga questioned his mother on various points about the Christian faith. 'Are not Bohemond and Tancred the gods of the Franks?', he asked in the *Gesta Francorum*.[114] Robert made a slight but crucial alteration: 'Are Hugh the standard-bearer and the Apulian Bohemond, and the Knight Godfrey [of Bouillon] their gods?'.[115] The substitution of Hugh's name for Tancred's is a clear attempt to associate the King's brother with two genuine, proven heroes of the crusade. By the time Robert was writing,

Bohemond and Godfrey were the best-known crusaders. It is also worth remembering that Robert wrote just about four years after Bohemond had married Constance, a time when establishing a textual connection to the Norman hero would have been viewed by the royal court in a positive light. It was also a time, as we saw, that clerics at Reims were working hard to ensure the preservation of the coronation rite for their city. And thus, this passage, which joined together in battle the King's uncle and his brother-in-law, would have resonated powerfully with a northern French audience, and perhaps won favour for the abbey at the royal court.

Portraying Hugh as a crusading hero was no easy task. His widely known desertion would have to be addressed. The *Gesta Francorum* had noted Hugh's departure in a single, short sentence: 'Hugh went but he never came back.'[116] Such a gloss is understandable from the *Gesta*'s author, who was predominantly interested in Norman crusaders. But Robert was writing in a location close to Hugh's domain with the clear purpose of sanitizing his crusading exploits. Thus, he could not ignore the royal brother's departure. Robert did not disappoint, writing that 'once Hugh had carried out his mission to the Emperor, he died unexpectedly and could not return at the end of his life as planned'.[117] Obviously, Hugh did not die on his mission to Constantinople and, given his heavy reliance on the testimony of returning crusaders, it is unlikely that Robert was simply uninformed about the fate of the brother of the French King. Rather, the evidence supports a claim that Robert knew of Hugh's return to France in 1098, knew of his actual death in 1102 while trying to fulfil his original vow, but altered his chronicle to blur these episodes. Indeed, Robert conflated Hugh's experience on the two expeditions with the goal of erasing his earlier failure.

Guibert of Nogent's history is worth briefly considering alongside Robert's because, unlike his contemporary from Saint-Remi, Guibert was not a member of a community with an explicit connection to the royal house. In fact, Guibert displayed a marked disfavour toward the Capetians on several occasions.[118] Moreover, that he was so emphatic in noting that much of his information was gathered from returning crusaders suggests that the stories that appear in the *Dei gesta per Francos* reflect the sort of crusading lore circulating around northeastern France in the first decade of the twelfth century.[119] As noted earlier, when he discussed the background to the crusade, Guibert carefully couched the expedition in terms of French history, transforming Bohemond's Norman background into a French one to accomplish this task.[120] In terms of context, it should be noted that Guibert's chronicle was written shortly after Bohemond's

1106 marriage to Constance (probably around 1108), when writing about a French connection to a crusading hero would have been popular in northern France. Furthermore, if Guibert's portrayal of Bohemond is placed alongside his treatment of key members of the royal court, in fact, a manifest interest in northern French crusaders is clear. Like Robert, Guibert went out of his way to highlight Hugh of Vermandois's royal ancestry when he noted that Hugh's arrest in Dyrrachium at the beginning of the crusade was the result of his princely status.[121] However, the most telling part of Guibert's text is his description of Hugh's departure from the East, which he attributed to illness: 'who could claim that Count Stephen and Hugh the Great, who had always been honourable, because they had seemed to retreat for this reason [illness] were comparable to those who had always behaved badly?'.[122] Guibert wrote his narrative after Hugh had returned to the East as one of the leaders of the 1101 crusade, and separating Hugh from other deserters probably contributed to the redemption of Hugh's image that occurred throughout the twelfth century.

Each chronicler who undertook to produce a sanitized narrative of the First Crusade did so for different reasons, though probably they all hoped to secure a long-term position of favour for their abbey. But in the short term these chronicles bear witness to a more dramatic point: there was a widespread recognition among a group outside the royal court that the Capetian image was threatened by the King's failure to crusade. One might assert that the position of the French King in the first decade of the twelfth century was not as weak as this argument assumes, and that the French monarchy was on the precipice of a great leap forward in terms of its ability to project power. The reign of Louis VI would come to be remembered as a period of marked increase in the fortunes of the French monarchy, but this is not the point. However, the issue at hand is less one of fact – was the French King weak in 1100 and was his position about to improve? – and more one of perception – did the French King and those surrounding him believe that he was threatened? All the evidence marshalled above points to an affirmative answer to the latter question. The die was cast, linking crusading prestige with rulership and power. Soon enough, a deliberate effort to shape the crusading memory of the Capetians would begin from within the court itself, under the leadership of Abbot Suger of Saint-Denis.

### Notes

1 OV, Vol. VI, pp. 46–50; *VLG*, pp. 46–50; *Actes*, Vol. I, p. 43, no. 22.
2 Ralph B. Yewdale, *Bohemond I, Prince of Antioch* (Princeton, 1924), pp. 3–39.

3  *Archives d'Anjou: Recueil de documents et mémoires inédits sur cette province*, ed. Paul A. Marchegay, 3 vols (Angers, 1843-54), Vol. III, p. 242, no. 396. See also Nicholas L. Paul, 'A Warlord's Wisdom: Literacy and Propaganda at the Time of the First Crusade', *Speculum* 85 (2010), 534-66.
4  OV, Vol. VI, p. 68.
5  *Ibid.*, Vol. VI, p. 70.
6  'Historia belli sacri', in *RHC Oc.*, Vol. III, p. 206.
7  Paul, *To Follow in Their Footsteps*, pp. 90-133.
8  Albert Poncelet, 'Boémond et S. Léonard', *Analecta Bollandiana* 31 (1912), 24-44.
9  'Vita et miracula S. Leonardi auctore Waleramno Episcopo Namburgensi', *Acta sanctorum*, ed. Jean Bolland, Jean Carnedet, *et al.* (Paris, 1863, repr. Brussels, 1965),.*Novembris*, Vol. III (Paris, 1863), pp. 178-82, portion concerning Bohemond, pp. 173-82; William of Malmesbury, *Gesta regum anglorum: The History of the English Kings*, ed. and trans. R. A. B. Mynors, completed by Rodney M. Thomson and Michael Winterbottom (Oxford, 1998), p. 693. For Bohemond's itinerary in the West see Luigi Russo, 'Il viaggio di Boemundo d'Altavilla in Francia', *Archivio storico Italiano* 603 (2005), 3-42.
10  Yvonne Friedman, 'Miracle, Meaning, and Narrative in the Latin East', *Studies in Church History* 41 (2005), 123-34.
11  *VLG*, pp. 46-50.
12  John G. Rowe, 'Bohemond of Antioch, Paschal II, and the Byzantine Empire', *Bulletin of the John Rylands Library* 49 (1966-67), 165-202.
13  OV, Vol. VI, pp. 70-1.
14  David Crouch, *The Birth of Nobility: Constructing Aristocracy in England and France, c. 900-c. 1300* (London, 2005), pp. 30-7; Richard E. Barton, 'Aristocratic Culture: Kinship, Chivalry, and Court Culture', in *A Companion to the Medieval World*, ed. Carol Lansing and Edward English (Malden, MA, 2009), pp. 500-24 (pp. 504-11). It is helpful to consider this alongside Victor Turner's concept of 'root paradigms'; see Victor Turner, *Dramas, Fields, and Metaphors: Symbolic Action in Human Society* (Ithaca, NY, 1974); Victor Turner, 'Process, System and Symbol', *Daedalus* 106 (1977), 61-80.
15  Jonathan Riley-Smith, *The First Crusaders, 1095-1131* (Cambridge, 1997), map 4 and pp. 239-42.
16  See above, pp. 7-8.
17  See above, pp. 17-19.
18  Michael E. Moore, *A Sacred Kingdom: Bishops and the Rise of Frankish Kingdoms, 300-850* (Washington, DC, 2011), pp. 1-2. Consider for example the influence of Max Weber. See Pierre Clastres, *Society against the State*, trans. Robert Hurley (New York, 1989), pp. 7-13; Jean-William Lapierre, *Essai sur le fondement du pouvoir politique* (Aix-en-Provence, 1968). For alternative perspective consider Søren Kierkegaard, *Papers and Journals: A Selection*, trans. Alastair Hannay (London, 1996), esp. p. 235.
19  Matthew Gabriele, *An Empire of Memory: The Legend of Charlemagne, the Franks, and Jerusalem before the First Crusade* (Oxford, 2011), pp. 102-6 and 114-15. See also Janet T. Nelson, 'Charlemagne and Empire', in *The Long Morning of Medieval*

*Europe: New Directions in Early Medieval Studies*, ed. Jennifer R. Davis and Michael McCormick (Burlington, VT, 2008), pp. 223–34 (p. 232).

20 Geoffrey Koziol, *The Politics of Memory and Identity in Carolingian Royal Diplomas: The West Frankish Kingdom (840–987)* (Turnhout, 2012), pp. 560–1.

21 Karl-Ferdinand Werner, 'Das hochmittelalterliche Imperium im politischen Bewusstsein Frankreichs (10.–12. Jahrhundert)', *Historische Zeitschrift* 200 (1965), 1–160 (pp. 14–18); Gabriele, *An Empire of Memory*, p. 158; Marcus Bull, 'Overlapping and Competing Identities in the Frankish First Crusade', in *Concile de Clermont de 1095 et l'appel à Croisade: Actes du Colloque Universitaire International de Clermont-Ferrand (23–25 juin 1995) organisé et publié avec le concours du Conseil Régional d'Auvergne* (Rome, 1997), pp. 195–211.

22 RM, p. 6.

23 GN, pp. 88–9.

24 Bull, 'The Capetian Monarchy'; James Naus, 'The French Royal Court and the Memory of the First Crusade', *NMS* 55 (2011), 49–78; Jay Rubenstein, 'Putting History to Use: Three Crusade Chronicles in Context', *Viator* 35 (2004), 131–68.

25 Fulcher of Chartres, *Historia Hierosolymitana: Mit Erläuterungen und einem Anhange*, ed. Hans Hagenmeyer (Heidelberg, 1913), p. 168; *Die Kreuzzugsbriefe aus den Jahren 1088–1100*, ed. Hans Hagenmeyer (Innsbruck, 1901), p. 160; both cited in Elizabeth Siberry, *Criticism of Crusading, 1095–1274* (Oxford, 1985), p. 47. See also James Brundage, 'The Army of the First Crusade and the Crusade Vow: Some Reflections on a Recent Book', *Medieval Studies* 33 (1971), 334–44; and James Brundage, 'An Errant Crusader: Stephen of Blois', *Traditio* 16 (1960), 380–95.

26 Nicholas Paul, 'Crusade, Memory, and Regional Politics in Twelfth-Century Amboise', *JMS* 31 (2005), 127–141, esp. p. 139.

27 *VLG*, pp. 128–30.

28 Marcus Bull, *Knightly Piety and the Lay Response to the First Crusade: The Limousin and Gascony, c. 970–1130* (Oxford, 1993), pp. 250–81. On the martial elements of French kingship see Régine Le Jan, 'La sacralité de la royauté mérovingienne', *Annales: Histoire, Sciences Sociales* 58 (2003), 1217–41.

29 Bisson, *The Crisis of the Twelfth Century*, p. 2.

30 *Ibid.*, pp. 2–21.

31 *VLG*, p. 48.

32 *Ibid.*, p. 44.

33 Andrew W. Lewis, *Royal Succession in Capetian France: Studies on Familial Order and the State* (Cambridge, MA, 1981), pp. 44–77; Andrew W. Lewis, 'Anticipatory Association of the Heir in Early Capetian France', *American Historical Review* 83 (1978), 906–27.

34 OV, Vol. IV, pp. 264–5; *VLG*, p. 48. James Doherty has recently completed a Ph.D. thesis at Lancaster University on 'Count Hugh of Troyes and the Early Crusading Era'. Unfortunately, I was not able to consult this work before submitting this manuscript for publication.

35 Jan Dhondt, 'Sept femmes et un trio de rois', *Contributions à l'histoire économique et sociale* 3 (1964–65), 37–70 (53–5); Lewis, *Royal Succession*, p. 45.

36 *Recueil des actes de Philippe Ier*, pp. xvi–xxiii.
37 Jean Flori, *Bohémond d'Antioche: Chevalier d'aventure* (Paris, 2007), pp. 266–7.
38 GN, p. 106.
39 OV, Vol. IV, pp. 264–5; 'Historia regum Francorum monasterii sancti Dionysii', *MGH SS* 9, pp. 395–406 (p. 405); William of Tyre, *Chronicon*, ed. R. B. C. Huygens, 2 vols, *CCCM* 63 and 63A (Turnhout, 1986), Vol. I, p. 495.
40 *VLG*, pp. 38–40; Albert of Aachen, *Historia Ierosolimitana: History of the Journey to Jerusalem*, ed. and trans. Susan B. Edgington (Oxford, 2007), p. 614.
41 *La chronique de Morigny 1095–1152*, ed. Léon Mirot, 2nd edn (Paris, 1912), pp. 40–1.
42 Eric Bournazel, *Le gouvernement capétien au XIIe siècle 1108–1180: Structures sociales et mutations institutionelles* (Paris, 1975), pp. 31–4; Augustin Fliche, *Le règne de Philippe 1er, roi de France (1060–1108)* (Paris, 1912), pp. 320–3.
43 *VLG*, pp. 39–41.
44 Riley-Smith, *The First Crusaders*, pp. 144–88. Guy of Rochefort's nephew, Guy Trousseau, arranged a marriage between his daughter Elisabeth and Count Philip, the French King's youngest son. See OV, Vol. V, pp. 30 and 98; *VLG*, p. 36.
45 'Narratio quomodo reliquiae martyris Georgii ad nos Aquicinenses pervenerunt', *RHC Occ.*, Vol. V, pp. 248–52 (p. 251); 'Annales Aquicinctini', *MGH SS* 16, pp. 503–6.
46 Nicholas Paul has identified a number of charters, produced between 1100 and the Count's death in 1111, that make manifest reference to his experience in the East. See Paul, *To Follow in Their Footsteps*, p. 41.
47 OV, Vol. VI, p. 394.
48 Jean Laureau, 'Les seigneurs du Puiset à la Croisade', *Bulletin de la Société archéologique d'Eure-et-Loire* 62 (1999), 23–35; John L. LaMonte, 'The Lords of le Puiset on Crusade', *Speculum* 17 (1942), 100–18.
49 *La chanson d'Antioch*, ed. Susanne Duparc-Quioc (Paris, 1976), pp. 171 and 450; Albert of Aachen, *Historia Ierosolimitana*, p. 96.
50 Susanne Duparc-Quioc, *Le cycle de la croisade* (Paris, 1955), pp. 39–44.
51 Paul, *To Follow in Their Footsteps*, p. 148.
52 On French political transformation more generally see Poly and Bournazel, *The Feudal Transformation*; Achille Luchaire, *Histoire des institututions monarchiques de la France sous les premiers Capétiens (987–1180)* (Brussels, 1964); Robert Fawtier, *The Capetian Kings of France: Monarchy and Nation, 987–1328*, trans. Lionel Butler and R. J. Adam (London, 1960); Dominique Barthélemy, *L'ordre seigneurial: Xie–XIIe siècle* (Paris, 1990); Strayer, *On the Medieval Origins of the Modern State*; Bull, 'Introduction', in *France in the Central Middle Ages*, pp. 2–3.
53 Susan Twyman, *Papal Ceremonial at Rome in the Twelfth Century* (London, 2002), pp. 1–22; Kathleen Ashley, 'Introduction: The Moving Subjects of Processional Performance', in *Moving Subjects: Processional Performance in the Middle Ages and the Renaissance*, ed. Kathleen Ashley and Wim Hüsken (Amsterdam, 2001), pp. 7–24; Karl Leyser, *Rule and Conflict in Early Medieval Society: Ottonian Saxony* (Bloomington, 1979), pp. 94–105; Clifford Geertz, 'Centers, Kings, and Charisma: Reflections on the Symbolics of Power', in *Local Knowledge: Further Essays in Interpretive Anthropology* (New York, 1983), pp. 121–46.

54 Twyman, *Papal Ceremonial*, pp. 13–18; Michael McCormack, *Eternal Victory: Triumphal Rulership in Late Antiquity, Byzantium and the Early Medieval West* (Cambridge, 1990); Geoffrey Koziol, *Begging Pardon and Favor: Ritual and Political Order in Early Medieval France* (Ithaca, NY, 1992), pp. 289–324; Ernst Kantorowicz, 'The King's Advent and the Enigmatic Panels in the Doors of Santa Sabina', *Art Bulletin* 26 (1944), 207–31 (pp. 215–16).
55 Norman Anonymous, *Tractates*, ed. Heinrich Böhmer, in *MGH Libelli de lite* 3, pp. 642–87 (p. 667). Cited and discussed in Ernst Kantorowicz, *The King's Two Bodies: A Study in Medieval Political Theology* (Princeton, 1981), pp. 42–61.
56 Roger Collins, *Charlemagne* (Toronto, 1998), pp. 43–101.
57 For a review of the critical texts involved in this tradition see Gabriele, *An Empire of Memory*, Chapter 2, pp. 41–70.
58 'Annales Laureshamenses', *MGH SS* 1, pp. 22–32 (p. 35).
59 OV, Vol. VI, pp. 70–1.
60 Ralph of Caen, 'Gesta Tancredi', *RHC Oc.* 3, pp. 587–716 (p. 714); OV, Vol. V, pp. 170–1. Also see Riley-Smith, *The First Crusaders*, pp. 78–80.
61 Geoffrey Koziol, 'England, France, and the Problem of Sacrality in Twelfth-Century Ritual', in *Cultures of Power: Lordship, Status, and Process in Twelfth-Century Europe*, ed. Thomas N. Bisson (Philadelphia, 1995), pp. 124–48; Bernhard Töpfer, 'Tendenzen zur Entsakralisierung der Herrscherwürde in der Zeit des Investiturstreites', *Jahrbuch für Geschichte des Feudalismus* 6 (1982), 164–71.
62 Koziol, 'England, France, and the Problem of Sacrality', pp. 125–6; Ernst Kantorowicz, *Laudes regiae: A Study in Liturgical Acclamations and Medieval Ruler Worship* (Berkeley, 1946); H. E. J. Cowdrey, 'The Anglo-Norman *Laudes regiae*', *Viator* 12 (1981), 39–78.
63 Koziol, *Begging Pardon and Favor*, pp. 133–4. This should be read alongside Philippe Buc, *The Dangers of Ritual: Between Early Medieval Texts and Social Scientific Theory* (Princeton, 2001); Geoffrey Koziol, 'The Dangers of Polemic: Is Ritual Still an Interesting Topic of Historical Study?', *Early Medieval Europe* 11 (2002), 367–88; Philippe Buc, 'The Monastery and the Critics: A Ritual Reply', *Early Medieval Europe* 15 (2007), 441–54.
64 Bisson, *The Crisis of the Twelfth Century*, pp. 1–21.
65 RM, p. 4.
66 *Ibid.*, p. 6.
67 GN, p. 328.
68 Hugh of Fleury, *Liber qui modernorum regum Francorum continet actus*, ed. Georg Waitz, *MGH SS* 9, pp. 376–95.
69 *Die Briefe Heinrichs IV*, ed. Carl Erdman, *MGH Deutsches Mittelalter* (Leipzig, 1937), pp. 39–40. Discussed in Ian S. Robinson, *Henry IV of Germany, 1056–1106* (Cambridge, 1999), pp. 109–10.
70 William M. Aird, *Robert Curthose, Duke of Normandy (1054–1134)* (Woodbridge, 2008), pp. 191–202. For the possibility of an *adventus* ceremony at Rouen see OV, Vol. V, pp. 300–1, cited in Aird, *Robert Curthose*.
71 Cited in Christopher Tyerman, *England and the Crusades, 1096–1588* (Chicago, 1988), p. 23.

72 William of Malmesbury, *Gesta regum anglorum*, p. 703.
73 *Ibid.* Cited and discussed in Tyerman, *England and the Crusades*, pp. 22-3.
74 Henry of Huntingdon, *Historia Anglorum: The History of the English People*, ed. and trans. Diana Greenway (Oxford, 1996), p. 454.
75 *Ibid.*
76 Fliche, *Le règne de Philippe 1er*, pp. 36-77.
77 George Duby, *Medieval Marriage: Two Models from Twelfth-Century France*, trans. Elborg Forster (Baltimore, 1978), pp. 28-45.
78 *Ibid.*; Marie-Bernadette Bruguière, 'Canon Law and Royal Weddings, Theory and Practice: The French Example, 987-1215', in *Proceedings of the Eighth International Congress of Medieval Canon Law*, ed. Stanley Chodorow (Vatican, 1992), pp. 473-96.
79 Duby, *Medieval Marriage*, p. 30; *Sacrorum conciliorum nova, et amplissima collectio*, ed. J. D. Mansi, 55 vols (Paris, 1901-27), Vol. XX, p. 815; Robert Sommerville, 'The French Councils of Pope Urban II: Some Basic Considerations', *Annuarium historiae conciliorum* 2 (1970), 98-114; Augustine Fliche, 'Urbain II et la croisade', *Revue d'histoire de l'Eglise de France* 13 (1927), 289-306 (p. 300).
80 For Urban's itinerary see Alfons Becker, *Papst Urban II. (1088-1099)*, 2 vols (Stuttgart, 1964-88), Vol. II, pp. 435-58.
81 Christopher K. Gardner, 'The Capetian Presence in Berry as a Consequence of the First Crusade', in *Autour de la Première Croisade: Actes du colloque de la Society for the Study of the Crusades and the Latin East (Clermont-Ferrand, 22-25 juin 1995)*, ed. Michel Balard (Paris, 1996), pp. 71-81 (pp. 75-6).
82 Jay Rubenstein, *Armies of Heaven: The First Crusade and the Quest for Apocalypse* (New York, 2011), p. 21.
83 For conceptualization of this idea see Vincent Ryan, 'Richard I and the Early Evolution of the Fourth Crusade', in *The Fourth Crusade: Events, Aftermath, and Perceptions*, ed. Thomas F. Madden (Aldershot, 2008), pp. 3-14.
84 *VLG*, p. 10.
85 In practice this meant that Philip ensured the proper rituals were followed in the marriage, including the gift of a dowry and the celebration by the Bishop of Senlis. Duby, *Medieval Marriage*, p. 38.
86 Bruguière, 'Canon Law and Royal Weddings, Theory and Practice'.
87 Bull, 'The Capetian Monarchy', p. 26; Carl Erdmann, *The Origin of the Idea of Crusade*, trans. Walter Goffart and Marshall W. Baldwin (Princeton, 1977); Ian S. Robinson, 'Gregory VII and the Soldiers of Christ', *History* 58 (1973), 169-92; H. E. J. Cowdrey, 'The Genesis of the Crusades: The Springs of Western Ideas of Holy War', in *The Holy War*, ed. T. P. Murphy (Columbus, OH, 1976), pp. 9-32 (pp. 17-21).
88 *GN*, pp. 133-4; Bull, 'The Capetian Monarchy', 33-5; Matthew Gabriele, 'The Provenance of the *Descriptio qualiter Karolus Magnus*: Remembering the Carolingians in the Entourage of King Philip I (1060-1108) before the First Crusade', *Viator* 39 (2008), 93-117 (pp. 113-16).
89 Bull, 'The Capetian Monarchy', 34.

90 *Sacrorum conciliorum nova*, Vol. XX, p. 937; *La chronique de Saint-Maixent*, ed. and trans. Jean Verdon (Paris, 1979), p. 154.
91 Erdmann, *The Origin of the Idea of Crusade*, pp. 182–200.
92 Anna Comnena, *The Alexiad*, trans. E. R. A. Sewter (Baltimore, 1969), pp. 313–14.
93 *GF*, pp. 5, 18, 19, 20, 68, 70, and 72.
94 Cf. Albert of Aachen, *Historia Ierosolimitana*, pp. 340–2; *GF*, p. 72.
95 *Gallia Christiana in provincias ecclesiasticas distributa*, ed. Scévole de Sainte-Marthe and Louis de Sainte-Marthe, 16 vols (Farnborough, 1970), Vol. X, appendix, pp. 424–5 n. 57.
96 'Annales S. Benigni Divionensis', *MGH SS* 7, pp. 37–50 (p. 42). Cited and discussed in Bull, 'The Capetian Monarchy', 31.
97 OV, Vol. V, pp. 324–5.
98 Brundage, 'An Errant Crusader', pp. 390–2.
99 *VLG*, pp. 39–41; Fliche, *Le régne de Philippe 1er*, p. 320 n. 4; Bournazel, *Le gouvernement capétien*, pp. 31–4 and 46.
100 *VLG*, pp. 39–41.
101 Bournazel, *Le gouvernement capétien*, pp. 31–4.
102 Jonathan Phillips provides a brief introduction to the First Crusade literature in his recent discussion of the years leading up to the Second Crusade. Jonathan Phillips, *The Second Crusade: Extending the Frontiers of Christendom* (New Haven, 2010), pp. 17–36. For an alternative approach to the texts see Jean Flori, *Chroniqueurs et propagandistes: Introduction critique aux sources de la première croisade* (Geneva, 2010).
103 Jonathan Riley-Smith, *The First Crusade and the Idea of Crusading* (Philadelphia, 1986), pp. 132–52; Susan Edgington, 'The First Crusade: Reviewing the Evidence', in *The First Crusade: Origins and Impact*, ed. Jonathan Phillips (Manchester, 1997), pp. 57–77.
104 John France, 'Use of the Anonymous *Gesta Francorum* in the Early Twelfth Century: Sources for the First Crusade', in *From Clermont to Jerusalem: The Crusades and Crusader Societies, 1095–1500*, ed. Alan V. Murray (Turnhout, 1998), pp. 29–42; Rubenstein, 'What Is the *Gesta Francorum*?'; France, 'The Anonymous *Gesta Francorum*'; Colin Morris, 'The *Gesta Francorum* as Narrative History', *Reading Medieval Studies* 19 (1993), 55–71; Kenneth B. Wolf, 'Crusade and Narrative: Bohemond and the *Gesta Francorum*', *JMH* 17 (1991), 207–16; Harari, 'Eyewitnessing in Accounts of the First Crusade'.
105 For manuscript identification see Friedrich Kraft, *Heinrich Steinhöwels Verdeutschung der 'Historia Hierosolymitana' des Robertus Monachus: Eine literarhistorische Untersuchung* (Strasbourg, 1905). Although Knoch identified more than 100 manuscripts, Damien Kempf and Marcus Bull have revised that number to 80, allowing for translations of manuscripts; RM, p. lxv. For discussion of the text see Carol Sweetenham, 'Introduction' to Robert the Monk, *Robert the Monk's History of the First Crusade: 'Historia Iherosolimitana'* (Aldershot, 2005), pp. 1–47; Edgington, 'The First Crusade'; Georg Marquardt, *Die 'Historia Hierosolymitana' des Robertus Monachus: Ein quellenkritischer Beitrag zur Geschichte des ersten Kreuzzugs* (Königsberg, 1892); Luigi Russo, 'Ricerche sull'

"*Historia Iherosolimitana*" di Roberto di Reims', *Studi medievali* 43 (2002), 651–91.
106 RM, p. 3.
107 Peter Knoch, 'Kreuzzug und Siedlung: Studien zum Aufruf der Magdeburger Kirche von 1108', *Jahrbuch für die Geschichte Mittel und Ostdeutschlands* 23 (1974), 1–33.
108 RM, pp. xvii–xli.
109 Hincmar of Reims, *Vita sanctii Remigii*, PL 125, cols 1129–88. It is also possible that Ralph the Green was particularly upset that the Archbishop of Sens was responsible for the coronation of Louis, as the two bishoprics had been at odds over the right of coronation for several centuries by this point.
110 *GF*, pp. 56–7.
111 For what follows see Bull, 'The Capetian Monarchy', 36–40.
112 As evidence of this, see a charter produced around 1100 at the abbey of Molesme in which a departing crusader describes his intention to follow Hugh to the East as part of the 1101 expedition. *Cartulaires de l'abbaye de Molesme*, ed. Jacques Laurent, 2 vols (Paris, 1907–11), Vol. II, p. 13, no. 7.
113 RM, p. 740.
114 *GF*, pp. 55–6.
115 RM, p. 813.
116 *GF*, p. 72.
117 RM, p. 837.
118 Jay Rubenstein, *Guibert of Nogent: Portrait of a Medieval Mind* (New York, 2002), pp. 87–95.
119 GN, p. 82. In fact, Guibert included several negative comments about Philip I and his relationship with the French Church. He was, for instance, the only one of the early-twelfth-century chroniclers to point out that Philip was excommunicated at the Council of Clermont, which certainly was not a move intended to ingratiate himself with the King. Guibert may well have disliked Philip, particularly his relationship with the Church, but the way that the monk treated members of the royal entourage shows that stories about these men were what people wanted to hear around 1108.
120 *Ibid.*, pp. 105–6.
121 *Ibid.*, p. 35.
122 *Ibid.*, p. 228.

# Part II

## Response

# 3

# Suger of Saint-Denis and the ideology of crusade

Around 1100 a monk at Fleury added new material to a much older manuscript.[1] The original manuscript – produced in the ninth century – contains an abbreviated version of Bede's *Chronica*, a popular text in the Carolingian period that recounted the Six Ages of the World beginning with Adam.[2] To that text, the monk added a genealogy of the French kings that attempted to link the present King (Philip I) back to Adam and the First Age of the World. The genealogy, which occupies a full three folios of the manuscript, employs a specific Latin formulation designed to highlight the legitimacy of the transfer of power from one king to another ('ab … usque …').

> When Adam was 130 years old he begot Seth …
> From Justinian to Pippin II
> From Louis [the last Carolingian] to Hugh [Capet]
> From Hugh to Robert
> From Robert to Henry
> From Henry to Philip[3]

The genealogy, of which this is a small excerpt, lists the Roman emperors, the Christian Latin emperors up to Justinian, and then jumps to Pippin II and the early Capetians. It is interesting that the Fleury genealogy omits the Robertian kings, moving directly from Charles the Fat to Charles the Simple, and then to Rudolf (thus skipping Odo of Paris and Robert I). It is unlikely that a monk at Fleury was simply unaware of these kings, since they had had a particularly close relationship to the monastery when they ruled.[4] A more likely explanation is that the monk knew about the illicit nature of the Robertian takeover and wanted to avoid highlighting it in the portion of a text manifestly dedicated to proving dynastic legitimacy. There is no question, the text seems to say, of the current King's legitimacy.

The production of genealogical literature decreased with the demise of the Carolingians, and was not revived until the late eleventh century. Georges Duby took this as evidence of the growing power of the aristocracy in this period, and he explained the comparative absence of French genealogical literature by arguing that the King circa 1100 did not have the need to prove his dynastic validity.[5] The Fleury text argues against this point, and its production in the year following the successful capture of Jerusalem by the first crusaders may help to explain its significance. As we saw in Chapter 2, at precisely the time this text was composed, the Capetian court was in a period of crisis. Philip I had not joined the First Crusade, and his brother Hugh had (in 1100) come home in shame, having deserted the crusading host and not yet returned as part of the crusade of 1101. Thus, after several hundred years of little interest in producing genealogical literature, it is highly significant that a monk at Fleury – a religious house that had for quite some time been concerned with the health of the Capetian image – was now producing a defensive text that, in effect, sought to prove through genealogy the sacred status of the Capetian kings.

It is, of course, not possible to know the impact this had at the royal court, though it is worth noting that Philip I violated a well established practice by choosing to be buried at Fleury rather than Saint-Denis, the traditional necropolis of the French kings.[6] This was no small matter, either. Elizabeth Hallam has demonstrated that the King's selection of his burial location and the accompanying funerary rites could bring tremendous prestige and real power to an abbey.[7] Thus, Philip's decision to be buried at Fleury caused quite a stir in French royal politics at the time. It helps explain why monks at Saint-Denis began jockeying to reassert their relationship with the French throne. And given the new connection between prestige and crusading, it is not surprising that this proved fertile ground on which to do so.

## Saint-Denis and the Capetian image

Scholars have long recognized that it was Suger, more than anybody else, who fashioned the Capetian image in the first half of the twelfth century. Part of this programme included moulding the Capetian image to generate currency in the new economy of crusading status. As we will see, this effort manifested itself in a seemingly paradoxical way, with Suger arguing in texts against the need to possess crusading virtues while, often in close proximity, attempting to attach precisely these attributes to his subject. It was as if he were trying to demonstrate that the French kings had the virtues of a crusader, while simultaneously making the case that such virtues were not that important. The contradiction can be reconciled if we approach the Abbot on his own terms, as a man trying to compete on behalf of his abbey in an ever-changing political world. One should not have to struggle too much with this paradox. Modern political candidates regularly employ the same sort of intellectual flexibility in pursuit of their electoral goals.

Above all else, Suger was a great negotiator of the contested space between an ideal vision of kingship and the realities of politics in the twelfth century. He was a practical thinker who promoted the King as a great leader and warrior not because, as some have suggested, he anticipated a modern vision of hierarchically ordered kingship, but because his beloved abbey of Saint-Denis had much to lose if the French kings could not compete in the twelfth-century power structure.[8] As the first chapter demonstrated, the abbey's fortunes were indivisibly tied to the strength of the royal court, and had been so since Merovingian times. That connection, however, had been strained since Philip I ascended the throne in 1060, when a host of other religious houses began competing for the favour of the King, and Saint-Denis was forced to find support elsewhere.[9] To many contemporaries it must have seemed as if Saint-Denis's influence on the French royal court was on the decline, particularly since Philip I displayed a marked disdain for the abbey. If judged by donations, then Fleury and Saint-Remi come out on top.[10] Philip also showed a keen interest in Compiègne, a religious house favoured by his Carolingian predecessors.[11] Among other things, he presided over the translation of the house's prized relic, the Shroud of Christ.[12] The important point to stress is that he disfavoured Saint-Denis, and as a result, throughout the late eleventh and early twelfth centuries, the abbey was forced to find support outside the Capetian-dominated Ile-de-France. Philip struck his most powerful blow to Dionysian prestige in 1108 when he decided to be buried at Fleury, becoming the first of the Capetian dynasty not to be interred at Saint-Denis.[13]

From this perspective, it is clear that Suger was not operating from a position of strength. In fact, it was just the opposite; he was anxious to protect his abbey from further loss, and worked to regain what was lost. It is, of course, difficult to measure with precision the impact of the deterioration of the relations with the Capetians, but some circumstantial evidence does exist. Later in his life, Suger recalled the poor state of the Dionysian holdings early in his career.[14] Suger's comments no doubt reflect his constant desire to celebrate his own achievements, but their veracity is partly supported by the above-referenced negative comments about the level of corruption in Abbot Adam's administration.[15] These are crucial episodes that demonstrate the magnitude of the challenge faced by Suger. Indeed, it was in the context of having to react constantly to perceived indignities against Saint-Denis's prestige that Suger dedicated his career to placing his abbey, as one scholar puts it, 'in a position of such (literally) monumental importance to the monarchy that it could never be dislodged'.[16]

The various practical manifestations of this are well known. At some point in the first decade of the twelfth century, the scriptorium at Saint-Denis began producing royal historiography in a new way and at an unprecedented rate.[17] This is best exemplified in the Abbot's histories of Louis VI and Louis VII. Suger also did much more. In the later part of his career, he embarked on a major renovation campaign at the basilica, incorporating elements of manifestly secular and royal meaning into the western façade of the church, including Roman triumphal arches, crenellated walls and towers, and statues of several of the Merovingian and Carolingian kings buried within.[18] He also commissioned a stained-glass window for the new basilica, which combined images of a French king leading an eastern expedition with depictions of Charlemagne's legendary exploits and actual scenes from the First Crusade, thus creating a master narrative of French crusading tradition (Figure 1).[19] Every aspect of his design and historiographical programme was designed to maximize the connection between abbey and court, hopefully drawing royal attention back to Saint-Denis and away from the competition. It so happened that one key way in which this was accomplished was to boost the Capetian crusading credentials.

In addition to crafting the historiographical and architectural crucible in which French kingship would be shaped for much of the central Middle Ages, Suger (and Adam, until his death in 1122) worked hard to re-establish the abbey's claim to be the royal necropolis, which was in doubt since King Philip's burial at Fleury in 1108. It was essential for the abbey's future well-being to ensure that Louis VI would return to Saint-Denis for his burial, and it was not clear that he would. Fleury had, as we saw, convinced King Philip I to be buried there, and the monks attempted to convince his son to do the same. Writing in the first decades of the twelfth century, Hugh of Fleury composed a text – which he dedicated to Louis VI – that set out Fleury's historical role in promoting royal legitimacy.[20] Suger and Adam, therefore, had their work cut out in terms of trying to convince Louis to return to Saint-Denis. Shortly after Philip's death, Adam instituted an annual celebration on the anniversary of the death of King Dagobert, the legendary founder of the abbey.[21] The implementation of the anniversary

Figure 1  The 'Crusading Window' of Saint-Denis. Photo by Hans Fischer. Courtesy of Glencairn Museum, Bryn Athyn, Pennsylvania.

was designed to remind Louis of the benefits of eternal rest under the protective watch of St Dionysius. The annual celebration was a major event at the abbey, and may have played a crucial role in Louis's decision in 1112 to confirm the concessions to Saint-Denis. Whatever the case, it must have worked since Louis decided he would not follow his father's example, but instead would be interred at Saint-Denis upon his own death, which came in 1137. And just to make certain that nobody misinterpreted Saint-Denis's status as royal necropolis, near the end of his life, an ageing Suger convinced Louis VII and Pope Eugenius III to place Saint-Corneille – a favoured burial spot for several Carolingian kings – under his control.[22] Claiming to be acting in the interest of reform, he removed the canons from Saint-Corneille and appointed one of his own monks, his young protégé (and recently returned crusade chaplain) Odo of Deuil as abbot.[23] With this move, Saint-Denis was in charge of most dead French kings.

### Suger's *Gesta Ludovici Grossi* and the crusades

The preceding discussion makes a case for approaching Suger's historiographical, architectural, and political programmes as part of a broad agenda to improve the status of his abbey by improving the status of the kings on whose support the abbey relied.[24] While this perspective has achieved a consensus status in recent years, no scholar has considered the place of early crusading in Suger's programme, despite the fact that repairing the tarnished crusading image of the French kings fitted naturally within other ambitions of this programme. Seen from this perspective, Louis VII's departure ceremony marked the fulfilment of Suger's ambition to create a crusader king for France to take his place properly as the leader of the Franks and defender of Christendom (not to mention Saint-Denis). Until Louis VII's departure for the East, of course, that vision was confined to the abstract, mainly to texts emanating from the abbey's scriptorium and works of art installed in the church. Given Suger's developed use of the crusade as a conduit by which to advance Louis VII's claim to sacral kingship, we should not be surprised to find the birth, gestation, and deployment of these ideas in his most substantial creations: the *Vita Ludovici Grossi* – Suger's history of Louis VI and arguably the most famous text to come from Saint-Denis – and his renovation of the Saint-Denis basilica.

The *Vita Ludovici* is well known to scholars, and is most often drawn upon as a chronological record of Louis VI's gradual political triumph over the mid-ranking nobles of northern France. It was widely read in the Middle Ages, and survives at present in at least ten manuscripts originally from northern France.[25] Despite powerful challenges to literal interpretations of texts being raised by scholars since the 1970s, only a handful of scholars have sought to move beyond the chronological framework of the *Vita*, peeling away the complex layers of the text to reveal an intricate political, social, and cultural substrate.[26] None has considered it from the perspective of the new crusading economy of status. In terms of the *Vita Ludovici*, such a review is well justified, and one does not have to go deep into the text to see that it is much more than it first appears.

A well-known charter produced at Saint-Denis noted that late in the summer of 1120, King Louis VI travelled to the basilica along with his queen, several members of his court, and the papal legate Conon.[27] When he arrived – presumably under the approving eyes of Abbot Adam and his protégé Suger (abbot from 1122) – the King returned the crown of his father, which, 'in accordance with the right and custom of the French kings', should have been done twelve years earlier, directly after his own coronation.[28] Louis was notorious for his reluctance to warm to the French Church, and the King's return of the regalia to its customary place at Saint-Denis is therefore best approached as evidence of a thaw in the Church–State relationship.[29] Given his presence during the King's trip to the abbey, it is puzzling that when Suger included the event in the *Vita Ludovici Grossi*, he erroneously dated it 1124, appending it to a list of gifts and privileges made by Louis to show his gratitude to St Dionysius for the saint's protection against a potential invasion by the German Emperor, Henry V.[30] It is possible, of course, that this anomaly was a simple error, but given the significance of the event in Dionysian history and Suger's well-known role in other forgeries, it is more likely that he purposely conflated these two events – the return of the regalia and the weakening of Henry V – into a single, victorious moment crafted specifically to establish the primacy of Saint-Denis throughout the French Church.

The artificially constructed nature of the 1120/24 episode in the *Vita Ludovici Grossi* is an excellent point of entry into a broader understanding of the text. Interpretations of it have tended to follow either the positivist approach of Achille Luchaire, who read the text as the faithful and chronological record of Louis's progressive victory over the castellans, or one that locates in the text an ideal, hierarchical vision of society, most likely rooted in the theology of Pseudo-Dionysius the Areopagite, the fifth-century writer whom the Dionysian monks erroneously identified with St Dionysius, their patron.[31] Both approaches risk an incomplete reading of the text because neither properly situates it in the political and social conditions of early-twelfth-century France. Given the selectiveness

RESPONSE

of events that Suger included (as evidenced by the 1120/24 episode), we can chart a better way forward by posing new questions about the historiographical aims and internal structure of the text, as well as about the cultural and political environment in which it was produced. Why did Suger include certain events and not others? What sort of values did the text impart onto Louis VI? Where did such ideas originate? Why do people and events of manifestly limited importance to the Capetian dynasty appear prominently in the text? The answers to these questions help illuminate some of the more confusing aspects of the *Vita* that have long confounded scholars.

For one thing, there is a clear focus on events early in Louis's reign. Suger added several chapters – those detailing the King's final illness, death, and burial at Saint-Denis – much later in his life.[32] In fact, they exist in a separate manuscript that is referred to in the *Chronicle of Morigny* and were probably intended to be used in the annual celebration on the anniversary of the King's death.[33] In other words, they were a memorial piece composed after the fact, and not part of the original text. Thus, if we remove these chapters, the *Vita Ludovici* records events only up to 1127, leaving a decade of Louis's reign untreated (he died in 1137). Suger also concentrated on events of limited importance to the overall arc of Capetian history in the twelfth century. Louis's capture of the castle of Sainte-Sévère was one of many equivalent episodes during his reign. Several of them were more important to the solidification of Capetian power in northern France, and yet appear nowhere in the *Vita*. On the other hand, Suger afforded the siege of Saint-Sévère a full chapter. In the same way, the most recent translators of the text find it difficult to explain the Abbot's detailed discussion of the murder of Guy of La Roche-Guyon by his brother-in-law William.[34] This event did not really involve the King at all except that Louis ended up issuing a formal condemnation after the fact. Examples of this sort can be parsed from almost any chapter in the *Vita*, which is sufficient to demonstrate the general point that Suger's history of Louis VI is not a chronological retelling of the King's reign in the style for which Saint-Denis would become famous in the later twelfth century because of writers such as Rigord.[35] We must be appropriately cautious not to read the organization of these later sources back onto an earlier period.

If we remove from consideration those duplicate chapters found in both the *Vita Ludovici* and the Morigny text, which was composed much later, then twenty-five of thirty-two chapters are predominantly concerned with the King's military deeds, and a further two recount the crusading exploits of men closely associated with the royal family, making a total of twenty-seven of thirty-four chapters with a military focus, several of which make specific reference to the First Crusade or rely heavily on crusading images and ideas. This point alone makes the *Vita Ludovici* unique. In addition, the text is not similar in style or content to other major examples of French royal biography readily accessible and well known at Saint-Denis.[36] Einhard's *Vita Karoli Magni* mimics the tripartite structure of Suetonius's *Lives of the Caesars*, while Helgaud of Fleury's history of Robert the Pious draws its inspiration from hagiography. The military focus of Suger's text has led some scholars to compare the *Vita Ludovici* with Norman chronicles such as William of Poitiers's *Gesta Guillelmi*, but the internal structures of the two texts are substantially different.[37] Whereas William's history is a reasonably accurate chronological account of the first years of the Conqueror's reign, Gabrielle Spiegel has demonstrated that each chapter of the *Vita Ludovici* is best conceptualized as a single 'event-unit', study of which reveals a 'virtually identical internal structure in which historical action is inaugurated by a disturbance to an existing situation, followed by the King's attempt to deal with the consequences of that disturbance, [concluding] with the restoration of "correct" order'.[38] What this means for our present discussion is that the *Vita Ludovici* deserves a fresh reading, one set firmly in the changing cultural world of crusading status discussed in the previous chapter.

Crusading themes and ideas penetrate the text on multiple levels. Most directly, Suger works hard to associate the Norman crusading hero Bohemond of Antioch with the Capetians, weaving his great deeds in the East into the history of the royal family, claiming him as one of their own. It is difficult to see any other reason for the Abbot's decision to give Bohemond his very own chapter in the *Vita*. We already considered above the passage in which Suger used Bohemond's deeds at Antioch to prove that he was a genuine crusading hero. From here, Suger goes on to highlight Bohemond's early successes wresting Greek territory away from Emperor Alexius. The combination of this and his crusading prowess was enough to qualify him for marriage to Constance, a French princess who was previously engaged to a leading French noble, but who 'was not seeking another marriage with somebody unworthy of her'.[39] Evidently Bohemond fitted the bill, and the 'threat of such a union frightened even the Saracens for the great valour of the kingdom of the French and the lord Louis was well known'.[40]

RESPONSE

A better way forward may be to consider the timing and purpose of Bohemond's trip to France. As the first crusaders passed through Constantinople, Emperor Alexius had forced them to swear oaths that any former Byzantine territory that they captured en route to Jerusalem would be returned to the Greeks.[41] As the crusaders moved further from Constantinople and, by extension, the Emperor's influence, relations between the Greeks and Latins became strained. By the time that the crusaders captured Antioch in 1098, they had broken down completely, and as a consequence, Bohemond secured possession of the city for himself.[42] Although not all the crusade leaders – especially Raymond of Toulouse – approved of Bohemond's violation of the oath to Alexius, they eventually accepted it, and moved on to capture Jerusalem in 1099. At this point, a majority of the surviving western knights returned home, which left Bohemond on his own, constantly having to fend off attacks from Muslims in the east and south, and from Greeks in the north.[43] After several years of skirmishing with the two sides (and a rather bizarre period of captivity at the hands of a Turkish atabeg), Bohemond decided that he needed to end the Greek threat once and for all. Thus, he sent his cousin, Richard of the Principality, in advance to meet King Philip of France and arrange Bohemond's marriage to Princess Constance.[44]

When he arrived in France in 1105, Bohemond arranged for his wedding to double as a recruiting platform for his upcoming expedition against Alexius. According to Orderic Vitalis, after being joined to Constance, 'the duke ... mounted the pulpit before the altar of the blessed Virgin and mother, and recounted all his deeds and adventures to the huge crowd that had assembled'.[45] He went on to 'urge those who bore arms to attack the Emperor with him, promising them wealthy towns and castles' in return.[46] Suger tells much the same story in his Bohemond chapter, adding an explicit reference to the 'crusading' nature of Bohemond's trip with his remark that 'the lord pope Paschal had sent him [the papal legate, Bruno of Segni] in the company of the lord Bohemond to summon and urge people to make an expedition to the Holy Sepulchre'.[47] No matter one's position in the debate over whether this expedition was a legitimate crusade, the fact remains that there would have been no reason to draw a connection with the 'Holy Sepulchre', since the venture was aimed at Byzantium.[48] It is highly unlikely that Suger simply was mistaken either, since he was a purposeful writer. There was a more deliberate plot at work. He sought to link the Capetians to the crusading movement through the vehicle of Bohemond's marriage to Constance, making the case, in essence, that the Norman's planned 'Crusade' against

Alexius I should be counted in favour of the French King and his family. This point gains credence given that, as observed previously, within a decade of the capture of Jerusalem in 1099, Philip arranged to have four of his five children married either to veteran crusaders or to their children. Suger's focus on Bohemond's crusading heroism and marriage to Constance is evidence of the realignments of power and status that the crusade entailed.

Crusading ideas exist in the text at a deeper, more fundamental level as well, shaping its very structure. The continued focus on Louis's military service, undertaken for a just cause and with clear ecclesiastical sanction, shares a number of features with the second-generation narrative crusade chronicles that were produced in the decade and a half after the First Crusade. We have already seen the extent to which Benedictines such as Robert the Monk and Guibert of Nogent revised and adapted the *Gesta Francorum* to fit better into a Western European theological framework. A large part of this programme was to provide a more refined version of the Council of Clermont, where Pope Urban II had initially called the First Crusade in 1095. While eyewitness accounts such as the *Gesta Francorum* provide only the most basic details, focusing most of their attention on the progress of the expedition itself, the French monks were eager to demonstrate how Urban II had successfully redirected the martial energy of western knights from fighting *against* one another to fighting *for* the Church and Christendom. Indeed, this is what made crusading such a potent shaper of the European power structure.

In his account of Urban's speech, Baldric of Bourgueil concentrated on the theme of justice and ecclesiastically sanctioned violence – that is to say, what made the crusade a legitimate military action in the Church's opinion. As Baldric tells it, the Pope reproached Christian knights for constant in-fighting amongst themselves, and then urged them to seek redemption by joining the ecclesiastically endorsed expedition to the East.

> You, secured with the badge of knighthood, are arrogant with great pride. You fight against your brothers and cut one another to bits ... You should shake, brothers, shake at raising a violent hand against Christians. It is less evil to use your sword against Saracens. It is the only righteous warfare.[49]

Robert the Monk largely echoes Baldric's remarks when he recalls Urban's admonishment to the crowd gathered at Clermont: 'so let therefore hatred depart from between you, let your fighting end, let battles cease, and let all conflicts and controversies fall to rest. Set out upon the road to the Holy

Sepulchre, deliver the land from a wicked race and take it yourselves.'[50] For both authors, it was a consequence of the First Crusade's success that the crusading vocation became revered by many as the fulfilment of the Church's ambitions for peace in Europe. Thus, the prestige, valour, and heroism attached to the returning veterans were imbued with a uniquely Christian ethic, part of what made them such powerful challengers to the ruling elite. It follows, then, that in virtually all of these second-generation chronicles, the ultimate success of the first crusaders is seen as 'the literal fulfilment of certain prophecies in scripture'.[51] The knights were doing the work of God, as the title selected by Guibert of Nogent for his crusading chronicle illustrates: *The Deeds of Good through the Franks (Dei gesta per Francos)*. Guibert's title also introduced another common feature among crusading chronicles, both second-generation and eyewitness. There was a clear attempt to situate the First Crusade alongside the legendary Eastern expeditions of Charlemagne.

The eyewitness and second-generation histories of the First Crusade were quite popular, and Suger probably was familiar with at least a few of the better-circulated ones.[52] Given the monumental impact of the Benedictine texts on western intellectual tradition, it is nearly impossible to believe that copies did not flow into the Dionysian archives. Indeed, in a letter written later in his life to King Louis, Suger used identical phrases to ones found in two different First Crusade chronicles. Moreover, Suger was also aware of the many artistic and architectural records of the First Crusade appearing around this time, since he incorporated the design elements into his own work.[53] Thus, it does not require much of an intellectual leap to propose that as he sat down to write a history of Louis's reign, aware of the decline in authority suffered by the Capetians since 1099, his thoughts would have focused on the powerful image of heroic crusaders publicly turning their attention from fighting each other to fighting for God, following in the footsteps of Charlemagne and his legendary Frankish army. He would have naturally wanted to give his subject the same gravitas in the new economy of status. Therefore, in the *Vita Ludovici*, he fused traditional Carolingian ideas of sacral rulership with newer ideas inspired by crusading to create a highly selective narrative of Louis's reign that stressed military actions undertaken to preserve justice and within the defined limits of ecclesiastical sanction. In effect, Suger manipulated the unknown future of the crusades to create a mould in which could be forged an ideal image of Capetian kingship, one that embraced the 'old' of Charlemagne and the 'new' of crusading.

At some point before March 1111, Count Theobald of Chartres visited the King to complain of the 'dishonourable deeds' being perpetrated by Hugh of Le Puiset and various members of his family.[54] According to Theobald, for a long time Hugh had been 'delighted for having gone unpunished while he brutally tyrannized needy churches and monasteries' throughout the Beauce.[55] Hugh had done much worse, including plundering the poor at every chance and inflicting several unnamed (through surely horrific) hardships on widows and orphans. The King was appropriately moved by Theobald's request for aid and immediately prepared to do battle with Hugh. Before departing for the Beauce, though, Louis 'set a day to take counsel', and on 12 March 1111 he convened a meeting of several leading Church officials at Melun to hear their opinions of Hugh's actions.[56] The high rank of those in attendance – Suger, the Archbishop of Sens, the Bishop of Orléans, and Ivo of Chartres – indicates that this was no mere formality designed to assuage the fears of squeamish churchmen; Louis needed their advice, and, perhaps more crucially, their endorsement. Once assembled, the clerics 'pleaded that the king make free what belonged to God, whose image he maintained and kept alive in his own person'.[57] Louis agreed, and took appropriate action, which amounted to capturing Hugh. He eventually released him, and Hugh went back to his old, nasty ways. It is not the outcome but the sequence of events that is important. Louis proceeded with punitive measures against Hugh only *after* he obtained the approval of the Church.

Suger's description of Louis's attack on Hugh's castle was crafted in sufficiently thrilling prose that it would earn any knight's approval (and perhaps envy). 'What a sight to behold', he wrote, 'arrows rained down, sparks of fire flashed from countless blows atop shimmering helmets'.[58] The enemy was pushed back into the castle, but not before the will of the attacking army was broken. Of course, descriptions of a brave and heroic king were nothing new to a medieval audience. Charlemagne's deeds circulated in all sorts of formats, and his is only the most widespread example. But there is something different in Suger's writing; he strove to set Louis's deeds into a framework of divine intervention *and* clerical endorsement. This combination does seem to be new. In fact, it follows a remarkably similar pattern to the structure set out in the histories of the First Crusade: a military action is initiated by the Church in response to the interruption of the right Christian order and is followed by a unified army of Franks restoring that order. This schema, it might be noted, fits within the internal structure of the *Vita Ludovici* set out by Spiegel, while adding nuance concerning the particular social, cultural, and political *milieu* of twelfth-century France.

Indeed, Suger followed the same pattern when he discussed a majority of Louis's adventures. Writing about the defeat of Thomas of Marle, for instance, Suger declared that the King 'took a similar revenge, pleasing to God and celebrated among men'.[59] As the episode unfolded, representatives from several local churches approached the King, who consequently ventured to Laon to take revenge on behalf of the Church at large. As he had done in the case of Hugh at Le Puiset, before he undertook any military action Louis sought advice from available prelates. They urged quick and decisive action, and so Louis put the castle to siege, wounding Thomas in the process and claiming all his property for the royal court. In a similar instance, the Bishop of Clermont was forced to seek refuge with Louis after the Count of the Auvergne had laid siege to his city and fortified the cathedral 'like a tyrant'.[60] The Bishop called upon Louis to free the 'enslaved church from its bondage and curb that unfettered tyrant with the sword of his royal majesty'.[61] Predictably, Louis ventured to the Auvergne and effected quick justice on behalf of the Bishop.

In one of the more famous episodes from the *Vita Ludovici*, Suger recorded Louis's preparations for an invasion by Emperor Henry V of Germany.[62] By 1123, Louis's relationship with the English King Henry I had reached a nadir, and as a consequence the English King convinced his son-in-law, Emperor Henry V of Germany, to invade northeastern France. The Emperor set his sights on the city of Reims, which had an obvious strategic advantage, and perhaps a psychological one as well, since it was here that Pope Calixtus II, under French protection, had excommunicated him. Whatever the reason, Louis learned of the Emperor's plans from his close advisors, and was forced into action. Suger chronicled the King's response in one of the longer chapters in the *Vita*. After meeting leading nobles from northern France, Louis 'hurried to the blessed Dionysius … Offering prayers and gifts, he begged him [St Dionysius] to defend his kingship, to keep safe his person, and to resist the enemy in his customary way.'[63] Before returning home, 'he took from the altar the standard belonging to the county of the Vexin', thus becoming the first French king to ride into battle carrying the abbey's banner. The King then 'sent forth a mighty call for all of France [*tota Francia*]' to follow him into battle.[64] Nobles took heed of the King's wishes, showing up at Reims in droves. As the day of battle neared the King and his advisors divided the assembled host into battle lines. As Suger wrote: 'One, over 60,000 strong, was made up of knights and foot soldiers from Reims and Châlons. The second, comprising the men of Laon and Soissons, was no smaller; and the third included the men of Orléans, Etampes, and Paris, together with a large host from Saint-Denis.'[65]

As it happened, Henry V never showed up, and 'the French [*Francis*] went home, having won a grand and prestigious victory'.[66] If Suger is to be believed, the mere fact that the victory was the result of forfeit did not detract from its significance. And in a way he was correct. In Suger's view, what mattered was a unified Frankish host, which had assembled despite major political obstacles. While we might not be surprised that various magnates from the Ile-de-France, like the King's cousin, Ralph of Vermandois, showed up, it is remarkable that the Count of Flanders did. Although he was related to the King by marriage, many of his lands fell under the control of Emperor Henry V, and he sided with the King only at grave personal and political risk to himself. The same risk was undertaken by Theobald of Chartres, the nephew of Henry I, whose ire he would not have wanted to raise.

Given this realignment of the political leaders of France, what exactly did *tota Francia* mean? More to the point, how did Suger want his audience to understand it? Many scholars have found in this passage evidence for Suger's proto-modern vision of kingship and French nationhood. His claim that Louis stood as the head (*caput*) of France has been especially convincing to this end. But, taken as a whole, the narrative Suger offered his audience was not new at all. It was old, harking back to deeply entrenched memories of the Frankish *imperium* under Charlemagne. Such notions were embedded in the fabric of twelfth-century society, having underpinned the various First Crusade texts as well. As the eyewitness observer Fulcher of Chartres remarked, the crusading host was 'a multitude speaking many languages and coming from many regions'.[67] His point in doing this, of course, was not to highlight difference, but to emphasize the ultimate success of the unified army. Whereas the crusaders started out as members of a divided host (they did not even travel together for much of the time), when they met Kerboga in battle before the walls of Antioch they defeated him as a single force, diverse in language and nationality perhaps, but 'brothers in the love of God'.[68] Charlemagne would certainly have been proud of this moment, since, as Matthew Gabriele points out, 'this language is all but lifted' from the *Song of Roland*.[69] The first crusaders, whether by intention or not, had become the successors to Charlemagne.

The details were different, but the narrative offered to the audience was the same. Robert the Monk likened the first crusaders to the Israelites; following their stunning victory at Doryleaum, he wrote that they sang a hymn that recalled Moses's song of gratitude in Exodus after the destruction of the Egyptians in the Red Sea.[70] In the words of Gabriele, 'it should not surprise us that the participants in the First Crusade, even though they came from what we think of as such disparate regions, could rely on a common political culture, using it to harken back to older, eighth- and ninth-century conciliar models in order to govern the armies as they marched to Jerusalem'.[71] Charlemagne had done the same thing, and nobles in the early twelfth century would have known it. This is why it was so critical for Suger to imbue Louis with the same qualities: leader of the *populus Christi*, defender of the Church, champion of Christendom. These were pervasive ideas in the twelfth-century imagination; they were what made crusading status such a potential political force, and they were the vehicles by which Suger meant to elevate the King to his rightful place. Louis VI never went on crusade. But in a sense he never had to. He achieved the same virtues as a crusader while staying in France.

## Architecture, art, and the Capetian image

No matter how pervasive the crusading ideas are in the *Vita Ludovici*, and no matter how impressive the figure cut by the King in those chapters, in the Middle Ages ideas contained in a Latin text could only penetrate the imaginations of a small number of people. In Suger's favour, the nobility were the most likely to be receptive to the ideas contained within the *Vita*, and it was their acquiescence to Capetian kingship that mattered most. Still, Suger was motivated to promote his images concerning kingship to a wider audience, the majority of whom were illiterate by any modern definition. He did this in a number of ways. In addition to his widely discussed textual programme, he was also a keen designer of buildings and commissioner of artwork. In his vast building and art projects at Saint-Denis, begun around 1135 and continuing throughout the 1140s, crusading themes and images were integral.[72] Indeed, it is impossible to separate the crusade-specific themes from his larger construction programme, since they were a foundational element in his vision of French kingship.

When Suger began construction, the basilica was in desperate need of repair. By the mid-1130s, the church had been in continuous use for nearly 350 years, drawing large crowds as a royal necropolis and prominent pilgrimage centre.[73] In his account of his administration, Suger explained that his decision to renovate vast sections of the church was driven by the need to accommodate the growing number of pilgrims who visited Saint-Denis, especially on holy days and the annual Lendit Fair, held in early June. Suger lamented the 'inadequacy which we often noted on feast days ... for the narrowness of the place forced the women to run toward the altar upon the heads of men as upon pavement with much dismay and noisy confusion'.[74] In another especially colourful episode, Suger recalled how several monks, who were displaying the Passion relic to some pilgrims, were overwhelmed by the crowd and, 'having no place to turn, with the relics [they] escaped through the window'.[75] These two passages connect the crusades and Suger's broader programme of construction and design at Saint-Denis. We have already seen in our discussion of the *Vita Ludovici* how crusading themes were factored into a broader framework of royal ideology. The same is true in the building and design projects. In essence, by about 1140, it is not possible to separate Suger's attempts to create the image of a 'crusader king' from his other attempts to support his monarchy and his abbey.

Despite the need to expand the interior of the church, this was not the first project to command Suger's attention. He first worked to renovate the western façade of the basilica. In 1145 he wrote a short account of his own administration of the abbey of Saint-Denis that contained discussion of his architectural and artistic patronage. In this short text, *De administratione*, he described the main features of the renovated western façade: the triple portals with bronze doors, the strong towers, and the crenellated roof.[76] Most are still visible in the modern church, though only one tower was ever completed. The portals clearly were intended to be the predominant feature, and although it is less obvious from centuries of caked-on pollution, the stone used in their construction was of a different colour and type than that used in the rest of the entrance, immediately drawing one's attention to the lower portion of the façade. The shape is the key to understanding their function in Suger's design. The three portals of Saint-Denis bear a striking similarity to a number of triumphal arches of ancient Rome. The Abbot's fondness for classical Roman design is well known. Several of the interior features of the Saint-Denis basilica were inspired by classical Roman structures, especially the churches of St Peter and St Clement in Rome, St Bartolomeo at Benevento, and St Nicola at Bari.[77] The Arch of Constantine, in particular, was a popular destination (as it still is) for visitors to the city. This was especially so in the mid-twelfth century, which experienced a great awakening in interest in Roman architectural ruins, a movement historians have named the *renovatio Romae*.[78] Suger visited Rome in 1123 – in the midst of the *renovatio* – to attend the First Lateran Council. He stayed for six months. He wrote in the *Vita Ludovici* about having the opportunity to visit several of the leading sites around the city, and we can be nearly certain that the Arch of Constantine would have been on any itinerary.

While in Rome, Suger also witnessed papal ceremonial, some of which was based on ancient Roman models and relied on the ancient structures around the city, such as the triumphal arches. Scholars of Republican and

Imperial Rome have often drawn attention to the *adventus* and *triumphus* ceremonies, which by the fourth century had been combined into a single, ritualized celebration meant to evoke a sense of victory. The Roman triumphal arch played a critical part in the ritual, and throughout the Late Antique period, it remained a key component for various ceremonies in Rome.[79] Indeed, the Emperor who passed through the arch was both celebrating a secular victory and demonstrating his quasi-divine being. The Ottonian and Salian emperors, over the tenth and eleventh centuries, began incorporating various aspects of classical design into their building programmes in a deliberate attempt to portray the Emperor as having a special relationship with God.[80] Such ceremonies were not limited to secular rulers; popes were keen participants in the *renovatio Romae*. A key attribute of the Pope's processional route through Rome was for him to pass beneath the major triumphal monuments. On the particularly important day of a pope's coronation, temporary arches were erected along the *via Sacra*, a clear imitation of the victorious Roman general.

Suger borrowed heavily in other aspects of Saint-Denis's design as well. The triple portals were flanked by columns of life-sized statues depicting several Old Testament prophets as well as various Merovingian and Carolingian kings. Unfortunately, the sculptural programme suffered badly during the French Revolution, forcing scholars to reconstruct many of the figures from drawings commissioned in the early eighteenth century. This is not true of all the statues, however. Gerson has argued convincingly that Moses was included among the Old Testament prophets, and Crosby has added King Solomon, King David, and, of course, St Dionysius to the list.[81] While the exact identities of these remaining statues is unknown, it is clear from the surviving fragments and drawings that many of them bear the trademark symbols of royals. One fragment, for example, depicts a bearded head wearing a crown.

The main design elements of the western façade had several purposes: extolling biblical iconography, supporting the link between French kings and St Dionysius, and, crucially, providing an ideal backdrop for a wide range of ceremonial and ritual activities. The initial motivation for expanding the church was to accommodate the number of pilgrims who flocked to the abbey. Most of them, of course, were not familiar with texts such as the *Vita Ludovici Grossi*. Yet they would all pass through the triple portals. They would make their way down the central aisle to the altar, and then walk around it to the ambulatory, where the link between the powerful French King and the crusades would be the most poignant. Here Suger installed the so-called 'Crusading Window of Saint-Denis'.

Most of the 'Crusading Window' does not survive. Of the original fourteen medallions of stained glass – probably installed in late 1145 or early 1146 – only the bottom two survived the destruction wrought by the French Revolution in the eighteenth century (Figure 1). Of the several reconstructions that have been proposed, Elizabeth Brown and Michael Cothren's is the most convincing. Drawing on eighteenth-century engravings of the lost medallions, Brown and Cothren arranged the fourteen medallions into a single lancet window that they believe to have been installed in one of the westernmost radiating chapels at Saint-Denis.[82] The window's location near the main altar, which housed the relic of St Dionysius as well as several royal tombs, ensured that it was prominently visible to pilgrims processing through the ambulatory. Considered in this context, the window was not intended solely for the King or the monks who worked in the basilica. It was an effective means of communicating a narrative message to a constant stream of pilgrims.[83] But what message did it send?

The meaning of the window can best be inferred by examining the authorship and iconographic structure of the piece itself. The bottom two medallions (the surviving ones) depict general scenes of crusading, with the image on the left picturing a king leading an army into battle, while the one on the right shows several dead crusaders receiving their crowns of martyrdom. Other twelfth-century windows at Saint-Denis, such as the Infancy of Christ Window, were intended to be read from left to right across each register, and then bottom to top.[84] Applying this schema to the Crusading Window, the bottom register communicated to its audience a message that if one followed a French king on crusade and died, one would receive martyrdom as a result. The specific ideas of crusader martyrdom were still being worked out at the time of the Second Crusade, of course, but many people (nobles and others alike) already believed the fallen First Crusaders to be martyrs.[85] Juxtaposing such an image against scenes of a French crusading king would serve to link the sacred status of the fallen crusader with that of the French King. In large measure, this register functions as a pictorial representation of what the *Vita Ludovici* sought to do in text.

The next register contains two medallions depicting images of Charlemagne's legendary expedition to the East: the initial request for aid and Charlemagne's subsequent meeting with Emperor Constantine. Of course, Charlemagne's appearance in a 'crusading' window stretches chronological fact; he had been dead for over 300 years at this point. But, in the Middle Ages this would not have posed a serious problem. We would be wise not to read too much concrete content into the iconographic structure of the window. In this light, Charlemagne's appearance in a crusading context makes sense; by the 1140s his legendary expedition to the East was already being associated with the early crusades, and Suger was at least familiar with one of the better circulated versions of the Charlemagne legend, called the *Descriptio qualiter Karolus Magnus*, since it was included in a historical text produced at his abbey around 1118.[86] Moreover, many of the First Crusade sources drew parallels with Charlemagne's journey to the East. The *Gesta Francorum*, for example, described how the route followed by the great army of Duke Godfrey of Bouillon and his brother Baldwin had retraced Charlemagne's footsteps as they marched across the Balkans toward Constantinople.[87] In his recollection of Urban II's speech at Clermont, Robert the Monk had Urban commanding his audience to 'remember the greatness of King Charles the Great ... most valiant soldiers and descendants of invincible ancestors ... recall the valour of your progenitors'.[88] We have already seen the extent to which Suger tried to cast Louis VI in the mould of Charlemagne, and here he was doing the same for Louis VII. Finally, the remaining ten medallions show specific scenes from the First Crusade, beginning with the siege of Nicaea and ending with the Battle of Ascalon, in the termination of the lancet.

Approached as a single artifact, it is difficult to assign authorship to the window. Based on the iconography of the window, Brown and Cothren concluded that it was probably installed in the late 1150s, during the abbacy of Odo of Deuil (1151–62), although the artistic evidence only permits advancing a mid-twelfth-century date of installation, meaning that the glass was the product of either Odo's abbacy or Suger's. Yet when set within the broader framework of Suger's use of crusading ideas to increase Capetian prestige, the window can more reasonably be placed alongside his other renovations. Indeed, since the goal of the Dionysian monks was always to reassert the basilica's historic connection to the French royal dynasty, it would not have seemed politically expedient for Odo of Deuil – who was Louis VII's chaplain in the East and who had, therefore, witnessed the failure firsthand – to install a window that reminded the King of his failed crusading past upon each visit. Moreover, while it is true that Suger's secretary, William, in his biography of the Abbot, remarked upon Suger's disdain for the Second Crusade, William was writing long after the Second Crusade had failed, and after Louis VII had refused to join another expedition as recompense. Thus, it is likely that he was working to remove his subject from the spectre of the failed crusade.

Suger's attitude toward the early crusades was crucial to his view of rulership. The 'Crusading Window' and the *Vita Ludovici* paint a picture of a reactive abbot who worked as best he could to promote the cause of his monastery by supporting the crusading image of the French monarchy. Crusade ideology could mutate and endure in the decades after the First Crusade, and under Suger's careful guidance, narrative texts and artwork were primary agents in the process. To bring this chapter back to where it began, from the Abbot's perspective, Louis VII's decision to join the crusading movement was monumental because it gave a tangible quality to what he had, for several decades, been trying to create in artwork and text. In Suger's mind, the presumed success of the Second Crusade was set to be the crowning achievement of the twelfth-century Capetians. We must remember that he sent Odo of Deuil, his young protégé, along with Louis to keep track of the King's deeds. The resulting text, then, was intended to form the basis for much of Suger's planned biography of Louis VII. The problem, of course, is that Louis VII's crusade was not successful, a point that threated to destabilize the royal family. It was one thing for Philip I not to have gone on a divinely inspired expedition, but it was quite another for his grandson to fail on his crusade, seemingly the result of divine disapproval. The reaction of the royal court to this challenge is the subject of the next chapter.

## Notes

1 Paris, Bibliothèque nationale de France, MS Lat. 5543, fos 91v–93v.
2 Ildar Garipzanov, 'The Carolingian Abbreviation of Bede's World Chronicle and Carolingian Imperial "Genealogy"', *Hortus artium medievalium* 11 (2005), 291–8.
3 Paris, Bibliothèque nationale de France, MS Lat. 5543, fos 91v–93v.
4 Paxton, '*Abbas* and *rex*'; Rosenwein, Head, and Farmer, 'Monks and Their Enemies', pp. 782–3.
5 Duby, *The Chivalrous Society*, pp. 149–57.
6 Erlande-Brandenburg, *Le roi est mort*, pp. 75–6.
7 Elizabeth Hallam, 'Royal Burial and the Cult of Kingship in France and England 1060–1330)', *JMH* 8 (1982), 201–14.
8 See Jean-François Lemarignier, *Le gouvernement royal aux premiers temps capétiens (987–1108)* (Paris, 1965), p. 7; Georges Duby, *Les trois ordres; ou, L'imaginaire du féodalisme* (Paris, 1978), pp. 277–8; Eric Bournazel, 'Suger and the Capetians', in *Abbot Suger and Saint-Denis: A Symposium*, ed. Paula Gerson (New York, 1987), pp. 55–72 (p. 60). For discussion of this point see Michel Bur, *Suger, abbé de Saint-Denis, régent de France* (Paris, 1991), pp. 8–9; Lindy Grant, *Abbot Suger of St-Denis: Church and State in Early Twelfth-Century France* (London, 1998), pp. 7–21.

9   Of particular interest to the monks was (re-)establishing connections in Normandy and England. Also worth noting is an apparent gift of a stone tower made by William I of England to Saint-Denis. While Guibert of Nogent is the only contemporary to mention this, excavations by Crosby have confirmed the tower's existence. See Crosby, *The Royal Abbey of Saint-Denis*, pp. 97–8.
10  Grosse, *Saint-Denis*, pp. 131–6. For Reims and the Capetians see Naus, 'The *Historia Iherosolimitana* of Robert the Monk', pp. 105–15.
11  Koziol, *The Politics of Memory and Identity*, p. 560. For Philip's acts in favour of Compiègne see *Recueil des actes de Philippe Ier*, pp. 297–300, 311–21, 378–9, and 401.
12  *Recueil des actes de Philippe Ier*, pp. 318–21; *Genealogiae comitum Flandriae*, ed. L. C. Bethmann, *MGH SS* 9, pp. 302–36 (p. 307). Discussed in Koziol, *The Politics of Memory and Identity*, pp. 560–1.
13  *VLG*, pp. 82–4.
14  *Oeuvres*, Vol. I, pp. 54–5.
15  See above, p. 80.
16  Koziol, *The Politics of Memory and Identity*, p. 561.
17  Spiegel, *The Chronicle Tradition of Saint-Denis*, pp. 39–52; Grant, *Abbot Suger*, pp. 32–45.
18  For relevant images see Crosby, *The Royal Abbey of Saint-Denis*, p. 166 Fig. 68; 180 Fig. 77; and 200 Fig. 90. For the western façade see Sumner McKnight Crosby and Pamela Z. Blum, 'Le portail central de la façade occidentale de Saint-Denis', *Bulletin monumental* 131 (1973), 209–66 (pp. 211–12); Stephen Gardner, 'The Influence of Castle Building on Ecclesiastical Architecture in the Paris Region, 1130–1150', in *The Medieval Castle: Romance and Reality*, ed. Kathryn Reyerson and Faye Power (Dubuque, IA, 1984), pp. 97–123. For statues see Crosby, *The Royal Abbey of Saint-Denis*, pp. 192–201. For Suger's interest in imperial secular ceremonial see Peter C. Claussen, '*Renovatio Romae*: Erneuerungsphasen römischer Architektur im 11. und 12. Jahrhundert', in *Rom im hohen Mittelalter: Studien zu den Romvorstellungen und zur Rompolitik vom 10. bis zum 12. Jahrhundert. Reinhard Elze zur Vollendung seines siebzigsten Lebensjahres gewidmet*, ed. Bernhard Schimmelpfennig and Ludwig Schmugge (Sigmaringen, 1992), pp. 87–125.
19  See below, pp. 76–8.
20  Hugh of Fleury, *Liber qui modernorum regum Francorum continet actus*.
21  Robert Barroux, 'L'anniversaire de la mort de Dagobert à Saint-Denis au XIIe siècle: Charte inédite de l'abbé Adam', *Bulletin philologique et historique de comité des travaux historiques et scientifiques* (1942–43), 131–51.
22  *Cartulaire de l'abbaye de Saint-Corneille de Compiègne*, ed. Emile Morel and Louis Carolus Barré, 3 vols (Montdidier, 1904–77), Vol. I, pp. 118–19.
23  Koziol, *The Politics of Memory and Identity*, p. 562.
24  Grant, *Abbot Suger*, pp. 3–49.
25  For a bibliography of the text see 'History as Enlightenment: Suger and the *Mos Anagogicus*', in Spiegel, *The Past as Text*, pp. 163–77 (p. 164 n. 7). Henri Waquet discusses the manuscript tradition in his edition of the *Gesta Ludovici*; see *VLG*, pp. xvii–xxvi. Spiegel has identified three additional manuscripts, unknown to

Waquet, which are: Rome, Bibliotheca Apostolica Vaticana, Reg. Lat. 550 and Reg. Lat. 624; and Chantilly, Musée Condé, MS 869.
26 Cf. Spiegel, 'History as Enlightenment'. For an interesting discussion of the text see Suger, *Vie de Louis le Gros par Suger suivie de l'Histoire du roi Louis VII*, ed. Auguste Molinier (Paris, 1887), p. xiii. For theoretical discussion see Geoff Eley, 'Is All the World a Text? From Social History to the History of Society Two Decades Later', in *Practicing History: New Directions in Historical Writing after the Linguistic Turn*, ed. Gabrielle M. Spiegel (New York, 2005), pp. 36–61 (pp. 36–54). See also Spiegel's introductory remarks, pp. 1–26.
27 *Actes*, Vol. I, pp. 334–8, no. 163. For what follows see Grant, *Abbot Suger*, pp. 97–105.
28 *Actes*, Vol. I, p. 338.
29 At this precise time, Pope Calixtus II and his legate Conon were stranded in France, prevented by Henry V from travelling to Rome. Louis recognized the advantage to supporting the Pope, and was, as a consequence, notably more generous to the French Church from then onwards. See OV, Vol. VI, pp. 252–76.
30 *VLG*, pp. 226–8. See also Grant, *Abbot Suger*, p. 105; Françoise Gasparri, *L'écriture des actes de Louis VI, Louis VII et Philippe Auguste* (Geneva, 1973), pp. 21–5.
31 Achille Luchaire, *Louis VI le gros: Annales de sa vie et de son règne (1081–1137)* (Paris, 1890). For discussion of Luchaire's approach to the text see Spiegel, 'History as Enlightenment', pp. 163–5.
32 For the dating of the text generally see Grant, *Abbot Suger*, pp. 32–49.
33 *La chronique de Morigny*, p. 69. For the text of the additional manuscript see *PL* 186, cols 1342–6.
34 Suger, *The Deeds of Louis the Fat*, trans. Richard C. Cusimano and John Moorhead (Washington, DC, 1992), p. 79 n. 7.
35 Suger's writing shares few stylistic parallels with Rigord's *Gesta Philippi Augustus*, produced at the abbey only a few decades later. See Spiegel, 'History as Enlightenment', p. 166. For an alternative view see William J. Brandt, *The Shape of Medieval History: Studies in Modes of Perception* (New Haven, 1966), Chapter 7.
36 A ninth-century manuscript containing Einhard's text, now catalogued as Paris, Bibliothèque nationale de France, MS Lat. 4628A, was housed in the library at Saint-Denis during Suger's lifetime. See Donatella Nebbiai-Dalla Guarda, *La Bibliothèque de l'abbaye de Saint-Denis en France du IXe au XVIIIe* (Paris, 1984), p. 215. Also, Fleury and Saint-Denis maintained close connections, and were known to trade manuscripts frequently, making it very likely that Suger was also aware of Helgaud's text and could easily have had access to it.
37 See Grant, *Abbot Suger*, pp. 40–2; Lindy Grant, 'Suger and the Anglo-Norman World', *Anglo-Norman Studies* 19 (1997), 51–68.
38 Spiegel, 'History as Enlightenment', p. 166.
39 *Ibid.*, p. 48.
40 *Ibid.* Also see Paul, 'A Warlord's Wisdom'; and Yewdale, *Bohemond I*, pp. 108–15.
41 Albert of Aachen, *Historia Ierosolimitana*, pp. 84–7; *GF*, pp. 11–12. For discussion of the oaths see John H. Pryor, 'The Oath of the Leaders of the First Crusade to the Emperor Alexius Comnenus: Fealty, Homage', *Parergon* 2 (1984), 111–41;

RESPONSE

    Jonathan Shepard, 'When Greek Meets Greek: Alexius Comnenus and Bohemond in 1097-8', *Byzantine and Modern Greek Studies* 12 (1988), 185-277.
42 Yewdale, *Bohemond I*, pp. 78-87.
43 The Greeks, in particular, were a thorn in Bohemond's side, believing that he illegally held the city. According to a letter preserved in the *Alexiad*: 'You are aware of the oaths and promises made to the Roman Empire, not by you alone, but by all the outer counts. Now you are the first to break faith. You have seized Antioch and by underhanded methods gained possession of certain other fortified places ... I bid you withdraw from the city of Antioch ... thereby doing what is right, and do not try to provoke fresh hostilities and battles against yourself.' Anna Comnena, *The Alexiad*, pp. 357-8. See also *Gesta triumphalia Pisanorum in captione Hierosolymae, RHC Oc.*, Vol. V, p. 368.
44 OV, Vol. X, p. 24.
45 *Ibid.*, Vol. XI, p. 12.
46 *Ibid.*
47 *VLG*, p. 48.
48 Brett E. Whalen, 'God's Will or Not? Bohemond's Campaign against the Byzantine Empire (1105-1108)', in *Crusades: Medieval Worlds in Conflict*, ed. Thomas Madden, James Naus, and Vince Ryan (Aldershot, 2010), pp. 111-25; Rowe, 'Bohemond of Antioch'; Yewdale, *Bohemond I*, pp. 106-34; Russo, 'Il viaggio di Boemundo'.
49 BB, pp. 8-9.
50 RM, p. 728.
51 Riley-Smith, *The First Crusade*, pp. 132-52.
52 Rubenstein, 'Putting History to Use'.
53 See below.
54 *VLG*, p. 132.
55 *Ibid.*, p. 130.
56 *Ibid.*
57 *Ibid.*
58 *Ibid.*
59 *Ibid.*, p. 250.
60 *Ibid.*, p. 232.
61 *Ibid.*
62 *Ibid.*, pp. 218-30.
63 *Ibid.*, p. 220.
64 *Ibid.*
65 *Ibid.*, p. 222.
66 *Ibid.*, p. 226.
67 Fulcher of Chartres, *Historia Hierosolymitana*, pp. 306-7.
68 *Ibid.*; Gabriele, *An Empire of Memory*, p. 157.
69 Gabriele, *An Empire of Memory*, p. 157. For parallel passages in Roland see *Chanson de Roland*, ed. Gerard J. Brault, *The Song of Roland: An Analytical Edition* (University Park, PA, 1978), lines 2322-34, 3026-95, and 3700-4.
70 RM, pp. 27-8.

71 Gabriele, *An Empire of Memory*, p. 158.
72 On the dating of the construction programme see Grant, *Abbot Suger*, p. 239; and Crosby, *The Royal Abbey of Saint-Denis*, p. 121. For an alternative view see Otto G. von Simson, *The Gothic Cathedral: Origins of Gothic Architecture and the Medieval Concept of Order* (Princeton, 1988), pp. 90–1.
73 Jules Formigé, *L'Abbaye Royale de Saint-Denis: Recherches novelles* (Paris, 1960), pp. 2ff.
74 *Gesta Suggerii Abbatis*, in *Oeuvres*, Vol. I, p. 112.
75 *Scriptum consecrationis*, in *Oeuvres*, Vol. I, p. 10.
76 *Gesta Suggerii Abbatis*, pp. 112–22.
77 Grant, *Abbot Suger*, pp. 256–7.
78 Twyman, *Papal Ceremonial*, pp. 3–7; Herbert Bloch, 'A New Fascination with Ancient Rome', in *Renaissance and Renewal in the Twelfth Century*, ed. Robert L. Benson and Giles Constable (Cambridge, MA, 1982), pp. 615–36; Claussen, '*Renovatio Romae*'.
79 Twyman, *Papal Ceremonial*, pp. 6–9; Sabine MacCormack, *Art and Ceremony in Late Antiquity* (Berkeley, 1981), pp. 34–5.
80 Twyman, *Papal Ceremonial*, pp. 12–13.
81 Paula Gerson, 'The West Façade of St Denis: An Iconographic Study', Ph.D. dissertation, Columbia University, 1970, pp. 150–3; Paula Gerson, 'Suger as Iconographer: The Central Portal of the West Facade of Saint-Denis', in *Abbot Suger and Saint-Denis: A Symposium*, ed. Paula Gerson (New York, 1987), pp. 183–98; Crosby, *The Royal Abbey of Saint-Denis*, pp. 192–201.
82 Elizabeth A. R. Brown and Michael W. Cothren, 'The Twelfth-Century Crusading Window of the Abbey of Saint-Denis: *Praeteritorum enim recordatio futurorum est exhibitio*', *Journal of the Warburg and Courtauld Institutes* 49 (1986), 1–40. The literature on the window is diffuse and legion. Much of it centres on the question of dating. Of particular note is Louis Grodecki, *Les vitraux de Saint-Denis: Etude sur le vitrail au XIIe siècle* (Paris 1976), esp. pp. 115–21; Jane Hayward, *Radiance and Reflection: Medieval Art from the Raymond Pitcairn Collection* (New York, 1982), pp. 90–7; Phillips, *The Second Crusade*, pp. 122–4.
83 Wolfgang Kemp, *The Narratives of Gothic Stained Glass*, trans. Caroline D. Saltzwedel (Cambridge, 1997), p. 4.
84 See Michael Cothren, 'The Twelfth-Century Infancy of Christ Window at Saint-Denis: A Re-evaluation of Its Design and Iconography', *Art Bulletin* 68 (1986), 398–420.
85 H. E. J. Cowdrey, 'Martyrdom and the First Crusade', in *Crusade and Settlement: Papers Read at the First Conference of the Society for the Study of the Crusades and the Latin East and Presented to R. C. Smail*, ed. Peter Edbury (Cardiff, 1985), pp. 46–56; Jonathan Riley-Smith, 'Crusading as an Act of Love', *History* 65 (1980), 177–92 (pp. 191–2).
86 The *Descriptio*'s narrative appears in a text completed for Saint-Denis around 1118. For discussion see Gabriele, *An Empire of Memory*, pp. 51–6; Brown and Cothren, 'The Crusading Window', pp. 14–15. The manuscript survives as

Paris, Bibliothèque Mazarine, 2013, and is described in Jules Lair, 'Mémoire sur deux chroniques latines composées au XIIe siècle à l'abbaye de Saint-Denis', *Bibliothèque de l'Ecole des Chartes* 35 (1874), 543–80 (567–8).
87 *GF*, p. 2.
88 RM, p. 6.

# 4

## Louis VII and the failure of crusade

One afternoon in early June 1147, Abbot Suger of Saint-Denis stood alongside Pope Eugenius III on the steps of the Saint-Denis basilica, awaiting the arrival of King Louis VII. The King was travelling to the church to mark his departure on the Second Crusade. Upon his arrival, Louis expected to receive the pilgrim's script and a blessing from the Pope.[1] Louis also was going to receive Saint-Denis's legendary battle standard, the *oriflamme*, to carry with him to the East – a ritual that had come to symbolize St Dionysius's protection of the French King and his kingdom since Louis VI had initiated the rite in 1124.[2] This was a shrewd move on the part of Suger – who orchestrated the entire visit – designed to link his abbey to the King's presumed crusading success. As a consummate planner of political ritual, the Abbot had coordinated every detail of the ceremony to take the greatest advantage of the prestige that came through involvement with crusading, even down to the timing. Louis's visit coincided with the Lendit Fair, the largest annual gathering at Saint-Denis.[3] Since it was a rare event for the average Parisian to see a king in person (let alone one standing next to a pope) it is reasonable to assume that the crowd lining the seven-mile path from the city to the basilica was both legion and captivated. In the Middle Ages, as today, ritual procession conveyed a sense of social significance that demanded the observer's attention.[4] The presence of the King would have only heightened this effect.

Louis did not disappoint those who came to see him. According to Odo of Deuil, the Dionysian monk who reported the episode, upon entering a leper community just outside the city walls, 'Louis did an admirable thing, which few, if any, of his high rank could imitate.'[5] Odo does not reveal the specifics of what the King did, but his claim that the act could not be mimicked suggests that the King's stop was more than a simple charitable visit to a leper house, which in the twelfth century was commonplace among the nobility. It is likely that Odo was describing Louis's practice of the 'royal miracle', the exclusive rite of kings to heal diseases of the skin by touch.[6] If this is true, it means that Louis was curing leprosy and not scrofula, the malady of choice among curative kings. But these two diseases were commonly conflated before the thirteenth century, and the distinction probably did not matter, since early medieval men and women were inclined to associate leprosy with divine healing, which is what counted for the King.[7] The connection among leprosy, royal prestige, and crusade may have already had a place in Louis's mind. In the decade leading up to the Second Crusade, the King made several donations in favour of the Order of St Lazarus, a crusading organization devoted to the care of lepers.[8] Interpreted in this context, the stop was hardly spontaneous, and it may well be the case that Suger arranged the miracle as part of the sequence of the King's departure for the crusade. The use of the crusade ceremony as a space in which to bind sacral ritual with political theatre conjured exactly the sort of image that Suger would have wanted for Louis as he departed for the East: a divinely selected king leading the Frankish crusading army into battle while carrying the standard of Saint-Denis.

The King proceeded from the leper colony to Saint-Denis, where in front of the captive masses he received his purse and blessing from the Pope and the *oriflamme* from the Abbot, transforming him at once into a Christian pilgrim, protector of the abbey, and follower of Charlemagne. In the long term, this was an important moment in the history of France and its monarchy. Later French kings would employ crusading ideology and Carolingian descent to support their claims of dynastic legitimacy and right to use the title of 'most Christian' king.[9] Some of them, such as Philip Augustus in 1190, would follow in Louis VII's footsteps and select Saint-Denis as the site of their own departure on crusade.[10] For Louis and Suger, however, the moment had a more immediate significance. Louis had become not merely another crusader; he had become a crusader king – the first to come from France and the first to lead a major expedition to the East. For Suger, the leading creator and shaper of the royal image, who had worked so hard to support Louis VI in the face of the rising prestige of the castellans, this meant that Louis was better equipped to compete in the post-First Crusade economy of status.

As the first major royal leader of a crusade, Louis was sure to take pride of place among the storied heroes of the early crusades, whose deeds were widely celebrated in Latin and vernacular texts. From this point forward, it was hoped, Louis VII's deeds too would be recounted by future generations alongside those of Godfrey of Bouillon, Bohemond, and even Charlemagne, who by the 1140s enjoyed status as a legendary crusader. The problem, of course, was that the Second Crusade was not successful; in fact, it was a spectacular failure. Thus, as much as it had promised to boost the Capetian image, it now threatened to undercut it. Was Louis still fit to rule? Did he still enjoy divine approval? If so, why would God allow him to fail? It was one thing for Philip I not to have gone on the expedition in 1096. As we saw in previous chapters, Suger was able to deflect negativity away from the Capetians by painting Louis VI as a man who possessed the virtues of a crusader, even if he had not participated in any such enterprise. It was quite another thing for Louis VII to go on crusade and to fail. The reaction of Suger and the royal court to this challenge, and its impact on how French kings perceived and negotiated their relationship with crusading, is the subject of this chapter.

### The historical setting: Louis VII and the Second Crusade

Over the course of the 1130s, Zengi, the atabeg of Mosul and Aleppo, had been steadily gaining power by preaching *jihad* among the various Muslim communities in the Near East. Zengi had pledged to unify Muslims around a common goal of pushing the Franks out of the region, and he began this project in 1144 by attacking the Christian city of Edessa. Edessa had been the first crusader state to be founded (1098), and became the first to fall when Zengi's troops captured the city on Christmas Eve. The Muslim army sacked the city in what was remembered as a particularly brutal scene.[11] Edessa's fall had wide-ranging implications. The city had historical and religious significance, and also held strategic importance. The Christian East had benefited economically and politically from having Edessa as a buffer zone among various Muslim forces. The Franks in the East also relied on Edessa to keep peace in the northern Levant. More broadly, the loss of Edessa was a severe psychological blow to Christendom. The city's fall raised questions about the long-term security of the other crusader states, and Zengi's harsh treatment of Edessa's citizens was the cause of frustration and concern for Christian writers.[12] Over the following months, envoys began arriving in Western Europe from Jerusalem and Antioch, bringing news of Edessa's situation and appealing to their Christian brothers to travel once again to the East to liberate Christian territories. The messengers focused their attention on France, and particularly on recruiting Louis VII.[13] As the King of France, Louis ruled over the homeland of a majority of the First Crusaders, and the barons of the East hoped to appeal to ancestral prestige to generate interest.[14]

Louis's support of various Lazarine houses around Paris may have also contributed to the decision to approach the French King, since it demonstrated that he was sympathetic to the plight of the Holy Land.

Louis's motive for taking the cross has been a topic of considerable interest to scholars, whose differing interpretations reflect the wide divergence in the sources.[15] Otto of Freising wrote that Louis's decision to go to the East stemmed from a vow made by his older brother, Philip, whose premature death made its fulfilment impossible.[16] Hoping to take on his brother's burden, Louis set off for the East. A continuator of Sigebert of Gembloux's chronicle asserted that Louis was drawn to take the cross by the extreme guilt he felt for ordering the burning of the church at Vitry in 1144, the infamous culmination of his ongoing war with Theobald II of Champagne.[17] Odo of Deuil is more vague, describing 'the secret in his heart', which Louis hoped to share with his nobles.[18] He says nothing of the genesis of the secret, or even its true meaning, though contextual clues hint that the King had wanted to go to the East for some time, and the fall of Edessa gave him the excuse he needed to mount an expedition. The *Chronicle of Morigny* suggests that the fall of Edessa had a profound impact on Louis, directly motivating his decision to travel to the East.[19] Given the disparity in the sources, Jonathan Phillips concludes that the best explanation is one that takes them all into consideration, meaning that events such as his brother's vow and the Vitry burning all probably influenced the King, making plain his need to make amends with the Church and thus predisposing his eagerness to join the Second Crusade when the news of Edessa's fall eventually reached him.[20] What is clear is that when news did reach the King, he reacted very quickly. The envoys from the East probably reached France sometime in the summer of 1145.[21]

By Christmas of that year, Louis had summoned an unusually large number of nobles to Bourges for his annual Christmas coronation. The King was certainly planning to use the occasion to promote the expedition, but as it happened, Bourges turned out to be a false start. The nobles may have been impressed by Louis's enthusiasm, but they ultimately baulked at his crusading plans, probably because the papal bull *Quantum praedecessores* had yet to reach France, and they wanted some assurance of papal benefits before committing to an enterprise as demanding as a crusade.[22] Crusade historians are often accused of reading back onto the early crusading period the canons and privileges of a later (thirteenth-century) era. In 1146, the privileges and expectations of a crusader were still concepts very much in flux. It would, in fact, be Eugenius III's treatment of the Second Crusade that paved the way for crusading principles to enter canon law. It is therefore perfectly natural that the potential recruits hesitated at Louis's request, wanting to understand the Pope's expectations before embarking on an arduous and dangerous crusade.

Louis summoned a new meeting at Vézelay at Easter 1146, and this time he made sure to have the bull in hand. Roused by a series of powerful sermons delivered by Bernard of Clairvaux, Louis and a large number of nobles took the cross. In the months that followed, while Louis and his nobles made their preparations in France, Bernard travelled throughout Germany on a preaching trip, one that ultimately convinced Emperor Conrad III to take the cross. Conrad's decision to become a crusader meant that the Second Crusade would be led by the two most powerful rulers in the West. Conrad was the first to depart, leaving Regensburg in May 1147 and arriving at Constantinople in September of that year. The Byzantine Emperor, Manuel I Comnenus (r. 1143–80) was nervous about the presence of a well-armed German army in his city, and particularly unhappy about the poor way its members had behaved during their march through Byzantine territory in the Balkans. Thus, as quickly as possible the Emperor ushered the German army across the Bosphorus to Asia Minor. The original plan was for Conrad to wait for Louis's army at Constantinople, which he should have done. Nevertheless, perhaps propelled forward by a sense of national pride, he decided to march to Antioch and wait for the French King there. Events proved difficult for Conrad. Soon after he departed from Nicaea, the German Emperor met a Turkish army at Dorylaeum, the same place the first crusaders had vanquished Kilij Arslan's Seljuk forces in 1097. Things did not go nearly as well the second time around. The vast majority of the German army were destroyed by the Seljuks, and Conrad was lucky to escape with his life. He quickly retreated back to Nicaea, where he awaited the arrival of the French.

Louis VII and his army departed in early June 1147, and arrived in Constantinople in October, about a month behind Conrad. After spending a short period of time in the Byzantine capital, the French army crossed the Bosphorus and Louis met Conrad at Nicaea. Louis must have been surprised by the state of the German host. Since a majority of German knights had died at Dorylaeum, leaving Conrad only a small force, it was clear that if the crusade were to go forward, it would have to become a largely French expedition. Indeed, it did go forward, with Louis and Conrad opting to march along the coast of Asia Minor so as not to risk the shorter, but more perilous, march through Turkish-controlled territory in Asia Minor. Within a matter of weeks, Conrad fell ill and opted to return to Constantinople, where he was cared for in the imperial palace. When his health had

# RESPONSE

improved, he transshipped directly to Jerusalem. While the German Emperor convalesced in Constantinople, Louis and his army endured a harrowing march along the Anatolian coastline. Though Manuel had sent along Byzantine troops, they were more concerned with protecting Greek possessions than defending against the Turks, who harassed the French army on a daily basis. When he reached the city of Adalia (modern Antalya), Louis had had enough. He wrote to the Emperor and ordered a fleet of ships to transport him and his army directly to Antioch. Unfortunately, there were not enough ships in the region to accommodate the French force. On the small number of vessels that did arrive, Louis put the clergy, himself, his family, and a select group of his nobles. For the rest of the army – the bulk of the crusading force, in fact – he left behind money and provisions, promising to meet them in Antioch. Louis arrived safely, but only a small number of his force survived the perilous march through the southern coast of Asia Minor. Most were killed very soon after the King's departure, when Turkish forces attacked them at Adalia. By this point, it was clear that the Second Crusade would not be able to retake Edessa.

After a series of familial disagreements with Raymond of Antioch (who happened to be Eleanor of Aquitaine's uncle), Louis eventually arrived in Jerusalem in June 1148. He and Conrad convened a war council to decide how to proceed, and eventually the group decided to attack the city of Damascus. The problem here was that while Damascus was a Muslim city, it was nevertheless a close ally of the Kingdom of Jerusalem. In spite of this, and illustrative of the difference in mindset between crusaders from the West and settlers in the East, Louis and Conrad believed that by attacking Damascus they could pre-empt any attempt by Nur-al-Din (who had replaced his father, Zengi, in 1146) to do the same. The siege of the city began in earnest in late July 1148, and it did not last long. After only four days the largest Christian army ever assembled in the East was forced to retreat. Conrad sailed for home soon after. Louis stayed behind in Palestine until 1149, returning home at Easter that year. The Second Crusade was over in less than two years. Its spectacular failure shocked the West, and in the longer term threatened the reputations and careers of those who had participated.

## The spectre of failure

In 1146, long before any omens of failure had appeared on the horizon, the Second Crusade was expected to equal, if not surpass, the divine achievements of the 1096 campaign. The communally felt reverence for, and in many cases direct familial connections to, the First Crusade were a powerful theme employed by those hoping to spur men to action in 1146.[23] It is worth remembering that although the First Crusade was nearly fifty years in the past, it continued to hold a special place in the European imagination on a level that was unmatched by other medieval events. Across Europe authors heralded the new expedition as the rightful successor to the First Crusade, describing the presumed success of its participants in the same providential framework in which writers such as Robert the Monk, Baldric of Bourgueil, and Guibert of Nogent had set the earlier expedition. The number of crusade-related stimuli that surrounded men and women on a daily basis to remind them of the event is staggering. In addition to the proliferation of eyewitness and second-generation chronicles, nobles commissioned family histories cataloguing the contributions of their crusader ancestors, and the western landscape was literally filled with crusading memorabilia and artwork.[24] Round churches, such as the one that still stands in the city centre of Cambridge (c. 1130), were built in the shape of the Holy Sepulchre. The First Crusade was even memorialized in ceremonies such as annual feasts celebrated to mark the capture of Jerusalem in 1099.[25]

Pope Eugenius III began the crusading bull *Quantum praedecessores* by comparing the divine success of the First Crusade with the expectations of the new endeavour. He promised the potential crusaders that 'it will be seen as a great token of nobility and uprightness if those things acquired by the efforts of your fathers are vigorously defended by you, their good sons'.[26] In the weeks leading up to the departure of Louis's army, Peter the Venerable, abbot of Cluny, delivered a sermon at Paris in which he presented a more nuanced version of the same argument. Expounding on the miraculous achievements of the first crusaders he told the audience that 'you went not as enemies, but as His creations, as servants, as redeemed men ... by these sacrifices [you], like the prophets and the angels, had declared that the Holy Sepulchre was more glorious than all earthly places'.[27] Peter described 1146 as a special time in the history of the world. Miracles such as the Divine Easter Fire, since they had been 'granted to our times ... can fully take the place of all those other [ancient] miracles'.[28] In other words, the Second Crusade was a divinely inspired enterprise. Earlier in the same year, Peter had written a letter to Louis comparing the knights of the Second Crusade to the armies of Moses and Joshua. He was certain that ancient prophetic miracles were being replayed in the twelfth century.[29] In this schema, the crusaders were more than a mere army of

Christian knights; they were an instrument of prophetic translation, moving the age of miracles from the ancient world to the present. This was a rather stunning claim when set against the achievements of the First Crusade. For the new expedition potentially to better the first meant that it was destined to be a very special enterprise indeed. Perhaps those who participated would enjoy proportionally inflated reputations.

Suger was determined to capitalize on the anticipated success of the Second Crusade on behalf of the French kings. He had not been able to do this with the First Crusade, since Philip I had not taken part. He astutely recognized the threat posed by castellans gaining power on the basis of their crusading, and he wrote the *Vita Ludovici Grossi*, in part, to paint a balanced picture of Louis's virtues: his stewardship of France set alongside the virtues of a crusader. Since Louis VI had never been on crusade, though, there was little else Suger could do. Things were to be different with Louis VII, and early on Suger influenced his decision to take the cross. Although the Abbot's biographer, the monk William, claimed that Suger was opposed to the King's plan, this statement is often misinterpreted as evidence that Suger felt a level of disdain toward the institution of crusading.[30] For one thing, William wrote his text several years after the Second Crusade failed, and after the 1150 expedition, which might have achieved some recompense, failed to get off the ground. Knowing this information, it is likely that William sought to remove his subject from the spectre of failure. Moreover, William described Suger's opposition to the crusade in the particular context of Louis's selecting him to be the Regent of France, a position that brought with it significant political and financial responsibility. Throughout the 1140s, Suger was working hard on the renovation of Saint-Denis, which could not continue alongside his new responsibilities in government.

Louis's absence while in the East had proved very expensive for Saint-Denis. On several occasions, the King wrote to Suger asking him to repay various debts, and not infrequently the money to do this came directly from the abbey's coffers.[31] By 1145, the year in which he was selected for the position, Suger had been involved with royal politics and finances for several decades, and was well aware of the monetary implications that an extended royal absence would have. Indeed, financial hardship is one of the most common themes in the letters sent by Suger to Louis during the King's time in the East. Louis's venture represented an unprecedented challenge to French royal power. Never before had a King been absent for this amount of time, and it was natural for Suger to be concerned about the implications of this. And yet, as we will see, Suger was the main force behind trying to convince the King to return to the Levant in 1150, less than a year after his return from Jerusalem and during a period in which royal finances were at a nadir. Had the Abbot harboured a deep animosity for the institution of crusading, this would not have made sense. Thus, it is important not to equate concerns about whether the King had properly planned for his absence with an overall dislike of the crusade.

There is rather more evidence to suggest that Suger was an enthusiastic supporter, and even promoter, of the Second Crusade. The 1146 departure ceremony clearly was designed to link the crusading reputation of the King with the monastery of Saint-Denis. Louis's entrance into the church through the recently constructed triple portals evoked ancient imperial *adventus* ceremonies and fundamentally placed Saint-Denis at the core of royal power. By 1146, the abbey was becoming a keen promoter of the link between the Capetian and Carolingian dynasties, which would have worked well for Louis VII. Moreover, the Crusading Window, located in the ambulatory just behind the altar, would have provided a moving backdrop for those who filled the church to witness the King's reception of the pilgrim's purse and the *oriflamme*. Had Louis been as successful as hoped, the Crusading Window would have served as a constant reminder of the tripartite link among the Capetians, Saint-Denis, and crusade.

Of all Saint-Denis's programmes, the historiographical one was the most definitive shaper of the image and practice of French kingship in the twelfth and thirteenth centuries, and Suger planned to use Louis VII's crusading experience as the centrepiece for a history of the King's reign on which he had already been working for nearly ten years. The monk who accompanied Louis to the East as a royal chaplain, Odo of Deuil, was handpicked by Suger for the job. The Abbot, after all, was the Regent of France and had been a leading advisor to Louis VII for more than a decade. It is only natural that when the King sought a religious leader to accompany his expedition he would seek out the advice of his own leading religious advisor. It makes equal sense that Suger would designate one of his own monks from Saint-Denis. Little is known of Odo's life and career before the crusade, though his selection for this important mission suggests that he was a monk of some importance at Saint-Denis.[32] In the years following Louis's return from the East in 1149, Odo wrote an account of the King's two years on crusade, a text called *De profectione Ludovici VII in orientem* (*The Journey of Louis VII to the East*). The text is well known to historians of the crusading movement, who commonly point to Odo's anti-Greek rhetoric as a way of explaining away the failure of the Second Crusade while still glorifying Louis.[33] The text has a further purpose as well: that of serving as a guide for future expeditions to the East. Much less attention has been paid to Odo by non-crusade specialists, perhaps because we know comparatively little about the rest of his life. Shortly after Odo return from the Second Crusade in 1149, Suger sent him to Compiègne, where he expelled the corrupt canons and replaced them with a group of monks from Saint-Denis.[34] He remained there as abbot. Then, upon Suger's death in 1151, Odo was elected abbot of Saint-Denis.[35] His tenure in that post was marked by scandal and attempted insurrection. This began early in his first year, when a group of dissatisfied monks attempted to have him deposed. He was saved only by the intervention of Bernard of Clairvaux, who intervened with the Pope on Odo's behalf in 1153.[36]

Given his controversial and unremarkable career as abbot, it is fair to state that what stands out about Odo is his history of the Second Crusade. Scholars are right to place great value on this text. It is the only eyewitness narrative dedicated to the Second Crusade. And yet, it is important to interpret Odo's work in the way he intended and in the context in which it was written. Of course, no medieval writer produced his text for the purpose of modern scholarly study, but neither did Odo plan for *De profectione* to be a stand-alone history of the expedition in line with the eyewitness chronicles of the First Crusade. Although he was exposed to several First Crusade chronicles in Saint-Denis's library and probably even used one as a guide during his time in the East, there is little evidence that Odo followed them as a model for his text. His purpose was not to explain and interpret the events of the Second Crusade in biblical and prophetic terms; his twin goals were to present his king in the most favourable light and to provide a guide for future crusades.

Odo produced his history of Louis's crusade experience in order to furnish Suger with the necessary material to complete a more comprehensive life of Louis VII – one similar in style to the *Vita Ludovici* – on which he had already begun work. The prefatory letter attached to the main text sets out this fundamental goal.

> I desire to demonstrate to you skillfully, with a view to your perpetuating them in writing, some facts about the journey ... I have enjoyed the glorified King Louis's generous favours and have been closely associated with him during the journey. I am eager to thank him; yet my powers are limited. Let this be the task of St Dionysius ... You have recorded his father's deeds, and it will be a crime to cheat future generations of knowing the son, whose entire life is a model of virtue ... Wherefore,

if anyone begins to depict this life only from the time of the journey to Jerusalem, he will cut off the greatest part of the example set forth by God for future kings ... Do you, therefore, to whom is justly due the honour of writing about the son, since you formerly made the father illustrious in literature.[37]

By the time Odo delivered his text (and this letter) to Suger, the Abbot had already been working on his history of Louis VII for the better part of a decade. Suger's new history of Louis VII was to serve a much broader (and older) purpose; it was going to do the same for Louis VII as the *Vita Ludovici Grossi* had done for his father. Indeed, as we have seen, Odo suggests as much in the prefatory letter.

Given this singularity of purpose, it is difficult to know whether Odo planned for *De profectione* to be read by a larger audience than Suger and perhaps the other monks at Saint Denis, though the manuscript evidence suggests that he may not have had such a goal in mind. There is only one known manuscript of Odo's chronicle, produced at Clairvaux in the late twelfth century.[38] Virginia Berry noted that Clairvaux was coming into its own at this time and already contained a small library. The monks often traded volumes with Saint-Denis for copying, and they may have been interested in Odo's text because of its connection to Bernard.[39] Whatever the case, the autograph copy of *De profectione* does not survive; nor do any copies survive from the library at Saint-Denis; nor was the text ever copied into the later histories of France produced at the abbey, like so many of the other texts would be. Henri Waquet, for instance, identified seven independent manuscripts of the *Vita Ludovici* while he was preparing his edition and translation, and it was a text that was widely copied into later volumes such as the *Grandes chroniques de France* – the monumental project begun during the reign of Louis IX to trace the history of France from its origins.[40] Even Suger's unfinished history of Louis VII enjoyed a level of popularity. It was copied into several twelfth-century manuscripts and also served as the base text for a portion of the *Grandes chroniques de France* dealing with the mid-twelfth century.[41] While it is curious that Odo's text did not share this fame, nevertheless, from the perspective of a standalone text emanating from Saint-Denis in the mid-twelfth century, it is reasonable to claim that *De profectione* was unpopular. This is surprising given the subject matter. And while the failure of the 1146 expedition may have dampened some enthusiasm for memorializing its events, it is significant that other crusade-related texts remained popular during times of Christian setbacks in the East. Bull and Kempf have demonstrated that

RESPONSE

Robert the Monk's *Historia Iherosolimitana* was widely copied in the aftermath of Saladin's 1187 conquest of Jerusalem; an illuminated copy was most probably intended for presentation to Emperor Frederick Barbarossa to commemorate his cross-taking for the Third Crusade.[42] Thus, a more likely explanation for the relative unpopularity of Odo's text is that it was intended from the beginning to be a sort of notebook for Suger, providing the raw material for a history of the reign of Louis VII. Thus, it lacked the panache and exempla-driven style of the more popular First Crusade narratives.

The text for which it provided the base material is known by scholars as *De glorioso rege Ludovico*. Suger died in 1151, before he could finish the work, but a small fragment of what he did produce survives in a late-twelfth-century manuscript.[43] The portion of *De glorioso rege Ludovico* that was completed is quite short, covering roughly the first year of Louis VII's reign (1137). It begins with the story of Prince Louis hearing about the death of his father, at which point he immediately travelled to the duchy of Aquitaine to prevent the typical scandals that follow a king's death.[44] The first substantive part of the text is a detailed discussion of the problems of succession that plagued the English and German monarchs, who often failed to produce male heirs. This stood, of course, in contrast to the Capetian dynasty, which had never faced this problem. Lindy Grant argued that this part of the text must have been written shortly after the events in question, since in the late 1130s, when Louis's marriage to Eleanor of Aquitaine was still solid, there was little concern about a Capetian heir.[45] Following the Second Crusade and the disintegration of the marriage, however, such a reference to the potential threat of not having an heir would have been politically damaging. Thus, Suger began *De glorioso rege Ludovico* in the late 1130s, and put it aside as his role in royal politics increased and peaked during the Second Crusade, intending to finish it with material provided by Odo of Deuil. In this schema, the history of Louis VII was intended to be based around the King's accomplishments in the East. It was, in a sense, the fulfilment of what Suger had tried to do in the *Vita Ludovici Grossi*. When the Second Crusade failed, however, the book was left unfinished. Suger was more concerned with managing the immediate risk of failure.

Writers across Europe decried the crusade and its participants. The *Chronicle of Morigny*, for example, dismissed the Second Crusade as 'having achieved nothing of value or worthwhile repeating'.[46] In addition to the general critics, many people sought to understand and to explain the failure of the Second Crusade, and particularly the Christian loss at Damascus.[47]

Some, such as Odo of Deuil, blamed the treachery of the Greeks, while others focused on natural disasters, and even the relationship between the eastern Christians and the Muslims.[48] The vast majority of those who wrote about the failure of the Second Crusade, though, blamed the sinfulness of the crusaders themselves. Elizabeth Siberry has shown that by the time of the Second Crusade, this had become the normal way of interpreting a defeat in the East.[49] Thus, in the years following the Christian failure at Damascus there appeared a host of texts that blamed the crusaders for their sins and made plain God's refusal to support them.[50]

For his role in championing the expedition, Bernard of Clairvaux was subjected to attacks from 'certain men [who] raised scandal against him'.[51] Comparatively little evidence survives to explain the character of these attacks. However, we know that Bernard was forced to explain the failure of the Second Crusade. Shortly after Louis's return to France, Bernard delivered a sermon in which he defined the failure as the result of the sins of man and divine judgement. He was careful not to offer any specific names, but preached more generally about the sins of mankind. He developed this theme further in a text composed at the behest of Pope Eugenius III, who was himself suffering the after-effects of supporting the failed expedition. In this short text, *De consideratione*, Bernard drew on biblical exempla to make the case for human sinfulness and divine judgement as the combined cause of the failure. 'It was as if the Lord, provoked by our sins', Bernard wrote, 'judged the world ... forgetful of his mercy'.[52] In the experience of the crusaders Bernard found Old Testament parallels. He recalled the story of Moses leading the Jews out of Egypt.

> He [Moses] did everything the Lord commanded, the Lord working with him, and confirming his work by signs. But those people, you say, were rigid, always stubbornly opposing the Lord and Moses, his servant ... Was there ever a time in their whole journey when they were not turning back into Egypt in their hearts? If they fell and perished ... can we wonder that our contemporaries with the same conduct have had the same experience? Was their fall contrary to the promises of God? No, nor has the fall of these latter [crusaders] been.[53]

In the same vein, Bernard recalled God's command to the Hebrews to fight the tribe of Benjamin, and how, relying on divine aid, they remained committed after twice being defeated so that God rewarded them with victory on the third attempt. Such exempla were widely used by authors seeking to explain the Second Crusade.

RESPONSE

Suger had a problem. We have seen above how authors in 1146 and 1147 had whipped up a widespread belief that the Second Crusade was destined to replay the deeds of the First Crusade. Since God wanted the new expedition, in other words, it would be victorious. Peter the Venerable had argued that the ancient miracles were being replayed in the present, and even Bernard himself in a letter to the English people had referred to those men who took the cross as 'a blessed generation', promising them that if they 'go with devotion … the gain will be God's kingdom'.[54] In the aftermath, writers were still drawing biblical parallels. However, the crusaders were now compared to the ungrateful Hebrews under Moses's command who were said to have failed to live up to the standard of the armies sent to meet the Tribe of Benjamin in battle. From Suger's perspective, it was the wrong set of biblical exempla drawing the wrong set of parallels for his king.

Louis was already being criticized for what was perceived by many writers as arrogance. When Bernard had delivered his *apologia* sermon, he had claimed that the army failed because of its pride. He did do Louis the courtesy of stopping short of naming him personally. Others did not hesitate. William of Saint-Denis, in a conversation alleged to have taken place between him and another monk, found parallels between the French army on the Second Crusade and the campaigns of Xerxes in the fifth century.[55] When describing Xerxes's Greek campaign, the Roman poet Seneca recalled how Demaratus had advised Xerxes that his army was too disorganized and would ultimately prove a burden to its commander.[56] Xerxes, of course, did not listen, and his forces were defeated at Plataea in 479 BCE. In much the same way, William chided Louis and Conrad for their overconfidence. Many other writers echoed this sentiment, attributing the crusade's failure to the hubris of the crusaders. Suger, of course, could not accept such an image of Louis VII. It threatened the carefully constructed narrative of French kingship toward which he had been working, and by extension, it also threatened the health of Saint-Denis itself. By 1150, the link between abbey and monarch was unbreakable. After all, Suger had put much on the line by organizing and hosting Louis's very public departure for the East. It was crucial for him to confront the failure of the Second Crusade.

### The non-crusade of 1150

What better way to negate the stained image of the Second Crusade than by orchestrating a new expedition to the East? A similar reason motivated men to join the crusade of 1101, and many saw their reputations rehabilitated as a consequence of their participation, despite the failure of the expedition. Stephen of Blois, for example, had agreed to go back to the East at the behest of his wife, who was quite concerned about the long-term health of his reputation. Though he died on the expedition, his willingness to fulfil his vow went a long way toward erasing his inglorious abandonment of the 1099 crusade. In the case at hand, for Suger and members of the royal court, the sooner a new expedition could get under way, the less time for public opinion to swing against the King. The spring of 1150 – just a matter of months after Louis VII had returned to France – presented the opportunity to consider such an option. The failure of the Second Crusade and the final departure of Louis from the East seem to have raised the confidence of Muslim leaders. According to William of Tyre's chronicle, until the Second Crusade the Muslim world was generally afraid of a massive western expedition coming to the aid of their eastern settlements, and they worked hard to prevent it from happening. After defeating the most recent crusaders, however, Muslim leaders steadily gained confidence in their ability to attack the Christian states. Since he was writing several years after the fact, it is difficult to know whether William was employing hyperbole for effect, but not long after Louis had left the East, Nur al-Din attacked Prince Raymond of Antioch. Raymond was killed shortly after, in late June 1149 at Inab. The loss of Prince Raymond was a serious setback to the Christians of the East. Not only had he been a respected military commander, but he had also provided a level of security to the northern Levant at a time when the Latin Kingdom of Jerusalem was facing internal discord because of feuds within the royal family. Moreover, Raymond's heir, Bohemond III, was only a child at the time and was unable to defend against further attacks by Nur al-Din.

It is in this context, we are told by William of Saint-Denis, that representatives from the King of Jerusalem, the patriarch, and the Templars visited Suger to request aid, most probably in the form of a new crusade.[57] According to William, Suger was sympathetic to their request, and even enthusiastic about the prospect of a new expedition to the East. The Abbot was 'tormented' by the failure of the Second Crusade, and particularly by the number of French knights who died in the East and the failure of those who did return home to achieve any glory.[58]

The key source for what followed is a series of letters sent among Suger, Bernard, Peter the Venerable, and Pope Eugenius. Though incomplete and fragmentary, they indicate that Suger was the driving force behind raising interest in the new expedition, the one commonly called by historians the 'crusade of 1150'.[59] Suger was the first to organize a meeting to discuss the possibility of launching a new crusade, though according to William of Saint-Denis – our only source for the meeting – none of the other principal clerics attended. The Abbot held it anyway, at Laon in March 1150, and while Bernard, Peter, and Eugenius failed to appear, Suger did convince King Louis and several leading French nobles to attend. Despite the Abbot's best efforts, however, the Laon meeting did not produce anything substantive. The King and nobles had only been back in France for a short time, and it is likely they needed significant convincing before marching off again to the East, though their willingness to at least entertain such a suggestion is demonstrated by their attendance at Laon. Most likely the meeting failed to gain traction because of the lack of a broader ecclesiastical support network. As had been the case at Bourges before the launch of the Second Crusade, French nobles typically wanted to understand the intentions and promises given by the Pope before committing themselves to such an undertaking. And while we know from letters that Eugenius was initially supportive of Suger's plan, he had not yet issued any kind of formal document (as he would do in the early summer), and thus the nobles and King may have been hesitating until they knew the Pope's intention.

Another meeting was scheduled, this time at Chartres in May. Suger's hope was to convince more churchmen to attend. Bernard, who was by this point quite supportive of the plan, wrote to Peter the Venerable in an attempt to convince the Abbot of Cluny to participate. 'Our fathers', he wrote, 'the bishops of France, with the king and the princes, are to meet at Chartres on the third Sunday after Easter [7 May] to consider this matter. I hope that we will be favoured with your presence.'[60] Bernard went on to play to Peter's vanity, remarking that the combination of his erudite advice and Cluny's prestige might be just the ticket for increasing the support of the French King and nobles. Peter nevertheless failed to appear – offering his apologies in a short letter to Bernard. The meeting at Chartres closed without accomplishing anything more in terms of noble recruitment, though Bernard indicated that he had been appointed leader of the planned expedition (much to his disapproval).

Suger remained enthusiastic about the new crusade, though Pope Eugenius began to express doubts. In a letter to the Abbot, sent shortly before the meeting at Chartres and probably not received until afterwards, Eugenius remarked that while he continued to support the expedition in theory, in practice he increasingly worried about the long-term consequence of more 'outpouring of Christian blood'.[61] Lamenting the blow to Christian prestige brought on by the Second Crusade, he wondered whether Christendom could survive another such blow. The Pope's hesitation piqued Bernard's attention, who enthusiastically encouraged Eugenius to support the crusade: 'The time has come for both swords to be deployed in defence of the eastern Church. You hold the position of Peter, and you should also to have his zeal.'[62] The Pope, it seems, remained unconvinced, though he did not terminate plans. Rather, he left the expedition's fate in Suger's hands. In a letter to the Abbot, Eugenius instructed Suger to evaluate the mental, physical, and financial condition of the King and other leading nobles, and thereby assess whether a new expedition was practical and likely to succeed.[63] The Pope also reissued *Quantum praedecessores*, promising the same privileges to those who signed up for the new expedition. Suger's response to this letter does not survive, though he must have believed the King capable and potentially willing, since he called yet another meeting to discuss plans. This time, the meeting was set for mid-July at Compiègne. We know this because, once again, Bernard wrote an emotionally charged letter to Peter the Venerable in an attempt to convince the Abbot to attend.

It is not clear whether the Compiègne assembly ever happened, though the Abbot was certainly in the city at the time, overseeing the reform of the canons at Saint-Corneille. At this point, discussion of the 1150 expedition disappears from the sources. The reason for the 1150 crusade's failure to launch is not clear, and many have simply assumed that it was not popular enough with Louis and other powerful nobles to gain any traction. Jonathan Phillips has also discussed various domestic political crises that prevented the King from leaving France even if he had wanted to. That may well be true but timing may also have played a role. The crusade was fundamentally Suger's brainchild, and he was an old man by 1150. By the autumn of that year, just a few months after the alleged Compiègne meeting, he was seriously ill, probably with quartan malaria. He finally died on 13 January 1151, and it is possible that he simply did not have the energy to sustain efforts to promote the new crusade. Indeed, his biographer, William, recalled that when recruitment efforts failed, the Abbot arranged for the Templars to transfer money from the abbey to the Holy Land, to be used in its defence.

The relevance of this small episode, therefore, is difficult to measure. The crusade of 1150 did indeed fizzle very quickly, never seeming to garner much more than lukewarm support from anybody other than Suger (and to some extent Bernard). And yet, its brief appearance is more than simply the tale of an unrealized plan. It offers a glimpse into the increasingly important function that crusading could play in discourses of political authority and cultural norms in France. Louis VII may not actually have been able to bring Suger's plan to fruition, but this point does not diminish the significance of the Abbot's use of crusade as a cultural and political mechanism in the first place. As the stillborn crusade of 1150 demonstrates, the institution of crusading was playing an increasingly important role in the formation of a royal identity in France. This would be one of Suger's key legacies in the second half of the twelfth century. Indeed, as domestic politics quieted and the situation in the Latin East deteriorated, Louis VII would once again plan to take the cross, and with an eye toward restoring royal dignity.

## Louis VII, Henry II, and Charlemagne

During the 1150s and particularly the 1160s, the political and military circumstances in the Latin East continued to decline markedly. As the strength of Nur al-Din's forces continued to grow, it became increasingly important to Christians that he should not get control of Egypt. Nur al-Din already ruled Aleppo and Damascus, and if he conquered Egypt it would create a massive Sunni-controlled territory that bordered the crusader states on three of four sides. Thus, during this period the leaders of the crusader states increased their efforts to seek military and financial assistance from the West. Louis VII remained a primary target for such requests, despite his association with the ill-fated Second Crusade.[64] That the King had remained in the Latin East for a year after the Second Crusade bespoke a genuine desire to help, and his early support of the crusade of 1150 demonstrated that he was at least willing to entertain the possibility of leading a new expedition to the Holy Land. Finally, since his return to France in 1149, Louis had continued to channel money to the Latin East, primarily through the Templars.[65]

Between 1163 and 1165, leaders in the East sent a number of letters to the King seeking financial and military aid.[66] Jonathan Phillips has studied this correspondence, and has concluded that it was driven by a widespread belief among the eastern rulers that Louis would, in the end, be willing and able to provide the necessary help.[67] Despite such high hopes, though, Louis ignored the multiple requests. Since no royal responses to any of the requests survive in the historical record, it is difficult to know the precise reason for the King's reluctance to send help, though his decision was almost certainly influenced by the domestic political situation in France and his tense relationship with the new English King, Henry II. Louis VII had been at odds with the English King since the spring of 1152, when Henry (then Count Henry of Anjou) married Eleanor of Aquitaine, the French King's ex-wife.[68] In 1154, in addition to being the greatest landholder in France, Henry became the King of England. During the rest of the 1150s, Henry's power and that of his family continued to expand, often at the expense of the French King. In the 1160s Louis began to enjoy limited success in his quarrel with Henry II. After the affair with Thomas Becket the French King's political leverage improved as the English King lost favour in the eyes of the papacy.[69] Nevertheless, Louis remained vulnerable, and thus, the political situation in France in the 1160s precluded the possibility of a crusade expedition that did not involve both monarchs.

The political and military conditions in the Latin East were deteriorating at a steady pace. By 1169, the military situation in the East had reached a nadir. Nur al-Din had gained control of Egypt and thus ruled all of the land bordering the crusader states. With the threat to the stability of the Latin states immeasurably higher, in 1169 the rulers of the states sent an embassy to the West with the task of inspiring a new crusade.[70] The group was led by Archbishop Frederick of Tyre, a northern European who had settled in the East and had risen to high standing in the Kingdom of Jerusalem. It is likely that the high rank of the envoys was meant to underscore the severity of the threat, as was the broad nature of the request, which was directed at Louis VII of France; Henry II of England; Frederick Barbarossa of Germany; and a number of leading nobles, most of whom had crusading connections of one sort or another. Louis VII, nevertheless, seems still to have held pride of place in the minds of the envoys, who targeted him particularly, perhaps relying on the Pope's close relationship with Louis's brother, Archbishop Henry of Reims, to pique the King's interest.

The envoys travelled to Paris in September 1169 to meet Louis in person. The King arranged for this meeting himself, and it is unlikely that he would have done so without knowing the exact purpose of the trip. If this is true, it suggests that the King was at least willing to consider formally the request for aid. The details of the gathering are known to us from the chronicle of Lambert of Watreloos, a canon at the monastery of Saint-Aubert in Cambrai.[71] Lambert was well informed about the issues discussed at the Paris meeting, including the somewhat obscure reference to an earlier, aborted embassy who had been forced to turn back after their ship was damaged in a severe storm. This story is independently confirmed by the chronicle of William of Tyre, which attests to the overall reliability of Lambert's account.

Archbishop Frederick of Tyre began his appeal to Louis by lamenting the threat faced by the Holy Land and then offering to Louis 'the keys to the gates of Jerusalem'.[72] He underscored the unique position of the French

King as the protector of the East before exhorting Louis to lead a new expedition to defend Jerusalem and the holy places: 'O king of the Franks, it is necessary for you and your people to end this anxiety by your zeal.'[73] The sequence of Frederick's appeal and the reference to the keys and gates of Jerusalem are significant. Nicholas Paul has argued that references to 'opening gates' and presenting 'keys' were metaphors for crusading in the East, connecting a present need to protect the ability of pilgrims to travel to the Holy City with the deeds of the first crusaders in 1099 (and before that of Emperor Heraclius in the seventh century).[74] Jonathan Phillips has argued for a more specific purpose: reminding Louis of the presentation by the patriarch of Jerusalem of several keys associated with the city that had been made for Charlemagne on the eve of his coronation in 800.[75] The story of Charlemagne receiving the keys was preserved in the *Annales regni Francorum*, a semi-official history of the Carolingian dynasty from the death of Charles Martel in 741 up to the beginning of Louis the Pious's political crisis in 829.[76] The text was popular throughout the Middle Ages, appearing in a number of monastic inventories, particularly in the lands of the former Frankish empire.

In addition, the story of Charlemagne's legendary pilgrimage to the East was well known by the 1160s. Variations of the story had circulated in Latin texts since the late eleventh century. Over the first half of the twelfth century, as European writers interpreted the events of the First Crusade, the story of Charlemagne's pilgrimage to the East took on a distinctly crusading flavour, inspiring a number of new vernacular treatments such as the Old French *Pèlerinage de Charlemagne*. Charlemagne's crusader status was also enshrined in the Latin chronicles of the First Crusade. The anonymous *Gesta Francorum* described how the first crusaders had 'travelled on the road which Charlemagne, heroic king of the Franks, had previously built to Constantinople'.[77] Robert the Monk built on this foundation, claiming that Urban II had used a reference to Charlemagne to spur men to action at the Council of Clermont: 'May the deeds of your ancestors move you and spur your souls to manly courage – the worth and greatness of Charlemagne ... '[78] In this way, crusaders were following Charlemagne's example and in his footsteps. Approached in this context, it is likely that Frederick of Tyre hoped to remind Louis of Charlemagne's legendary protection of the East and to offer an opportunity for the French King to renew the Frankish commitment to the Holy Land.

Such a claim may have found immediate purchase in the mind of Louis VII, who, we must remember, had a close relationship with Abbot Suger of Saint-Denis. Suger had worked hard to associate his abbey with the

Carolingians and even harder to associate the French King with the institution of crusading. The 1146 departure ceremony for the Second Crusade illustrates this point well. In addition to the traditional pilgrim's purse and staff, which the King received from Eugenius III, he had already received the *oriflamme* from Suger. In reality, it was little more than the Dionysian battle standard. According to legend, however, it was the same banner that Charlemagne had carried to the East on his own pilgrimage. Moreover, the Crusading Window that Suger installed in the ambulatory of Saint-Denis contained scenes linking Charlemagne to crusade. In particular, one set of scenes contains images of Greek envoys approaching the King to request his aid in the East, and another his arrival at Constantinople and meeting the Byzantine Emperor. Louis had been reared on such stories, and now Frederick and the other envoys were offering him a chance to follow in the footsteps of Charlemagne.

While Louis showed an initial enthusiasm for the new crusade – he surely would not have arranged to meet with the envoys otherwise – he insisted that he could not commit to the expedition so long as he remained locked in conflict with the English King. Thus, he suggested that the embassy meet Henry to broker a peace, at which point the two kings could work in tandem for the benefit of the Holy Land.[79] The specific elements of the brokered peace are difficult to put together because of the fragmentary evidence. However, it is clear that Frederick of Tyre played a key role in the process, his presence verified at most of the major meetings between English and French representatives. By the late autumn of 1169, relations had improved enough between the two kings that they agreed to meet in Paris to discuss plans for the upcoming crusade. Importantly, while in Paris Henry undertook a pilgrimage to Saint-Denis, where he and Louis spent a day in discussions.[80] Little record of the royal exchange survives. However, the particular choice of Saint-Denis may be important. Saint-Denis was a place steeped in both crusade and royal imagery. As Henry and Louis wandered around the basilica, they would have passed the tombs, many of them Carolingian. They would have also had time to view the Crusading Window, as well as the high altar, where Louis had received the signs of the crusader as well as the *oriflamme* in 1146. Though we cannot know for sure, it is likely that Louis used the time at Saint-Denis as a vehicle to reinforce his understanding and commitment to Capetian royalism, a viewpoint heavily steeped in a crusading tradition. By the time Henry left France, he and Louis had agreed that the new crusade should be ready to depart in 1171. Unfortunately, this crusade was never to be. In 1170, several of Henry's household knights murdered Thomas Becket as he prayed in the cathedral at Canterbury, plunging Henry into a long-term attempt to reach a settlement with the Church during which time he was not in a position (either practically or canonically) to go on crusade. So long as Henry did not go, neither would Louis.

In conclusion, crusading played a significant role in the life of Louis VII, a king who took the cross only for the Second Crusade, an expedition that was, by most accounts, a spectacular failure. It would seem that the King's strong support for the institution of crusading, and not his actual successes in the East, were what counted in terms of politics and prestige at home. Indeed, Louis VII had been the first French king to take the cross, but he would by no means be the last. In fact, he began a tradition of French kings being closely associated (if not always involved) with the crusading movement. For his son and heir, Philip II Augustus, this would be the driving force of his entire reign.

Over the course of the twelfth century the crusading movement played a crucial role in shaping and refining understandings of the obligations of sacral French kingship. The early crusades invested knights and nobles with the means to protect the Church and defend the helpless, thus offering them a means to participate in an ethical system previously reserved for kings. This provided the knights and nobles with the necessary prestige to challenge the social dynamics of the time. Kings, on the other hand, were late to the crusades, a consequence of the sundry expectations placed on rulers regarding their service to the Church. It was difficult for a king to commit to a crusade at the best of times. Prolonged absence from his country and the threat of death would place under stress the normal social and political structures of the time, and very often kings had to weigh circumstances at home against the prestige that might come from time spent in the East. It was no good going to Jerusalem if only to return home to a kingdom in crisis. In the wake of the First Crusade, therefore, European rulers had to redefine themselves in the wake of the crusade. In the case of France and her kings, a key group of advisors, most notably Abbot Suger of Saint-Denis, worked to lessen the prestige gap between heroic crusaders and stay-at-home kings. Through texts, artwork, and ritual celebration, Suger and others at Saint-Denis fused emerging crusade ideas with ancient notions of sacred kingship to create a new royal identity that was fundamentally connected to crusading but that allowed kings a necessary level of flexibility. They could participate in the crusading ethos, in a sense, by protecting the Church at home. By the end of the reign of Louis VII, what might be termed the 'broad interpretation' of a French king's relationship to crusading was a key element underpinning French political ideology.

The reign of Philip Augustus bears out this claim, and it thus remains the plan of the final chapter to consider French royal crusading in the years leading up to Louis IX.

## Notes

1 OD, pp. 15–19; 'Breve Chronicon ecclesiae Sancti Dionysii ad cyclos paschales', *RHGF*, Vol. XII, pp. 215–16; *Gesta Eugenii III papae*, *RHGF*, Vol. XV, pp. 423–5.
2 OD, p. 16. For the battle standard see Laura Hibbard Loomis, 'The Oriflamme of France and the War-Cry "Monjoie" in the Twelfth Century', in *Studies in Art and Literature for Belle da Costa Greene*, ed. Dorothy Miner (Princeton, 1954), pp. 67–82.
3 Léon Levillain, 'Essai sur les origines du Lendit', *Revue historique* 155 (1927), 241–76; Rolf Grosse, 'Reliques du Christ et foires de Saint-Denis au XIe siècle: A propos de la *Descriptio clavi et corone Domini*', *Revue d'histoire de l'Eglise de France* 87 (2001), 357–75.
4 Barbara Kirshenblatt-Gimblett and Brooks McNamara, 'Processional Performance: An Introduction', *The Drama Review* 29 (1985), 2–5 (p. 2); quoted in Ashley, 'Introduction', p. 14.
5 OD, p. 16.
6 Koziol, 'England, France, and the Problem of Sacrality', pp. 128–9; and Marc Bloch, *The Royal Touch: Sacred Monarchy and Scrofula in England and France*, trans. J. E. Anderson (London, 1973).
7 See Frank Barlow, 'The King's Evil', *EHR* 95 (1980), 3–27, esp. pp. 9–13; David Nierenberg, *Communities of Violence: Persecution of Minorities in the Middle Ages* (Princeton, 1998), pp. 58–60. Pope Gregory VII himself asserted in a letter to Bishop Hermann of Metz that those who could successfully cure lepers were imbued with divine grace. Letter translated and discussed in Bloch, *Royal Touch*, pp. 71–91. Indeed, Robert the Pious (r. 996–1031) was the first Capetian documented to have practised the royal touch, and he did so in a colony of lepers; Helgaud of Fleury, *Vie de Robert le Pieux*, p. 128.
8 Achille Luchaire, *Etudes sur les actes de Louis VII* (Brussels, 1964), pp. 101, 125, and 136. Also see David Marcombe, *Leper Knights: The Order of St Lazarus of Jerusalem in England, 1150–1544* (Woodbridge, 2003), pp. 6–15.
9 See Beaune, *The Birth of an Ideology*, pp. 172–93; Gaposchkin, *The Making of Saint Louis*, pp. 100–24. Also see the discussion of Philip Augustus visiting Saint-Denis on the eve of his departure for the Third Crusade, in Loomis, 'The Oriflamme of France', pp. 72–3.
10 *Oeuvres de Rigord et de Guillaume le Breton*, ed. Henri François Delabode, 2 vols (Paris, 1882), Vol. I, pp. 98–9.
11 Jonathan Phillips, *Defenders of the Holy Land: Relations between the Latin East and the West, 1119–1187* (Oxford, 1996), pp. 73–4. For description of Zengi's attack see Ibn al-Qalanisi, *The Damascus Chronicles of the Crusades*, ed. and trans. Hamilton A. R. Gibb (London, 1932), pp. 266–8.

12 Nerses Snorhali, 'Lament on Edessa', in *East and West in the Crusader States II: Contest, Contacts, Confrontations*, ed. Krijna N. Ciggaar and Herman G. B. Teule, trans. Theo Van Lint (Leuven, 1999), p. 75; cited in Phillips, *The Second Crusade*, prologue.
13 *La chronique de Morigny*, pp. 82–3.
14 Phillips, *The Second Crusade*, pp. 61–3.
15 See Aryeh Graboïs, 'The Crusade of Louis VII, King of France: A Reconsideration', in *Crusade and Settlement: Papers Read at the First Conference of the Society for the Study of the Crusades and the Latin East and Presented to R. C. Smail*, ed. Peter Edbury (Cardiff, 1985), pp. 95–104; Aryeh Graboïs, 'Louis VII pèlerin', *Revue d'histoire de l'Eglise de France* 74 (1988), 5–22.
16 Otto of Freising, *Gesta Friderici seu rectius Chronica*, ed. Georg Waitz and Bernhard Simson (Berlin, 1965), pp. 200–1.
17 Theobald was Count of Champagne from 1125. Before that he was Count of Chartres and Blois. Sigebert of Gembloux, 'Continuatio Praemonstratensis', *MGH SS* 6, pp. 447–56.
18 OD, p. 6.
19 *La chronique de Morigny*, p. 83.
20 Phillips, *The Second Crusade*, pp. 64–5.
21 *Ibid.*, p. 77.
22 *Ibid.*, p. 63.
23 *Ibid.*, pp. 17–36; Rubenstein, 'Putting History to Use', pp. 131–67.
24 For the narrative sources see Edgington, 'The First Crusade'. For objects and texts see Paul, *To Follow in Their Footsteps*, esp. pp. 90–133; Paul, 'Crusade, Memory, and Regional Politics'; Elizabeth Lapina, 'La représentation de la bataille d'Antioche (1098) sur les peintures murales de Poncé-sur-le-Loir', *Cahiers de civilisation médiévale* 52 (2009), 137–57.
25 Sylvia Schein, *Gateway to the Heavenly City: Crusader Jerusalem and the Catholic West (1099–1187)* (Aldershot, 2005), p. 31 n. 54.
26 Rolf Grosse, 'Überlegungen zum Kreuzzugsaufruf Eugens III. von 1145/46. Mit einer Neuedition von JL 8876', *Francia* 18 (1991), 85–92 (p. 90); Phillips, *The Second Crusade*, pp. 51–2.
27 'De laude dominici sepulchri', ed. Giles Constable, in *'Petri Venerabilis sermones tres'*, *Revue Bénédictine* 64 (1954), 234–54 (p. 247); Virginia Berry, 'Peter the Venerable and the Crusades', in *Petrus Venerabilis 1156–1956: Studies and Texts Commemorating the Eighth Centenary of His Death*, ed. Giles Constable and James Kritzeck (Rome, 1956), pp. 152–5.
28 'De laude dominici sepulchri', p. 251.
29 Peter the Venerable, Letter 130, in *The Letters of Peter the Venerable*, ed. Giles Constable, 2 vols (Cambridge, MA, 1967), Vol. I, p. 327; Phillips, *Defenders of the Holy Land*, p. 109; Berry, 'Peter the Venerable and the Crusades', pp. 148–50.
30 See Grant, *Abbot Suger*, p. 156.
31 Letter from Louis to Suger in *RHGF*, Vol. XV, p. 496.
32 Spiegel, *The Chronicle Tradition of Saint-Denis*, pp. 53–5. Also see Berry's introduction to her edition, OD, pp. xiii–xliv.
33 See Henry Mayr-Harting, 'Odo of Deuil, the Second Crusade and the Monastery of Saint-Denis', in *The Culture of Christendom: Essays in Medieval History in*

*Commemoration of Denis L. T. Bethell*, ed. Marc Anthony Meyer (London, 1993), pp. 225-41. Jonathan Phillips has produced a very sensible explanation; Jonathan Phillips, 'Odo of Deuil's *De profectione Ludovici VII in orientem* as a source for the Second Crusade', in *The Experience of Crusading*, ed. Marcus Bull, Norman Housley, Jonathan Phillips, and Peter Edbury, 2 vols (Cambridge, 2003), Vol. I, pp. 80-95.

34 Spiegel, *The Chronicle Tradition of Saint-Denis*, pp. 53-5. See also Koziol, *The Politics of Memory*, pp. 561-2.

35 Spiegel, *The Chronicle Tradition of Saint-Denis*, pp. 53-5.

36 *Ibid*. For Bernard's letter to Pope Eugenius see Bernard of Clairvaux, Letters 285 and 286, in *Sancti Bernardi opera*.

37 OD, pp. 3-5.

38 Montpellier, College of Medicine, MS 39, fos 15v-41. I have not consulted the manuscript, which is discussed by Virginia Berry in OD, pp. xxxii-xl.

39 OD, p. xxiii.

40 *VLG*, pp. xvii-xxiv. In his introduction Waquet refers to these as 'les sept principaux manuscrits' (the seven principle manuscripts), which suggests that he may have been aware of others. It is worth noting that Waquet was based in Paris, and was less aware of other archival holdings in France and Germany.

41 Georg Waitz, 'Ueber die Gesta und Historia regis Ludovici VII', *Neues Archiv der Gesellschaft für ältere deutsche Geschichtskunde* 6 (1881), 119-28; Léopold Delisle, 'Notes sur quelques manuscrits du Musée britannique', *Mémoires de la Société de l'Histoire de Paris et de l'Ile-de-France* 4 (1878), 183-238 (p. 209); Spiegel, *The Chronicle Tradition of Saint-Denis*, pp. 50-1.

42 RM, pp. xlv-xlvi. For discussion of Robert the Monk's appeal in Germany see Damien Kempf, 'Towards a Textual Archaeology of the First Crusade', in *Writing the Early Crusades: Text, Transmission and Memory*, ed. Damien Kempf and Marcus Bull (Woodbridge, 2014), pp. 116-26.

43 The manuscript tradition of this text is confusing, and essential for understanding what portion Suger completed. See Jules Lair, 'Fragment inédit de la Vie de Louis VII préparé par Suger', *Bibliothèque de l'Ecole des Chartes* 34 (1873), 583-96.

44 *De glorioso rege Ludovico*, in *Oeuvres*, Vol. I, pp. 158-60.

45 Grant, *Abbot Suger*, pp. 36-7.

46 *La chronique de Morigny*, p. 85.

47 Siberry, *Criticism of Crusading*, pp. 77-81 and 99-100.

48 *Ibid.*; OD, pp. 12-14 and 132.

49 Siberry, *Criticism of Crusading*, pp. 69-76.

50 *Ibid.*, p. 77. See Otto of Freising, *Gesta Friderici*, p. 65; Ralph Niger, *Chronica universalis*, *MGH SS* 27, pp. 327-43; '"Gesta abbatum Sancti Bertini Sithiensium": Continuation', *MGH SS* 13, pp. 635-63.

51 'Vita Prima S. Bernardi', *PL* 185, cols 225-426 (308-9).

52 Bernard of Clairvaux, 'De consideratione ad Eugenium papam', in *Sancti Bernardi opera*, Vol. III, pp. 410-11.

53 *Ibid.*, p. 412.

54 Bernard of Clairvaux, Letter 363, in *Sancti Bernardi Opera*.

RESPONSE

55 Cited and discussed in Siberry, *Criticism of Crusading*, pp. 26 and 99.
56 *Ibid.* Seneca, *De beneficiis*, vi.31. Also see Hubert Glaser, 'Wilhelm von Saint Denis: Ein Humanist aus der Umgebung des Abtes Suger und die Krise seiner Abtei von 1151 bis 1152', *Historisches Jahrbuch* 85 (1965), 257-323.
57 William of Saint-Denis, 'Sugerii Vita' in *Oeuvres*, p. 345.
58 *Ibid.*
59 See Phillips, *Defenders of the Holy Land*, pp. 100-39; Giles Constable, 'The Crusade Project of 1150', in *Montjoie: Studies in Crusade History in Honour of Hans Eberhard Mayer*, ed. Benjamin Kedar *et al.* (Aldershot, 1997), pp. 67-75; Timothy Reuter, 'The Non-Crusade of 1150', in *The Second Crusade: Scope and Consequence*, ed. Jonathan Phillips and Martin Hoch (Manchester, 2001), pp. 150-63.
60 Bernard of Clairvaux, Letter 364, in *Sancti Bernardi Opera*.
61 Eugenius III, 'Epistolae et privilegia', *PL* 180, col. 1414.
62 Bernard of Clairvaux, Letter 256, in *Sancti Bernardi Opera*.
63 Eugenius III, 'Epistolae et privilegia'.
64 Phillips, *Defenders of the Holy Land*, pp. 140-5.
65 *Ibid.*
66 Those cited by Phillips are found in Louis VII, 'Epistolae', *RHGF*, Vol. XVI, pp. 27-8, 36-40, 59-63, and 79-81.
67 Phillips, *Defenders of the Holy Land*, pp. 140-5.
68 Georges Duby, *Medieval Marriage*, pp. 54-65.
69 See Marcel Pacaut, 'Loius VI et Alexandre III', *Revue d'histoire de l'Eglise de France* 39 (1953), 5-45.
70 Phillips, *Defenders of the Holy Land*, pp. 168-70.
71 Lambert of Wattrelos, 'Annales Cameracenses', *MGH SS* 16, pp. 509-54 (p. 551). The embassy is also mentioned in William of Tyre, *Chronicon*, p. 991. Discussed by Phillips, *Defenders of the Holy Land*, pp. 172-3.
72 Lambert of Wattrelos, 'Annales Cameracenses', p. 550. For Lambert's career see Georges Duby, *The Chivalrous Society*, pp. 135-42.
73 Lambert of Wattrelos, 'Annales Cameracenses', p. 550. Cited in Phillips, *Defenders of the Holy Land*, p. 190.
74 Lambert of Wattrelos, 'Annales Cameracenses', p. 550.
75 Phillips, *Defenders of the Holy Land*, p. 191.
76 *Annales regni Francorum*, ed. F. Kurze, *MGH SS rerum Germanicarum* 6 (Hanover, 1895), pp. 1-178 (p. 112). For discussion see Aryeh Graboïs, 'Charlemagne, Rome and Jerusalem', in *Revue belge de philologie et d'histoire* 59 (1981), 792-809, esp. pp. 805-6; Philip Grierson, 'The Coronation of Charlemagne and the Coinage of Pope Leo III', *Revue belge de philologie et d'histoire* 30 (1952), 825-33.
77 *GF*, p. 2.
78 RM, p. 6.
79 Lambert of Wattrelos, 'Annales Cameracenses', pp. 550-1; Phillips, *Defenders of the Holy Land*, p. 193.

80 Paul, *To Follow in Their Footsteps*, pp. 224-5. For Henry's visit to Paris see Herbert of Bosham, 'Vita sancti Thomae', in *Materials for the History of Thomas Becket*, ed. James C. Robertson, RS 67 (London, 1875-85), Vol. III, pp. 155-534 (pp. 445-6); *The Correspondence of Thomas Becket*, ed. Anne Duggan, 2 vols (Oxford, 2000), Vol. II, p. 1047.

# 5

# Philip Augustus, political circumstance, and crusade

Philip II (r. 1180–1223) was crowned and anointed at Reims Cathedral on 1 November 1179, All Saints' Day.[1] While all coronation ceremonies were important demonstrations of the sacred attributes of the royal office, this one was especially meaningful. In addition to officially marking the beginning of Philip's reign, it also celebrated the young King's recent recovery from a life-threatening illness that had threatened the dynastic survival of the Capetians.[2] Philip and King Louis were thankful for his survival, and used the occasion of the coronation to acknowledge publicly their gratitude to God and to signal the young King's full readiness to rule.[3] For this reason, the crowd on hand to witness the coronation must have been both jubilant and large. It included representatives of all the major northern French magnates, including members of the houses of Flanders and Champagne, as well as King Henry II of England and three of his sons – Henry, Richard, and Geoffrey – who held territory in France.[4]

Exactly what they witnessed is difficult to piece together with any degree of certainty because the first coronation *ordo* specifically composed for the Capetians did not appear until the mid-thirteenth century, forcing historians to reconstruct previous coronations from a group of much earlier *ordines*.[5] While precision is not possible, enough common themes pervade the various *ordines* to allow general observations about the oaths Philip would have made during the ceremony. After being consecrated with oil and invested with the royal insignia by the Archbishop of Reims, Philip would have been reminded of his ancestors' service to the Church. At some point he would have been asked to formalize his acceptance of the obligation to the Church by promising to uphold the core values of French kings: preserving the peace of the Church and his subjects, preventing injustice, and showing mercy. Whatever the specific oath that Philip made, it undoubtedly encompassed some variation of these three precepts, which had defined French kingship since the time of the Carolingians.[6]

While Louis VII had fended off the expansionistic ambition of the Angevins with some success, even managing to make territorial gains for the French Crown at the expense of the major northern French magnates, the kingdom he left to his son was nevertheless fragile.[7] When Philip was crowned in 1179, the power of the French King was overshadowed by the Angevin rulers of England and western France. Even in the area around Paris, Philip had to tread carefully for fear of upsetting his powerful neighbours. The traditional enemies of the Capetians – the houses of Flanders to the north and east, and Blois-Champagne to the south and east – held territory just a few miles from the French capital, and the territorial princes from those regions easily matched, and on occasions exceeded, the French King in their ability to exercise real power, if not sacred status. By the time of Philip's death in 1223, however, France was transformed. He had destroyed the Angevin empire; consolidated royal territorial holdings; created a centralized bureaucracy; and, most crucially, asserted a powerful ideology that served as the foundation for the rapid expansion of French royal power in the thirteenth century.[8]

Philip's career and its broader place in the arc of Capetian history are encapsulated by a story recorded by the chronicler Rigord, whose *Gesta Philippi Augusti* recounts an often-discussed vision seen by Louis VII several years before the birth of his son.[9] In the vision, a young prince was holding out a chalice filled with the blood of French aristocrats to various assembled nobles, who all drank from it. Perhaps Louis VII had anticipated the future glory of his son, since he dramatically increased the power and prestige of the French monarchy. Many scholars have sought to explain the precise way in which Philip achieved this. Their explanations for the most part have been administrative and constitutional in nature. Less attention has been paid to Philip's relationship to crusading, despite the fact that four major expeditions were launched during his reign: the Third, Fourth, and Fifth Crusades, as well as the Albigensian Crusade. John Baldwin has considered the extent to which Philip's participation in the Third Crusade – including vis-à-vis his extended absence from France – had an impact on the growth of royal bureaucracy, but Baldwin's interest in the crusade was largely administrative in nature, and he did not consider whether the crusade might have had an impact on Philip's conception of monarchy.[10] This lack of attention is partly the consequence of Philip's failure to participate directly in the Fourth, Fifth, or Albigensian expeditions. It is also a result of the Third Crusade sources, which are overwhelmingly Anglo-Norman in provenance and tend, therefore, to favour Richard I of England.[11] This bias has shaped the opinion of many modern observers, who have denigrated Philip's role in the Third Crusade at the expense of his charismatic English counterpart. We are left with an image of a king who participated in one crusade, doing so only reluctantly, and, having failed at that, shunned the institution for the rest of his reign in favour of territorial aggrandizement at home.

In fact, King Philip's relationship to crusading was more complex than has hitherto been appreciated, and can be better understood when set in the context of the broader Capetian links to the crusades. As the heir of several decades of development of Dionysian political theology, Philip understood crusading to form a core element of his sacred obligation, an essential part of what it meant to be a French king. But, as with his father before him – and in line with the image of kingship set out by Suger in the *Vita Ludovici Grossi* – there were other obligations against which crusading always had to be balanced. Crusading remained an essential, if complicated to negotiate, part of French kingship.

### Coronation through the Third Crusade

Describing the Third Crusade army shortly after King Philip had departed from Acre in 1191 to return to France, the Anglo-Norman poet Ambroise contrasted the divided nature of the host with the unity of the first crusaders. He wrote:

> There was neither Norman nor French
> Poitivin nor Breton
> Mansel nor Burgundian
> Flemish nor English
> There was not the slightest gossip
> Nor insulting of one another
> Everyone returned with honour
> And All were called Franks ...
> When because of sin they disagreed
> The princes reconciled them.[12]

For Ambroise, the Third Crusade was hampered by internal disputes between the French and English kings, who allowed their territorial struggles in Europe to spill over to the crusade, weakening the possibility of cooperation in the East. There had been no kings on the First Crusade, of course, which makes this an inadequate comparison. Yet, the frustration apparent in Ambroise's lament bespeaks an inherent aspect of royal association with the crusade: it could never be divorced from the political and social climate in Europe. Any sort of reasonable settlement between the French and English kings was unlikely, and such an agreement was necessary for any major expedition to the East.[13] It must have been surprising to many that these kings agreed to participate in the first place, since in similar instances, such political struggles at home could mean that rulers were not able to contribute to expeditions. As we saw in the previous chapters, Louis VII was an enthusiastic supporter of crusading over the course of his life, but was only once able to take the cross himself. On many other occasions, thwarted by domestic politics and ongoing feuds, he was forced to provide financial and moral support in place of his leadership. The lesson is that we must be cautious in evaluating a king's relationship with the crusade solely on the criteria of participation and success. Suger had worked very hard to argue that a king could maintain the virtues of a crusader without ever travelling to the East by serving and protecting the Church at home. Philip put such ideas into practice.

Like his father, Philip only took the cross on one occasion, but there is evidence that he supported crusading from the beginning of his reign, believing that it was a core obligation of French sacred kingship. In 1184, five years after Philip's coronation, the Dionysian chronicler Rigord recorded the arrival at Paris of an embassy from Jerusalem that included Patriarch Heraclius and the Master of the Hospital.[14] They had travelled to the West with news of the rising threat of Saladin, who had recently defeated a large Christian force at Jacob's Ford, a strategic river crossing approximately 160 kilometres north of Jerusalem. The stunning speed and completeness of Saladin's victory were a stern warning to Christians in the crusader states, many of whom began to worry that his victory in 1179 presaged an eventual attack on Jerusalem itself. The envoys arrived at Paris and held a general council during which they described the defeat, and alerted the King and various nobles and clerics about the high stakes involved in Saladin's threat. Hoping to convince Philip to lead an army to the East, Rigord described how they offered him the keys to the city of Jerusalem as well as the Holy Sepulchre, before begging that 'he would, at God's instigation and out of love for the Christian religion, see his way to providing assistance to the land of the city of Jerusalem'.[15] Despite the arousal of Philip's 'paternal piety', Rigord argues, the King was unable to travel to the Holy Land because 'he had not yet received the desired heir from his wife'.[16] In his place, however, and at his own great expense, Philip sent several knights and foot soldiers.

Rigord's telling of this story is instructive on several levels, offering evidence of Philip's early support for the crusading movement as well as a glimpse into the continuing efforts of Saint-Denis (he was a Dionysian monk) to shape the crusading image of the French kings. Envoys from the East indeed stopped in Paris to make Philip aware of the escalating tensions with Saladin. However, Rigord's version of the episode is not complete, omitting the fact that the envoys also travelled to England, where they held a council at Clerkenwell and attempted to convince Henry II to the come to the East. As they had with Philip, they offered Henry the keys to Jerusalem. They also suggested a marriage between one of his sons and the heiress to the Kingdom of Jerusalem.[17] Henry demurred and decided instead to seek council with Philip. Thus, Henry and the envoys travelled to France, where they again met Philip (this time at Vaudreuil) and the two kings made their excuses for not travelling to the East, pledging financial aid instead, which they raised from a tax.[18]

Two things are evident in this episode. First, despite Rigord's selective retelling of the envoy's visit, Philip did indeed impose a tax to raise money for the defence of Jerusalem, thus demonstrating an early interest in the Holy Land and crusading. Second, the way in which Rigord recast the narrative – omitting any discussion of Henry II and excusing Philip's refusal to venture to the East on the grounds that he lacked an heir – is evidence that monks at Saint-Denis continued to fuse together ancient notions of kingship with newer crusade ideas. As it had been for Suger, the crusade was one of several obligations the French King had toward the Church. In Rigord's narrative, Philip supported the crusade – thus fulfilling his sacred obligation through financial assistance – but had to remain in France to protect the integrity of his dynasty. What would have happened, Rigord seems to be asking, if the French king were killed in the East with no heir to take over at home? Interestingly, this is precisely the situation that Suger had anticipated in his fragmentary history of Louis VII; the Capetians counted on dynastic continuity and it had to be protected above all else.[19] Moreover, this attitude fits Suger's vision of kingship set out in the *Vita Ludovici Grossi*. Suger had broken Louis's reign into sets of episodes, the King's resolution of which demonstrated his service to the Church. Harm to the Church happened in all parts of the world, not just the Latin East. A good king had to be alive to this fact, and follow a broad programme of protecting the Church.

A short while after the Jerusalem embassy, an episode involving another group of clerics demonstrated this point. Upon their arrival at court, they complained that Duke Hugh of Burgundy had been despoiling local churches, news that deeply upset the King. Rigord tells us that Philip, 'inflamed with zeal', interpreted Hugh's behaviour not only as a challenge to the local churches in question but also as an affront to the historical obligations of French kings to defend the Church en masse in France.[20]

> Charles and his successors, having expelled the Saracens as enemies of the Christian faith and, ruling in peace with much sweat and labour, founded with their hands many churches and monasteries in honour of our Lord Jesus Christ and Mary ... and assigned to them from their own rents adequate rents for an endowment so that the clergy, perpetually serving God in proper manner there, could obtain the necessary food. Some of them chose during their lifetimes to be buried in the church that they had founded, granting to them every kind of immunity.[21]

Philip's anger was partly the consequence of the longstanding Capetian policy of using control of churches in non-Capetian territory as a mechanism to expand political power. But there is perhaps more to Rigord's comments. When Hugh refused to make the reparations to the churches as Philip had demanded, the King used military action to bring the Duke to heel, and 'thus peace was restored, [and] King Philip Augustus returned to his palace in Paris, praising and magnifying the Lord'.[22]

Philip's conflict with Duke Hugh occurred in 1184, the same year in which the Jerusalem embassy had sought aid for the Holy Land. From a broad perspective, then, Rigord's narrative painted a picture of a king who supported the Church in the East while also protecting the Church in France, which was equally threatened by rogue barons such as Hugh. By the reign of Philip II crusading had been absorbed into the King's broader sacred obligation to the Church. French kings since the time of Charlemagne had indeed defended the Church and the peace in France. Since the reign of Louis VII, however, that role had expanded to include defending the Church externally through support of the crusade.

It would have been difficult for Philip seriously to consider journeying to the Latin East early in his reign. The years between the King's coronation in 1179 and his departure for the Third Crusade in 1190 were marked by a series of fluid alliances and constantly shifting conflicts in northern France as the young King struggled to negotiate his position.[23] The dominant power in the region was Henry II, who since the 1150s had been making significant territorial gains at the French King's expense. When Philip was crowned in 1179, Henry controlled Anjou to the west, Normandy to the north, and (through his wife, Eleanor), the duchy of Aquitaine to the south. King Louis, who always 'had hatred for the English King', recognized the potential menace to Capetian hegemony posed by the Angevins and warned Philip always to be wary of Henry and his sons.[24] In the first decade of his reign, therefore, Philip experienced competition with his leading adversaries in northern France: Count Philip of Flanders, his mother's relatives in Champagne, and Henry II and his sons.

This same set of political circumstances had occupied the final years of Louis VII's reign. Over the 1160s and 1170s, in response to the growth of Angevin power, King Louis had sought new allies to aid him in his struggle with Henry II. In particular he looked to Champagne and Flanders, both traditional enemies of the Capetian court. In 1160, Louis married his third wife, Adela of Champagne, and shortly afterwards appointed several of her close relatives to key positions in the court and French Church.[25] The connection to the house of Champagne provided a necessary counterweight to the rising prestige of the Angevins, especially since the two families had been contesting the city of Tours for several years and thus were unlikely to broker a peace agreement behind the King's back. In addition to seeking the support of his wife's family, Louis had already sought out the support of Count Philip of Flanders.[26] The county of Flanders was one of the wealthiest in France, and its close proximity to Normandy made Count Philip a natural ally in the conflict with Henry II. Count Philip remained a close confederate of the French King during the 1170s, and supported him in a number of actions perceived to be 'anti-Henry', including backing Thomas Becket in his fight with the English King, and accompanying Louis on a pilgrimage to Becket's shrine at Canterbury when young Prince Philip fell ill.[27]

While Philip was busy negotiating the tumultuous political world of northern France, news arrived of Saladin's capture of Jerusalem in 1187, the event that began the Third Crusade. The crusader states had been in a difficult position ever since the failure of the Second Crusade in 1149. In the immediate aftermath of that conflict, the Latin Kingdom of Jerusalem entered a bitter civil war as the young King Baldwin III struggled for control of Jerusalem against his mother, Queen Melisende. While the political struggle had ended by 1152, the fate of the Christian East did not improve much in the coming decades. Christians in the Latin East had long desired control of Egypt, and in the 1150s, the temptation of an easy victory proved difficult to resist. Unfortunately, the involvement of the crusader states in Egypt ended up pushing the Latin East into political and military difficulty, paving the way for the rise of Saladin by allowing him a way to expound the same type of *jihad* propaganda that Zengi and Nur al-Din had pioneered in the 1140s.[28] Saladin was a deeply religious man who dreamed of uniting the Muslim world under his banner, and he realized that he first needed to consolidate his power in the region. A four-year truce with the new King of Jerusalem, Baldwin IV, 'the Leper King', provided such an opportunity. By the time the truce was set to expire on 5 April 1187, Saladin had united an empire stretching from Egypt in the south to the Tigris river in the east. By the spring of 1187 he was in a position to move against the Christian states.

For much of the period of the truce, the Latin kingdom was mired in conflict. Baldwin IV's illness precluded the possibility of his producing a direct heir, and Guy of Lusignan and Raynald of Châtillon consequently fought for control of the kingdom.[29] As Guy consolidated his position in the Holy City, Raynald fled to his own territory in the Transjordan and declared it to be independent of Jerusalem and its king. The land Raynald controlled was important, in part because it was along a favoured trading route of the Muslim caravans travelling from Cairo to Damascus. In the winter of 1186–87, several months before the truce was set to expire, Raynald attacked one such caravan. With the period of peace coming to an end, Saladin demanded that Guy force Raynald to return the stolen items as well as to make suitable reparations. Raynald refused on the grounds that he was 'master of his own land, as Guy was of his, and he [Raynald] had no truce with the Saracens'.[30] The stage was set for open hostilities between Saladin and the crusader states.

Saladin entered Frankish territory late in 1187 with an army as large as 30,000 men.[31] The Christian force mustered by Guy, which numbered perhaps as many as 20,000, traversed the desert around Tiberias looking for an open stretch of land that would allow the Frankish knights to mount a cavalry charge. Manoeuvring around the desert is a hot and tiring business, however, and the Christians were not able to remain near a fresh water source. On 4 July 1184 Saladin's army surrounded the Christians at the Horns of Hattin, the site of an extinct volcano. With no water and no escape route, the Christian army was decimated.[32] Thousands of Christians were killed, and many others were taken prisoner. Saladin also seized the relic of the True Cross, which the first crusaders had discovered in 1099 and which the Franks had carried into battle ever since. From any vantage point, the loss at Hattin was devastating to the crusader states. The Christian army had drawn recruits from across the Latin East, and the large number of dead meant that it was no longer able to defend the territory. Over the remainder of the summer, Saladin captured many Frankish cities, including Tyre, Acre, Sidon, and Beirut. Jerusalem held out for a short period, but surrendered on 2 October 1187. Less than a century after its takeover by the first crusaders, the Holy City was back in Muslim control.

It did not take long for news to reach the West. Archbishop Joscius of Tyre set off in the early autumn of 1187, travelling on a ship with black sails, 'so that whenever the ship neared land those who saw it would know that it brought bad news'.[33] His first stop was in Sicily, where he convinced King William II to send a small number of troops to help defend the remaining Christian strongholds in the Holy Land.[34] Joscius made his way up the coast of Italy, eventually arriving in Rome, where Pope Urban III received him. News of Jerusalem's fall and the loss of the True Cross relic delivered a severe enough blow to the elderly Pope that he died of grief.[35] The coincidence of Urban's name was not lost on observers, one of whom noted that 'it was in the time of Urban II that Jerusalem was conquered, and it was in the time of Urban III that it was lost'.[36] The Pope was not the only one to be profoundly affected by the loss. Europe's ruling elite had been lukewarm to taking the cross since the failure of the Second Crusade. For nearly twelve years Henry II had ignored an order by the Church to undertake a penitential pilgrimage to Jerusalem as recompense for the death of Becket.[37] Only a few years before, as we saw, Henry and Philip had both refused to journey to the East, choosing instead to send financial aid. All of a sudden, however, men such as Henry and Philip were primed to act, and the new Pope, Gregory VIII, recognized this. For the Third Crusade to be successful it had to be led by kings. The stakes and expenses were otherwise too high. On this point, it is significant that virtually all of the major recruitment events in the regions that provided the bulk of crusaders happened only after the Pope secured a royal pledge from the corresponding ruler to support the expedition.[38] Indeed, one of the first things Gregory VIII did was to dispatch legates to the major European courts to drum up enthusiasm for the new crusade.[39]

The first prince to join the crusade was Henry II's eldest surviving son, Count Richard (soon to become King Richard I), who took the cross at Tours in November 1187.[40] Although Richard took the cross several months before any other European leaders, and quite independently of them, it is important to note that he was not yet king. Thus, the stakes were lower for him in committing to a lengthy absence. In addition, he was locked in conflict with his father, while still on friendly terms with Philip in November 1187, and perhaps he saw his assumption of the crusader's vow – one that his father had been neglecting for years – as a way for him to win support from the Church. Because of Richard's enthusiasm for taking the cross, scholars have been quick to charge Philip with delaying, but the evidence does not support this position. The French King had already demonstrated a willingness to help the Latin East in 1185 when he sent financial and military aid in the wake of the defeat at Jacob's Ford. Given the political climate in northern France in 1187, it was unreasonable for Philip to join the crusade before reaching some sort of peace with Henry II. The French King's seeming reluctance may also have been a reaction to Louis VII's false start at Bourges before the Second Crusade, the consequence of the lack of *Quantum praedecessores*. Philip may have wanted to have a sense of the papal plans as laid out in a crusading bull before either committing himself or asking his nobles to follow him. Finally, it is worth adding that Philip was probably nervous about his lack of an heir. Rigord had suggested as much in his description of Philip's refusal to go to the East in 1184. Louis was born in September 1187, a short time after news of Jerusalem's fall reached the royal court. Considering that Philip ultimately took the cross in January 1188, Prince Louis's birth was probably more than a coincidental precursor to Philip's decision. The French King was not a reluctant crusader; he was a cautious one.

The Pope issued *Audita tremendi* in the late autumn of 1187, authorizing a new crusade and setting out his expectations and the privileges to be enjoyed by those who took the cross. It began with a detailed recounting of Saladin's victory at Hattin, highlighting the loss of the True Cross, and his conquest of Jerusalem several months later. This much would be expected in any call to crusade, but the stakes were especially high with this appeal since Jerusalem was under Muslim control. Gregory needed royal support for his enterprise, and thus reminded Europe's rulers of their responsibility. Edessa was lost in 1144, he argued, because Christendom had sinned: 'For his anger is not quick, but he puts off the punishment, and gives time for repentance.'[41] Jerusalem was lost for the same reason; it was not the fault of those in the East, but rather the sins of those in the West: 'For we hear from every direction of scandals and conflicts between kings and princes, among cities, so that we lament with the prophet and are able to say, "there is no truth, no knowledge of God in the land, lying murder and adulterers abound, and blood pursues blood"'.[42] Much of the blame for the loss of Jerusalem fell squarely on the shoulders of Europe's rulers – like Philip and Henry – who constantly sinned against God by their incessant fighting. It naturally followed that if they had played a role in the loss of Jerusalem, then they should play a leading role in its recovery. We have already seen that Philip – perhaps more than Henry II – had expressed a willingness to provide aid to the

Holy Land, but he was not able to venture to the East if his major political enemies – Henry II, in particular – remained at home, free to attack his lands with impunity. Gregory understood this, and worked to broker a peace between the parties.

Archbishop Joscius of Tyre played the role of mediator. He caught up with Philip and Henry in a meadow near Gisors in January 1188 and, according to Roger of Howden, he worked 'to establish the strictest truce among all the princes of Christendom, to last for a period of seven years'.[43] The first move was to broker a peace between the two kings.[44] According to Joscius, he succeeded (if temporarily) in this goal, convincing both Henry and Philip to take the cross, which they did alongside many of the leading magnates from northern France.[45] This does not mean, as might be suggested, that when a king joined a crusade he entered a liminal state in which domestic political struggles were eclipsed by a sense of Christian unity and duty.[46] The stakes were too high for this. In the case of the Third Crusade, Roger of Howden recalled that while the army of the Third Crusade was united in general purpose, it was nevertheless split into distinct groups, reflecting various domestic territorial disputes raging in northern France. He wrote, 'the King of France and his men wore red crosses; the King of England with his, white crosses; while Philip of Flanders with his people wore green crosses'.[47] Roger does not go into great detail about the significance of the coloured crosses, though he does note that their purpose was to set apart the crusaders of various political loyalties, which suggests that the territorial disputes going on in northern France would carry over to the Syrian desert, at least in terms of shaping the allegiance of the troops.

Despite any crusading vows, the territorial conflicts continued to delay the kings' departure. Soon after Philip and Henry had taken the cross, Richard attacked the Count of Toulouse, who, by custom, appealed to Philip to intervene against the Angevins on his behalf. Though all the actors involved in this instance theoretically enjoyed the papal protections afforded to crusaders, Richard and Philip were unable to prioritize the crusade over their disagreements at home.[48] Indeed, it was only the death of Henry II at Chinon in July 1189 that freed Richard and Philip to move forward in their crusading preparations.

Much scholarship has emphasized the efficiency with which King Richard (after the death of his father) raised money and prepared for the crusade. Comparatively less attention has been paid to Philip's preparations, despite Rigord's recording the departing King's 'Testament' in his chronicle.[49] The document was designed to 'set down how the necessary business of the kingdom should be managed in our absence and to make final arrangements for our life in case we should end it on the way'.[50] The bulk of Philip's authority was vested in his mother, Adela, and his uncle, Archbishop William of Reims. The King had a particular fear of territorial aggrandizement by outside powers while he was away, and much of the Testament details the ways in which defence was to be organized should such an attack occur.[51] Baldwin had described the practical nature of this document, calling it the 'ordinary testament'.[52] It shows the logistical realities facing a king preparing to depart on crusade. However, it also points to Philip's profound anxiety about going off to the East at the expense of losing ground at home. This puts a new complexion on the King's seeming reluctance in taking the cross in the first place and his delay in departure, confirming the broader point about royal crusade introduced at the beginning of the chapter: it had to be weighed constantly against domestic political considerations.

Though Richard is commonly portrayed as the more eager crusader, it was actually Philip who took much of the initiative in organizing the kings and getting the expedition off the ground.[53] It is significant that he did so in a way that was in line with the established Capetian practice of using participation in the crusades as a way to promote sacred kingship. In the months preceding Philip's departure for the East, he followed a similar programme to the one used by Louis VII in 1146 as he prepared to depart on the Second Crusade. Indeed, it was almost as if Suger were planning the Third Crusade departure ceremony. On the Feast of St John the Baptist (24 June 1190) Philip travelled to Saint-Denis where he received the pilgrim's scrip and staff from his uncle, Archbishop William of Reims. The date may be significant, since the eve of the Feast of St John the Baptist marked the end of the Lendit Fair, which is when Louis VII had arrived at Saint-Denis for his own departure. Also like his father, in addition to the scrip and staff, Philip received the *oriflamme* from the altar. Rigord is clear that the King was following tradition: 'for the French kings had been accustomed since old that whenever they took up arms against their enemies they carried with them the banner from the altar of the Blessed Dionysius for their safety and protection'.[54] Also following the tradition – which was not so ancient, dating to Louis VI's 1124 war with Henry V – Philip prostrated himself before the altar at Saint-Denis, where he prayed to the holy relics for his safe return.[55]

Philip's departure ceremony was unquestionably patterned on the one used by Louis VII in 1146, which itself was based on Louis VI's 1124 visit to Saint-Denis to prepare for his upcoming fight with the German

Emperor.⁵⁶ Suger's legacy is evident in Philip's preparations for the Third Crusade, which were crafted with an eye toward the Capetian crusading image. The same was true of Philip's next major appearance at Vézelay, where he met King Richard in early July 1190. Located in the heart of Burgundy, equidistant from major zones of crusade recruit, Vézelay was a convenient point of muster for the two armies, but there was more to the two-day stopover than logistics might suggest. Vézelay had a clear connection to the Second Crusade as the place where Louis VII had stood alongside Bernard and convinced a huge number of French knights to follow him to the East. Philip already had his army, but he nevertheless used the backdrop of the cathedral at Vézelay to entrust 'the custody of the whole Kingdom of the Franks along with his most beloved son Louis to his very dear mother Adela and his uncle William, Archbishop of Rheims.'⁵⁷ Before the Third Crusade ever left France, King Philip had placed it within the royal French crusading tradition.

Domestic political squabbles continued to plague the Third Crusade once it was underway. The kings and their respective armies departed from Vézelay at the same time, made the journey across France together, and reached Lyon-sur-Rhône on the same day. The anonymous *Itinerarium peregrinorum et gesta regis Ricardi* recalled that Philip departed the city first, the weight of his army taxing the bridge over the Rhône river and causing it to collapse. The source is clear that Richard and his army were not any part of this group, since they only later learned of the event. Though a seemingly minor detail, this episode demonstrates that while travelling together with the French army, the Anglo-Norman force was recognized and treated by sources as a distinct and separate group.⁵⁸

Scholars have tended to follow the Anglo-Norman sources in highlighting Richard's contribution to the Third Crusade at the expense of Philip, who is portrayed as a reluctant participant always looking for a moment to return home.⁵⁹ The main eyewitness account of the Third Crusade is that of Ambroise, who was probably a Norman cleric in a minor order. His text, known as the *Estoire de la guerre sainte*, is highly complimentary of the Anglo-Norman crusaders, and shows hostility to those from the Ile-de-France.⁶⁰ For good or ill, Ambroise and the other Anglo-Norman writers offer the fullest coverage of the Third Crusade, and thus have been favoured by historians trying to reconstruct the events. In such cases, the bias of the sources has been allowed to shape modern treatments. Such approaches have also been influenced by an inclination to read history backwards, knowing the outcome of events. In this case, we know that Philip returned to France after the siege of Acre, and thus, we are more likely to believe that this was planned from the beginning. The evidence, however, does not support such a conclusion. Philip distinguished himself at Acre, and returned home early because political circumstances demanded it. The French King arrived at the port of Acre on 20 April 1191, long before Richard, who was bogged down on Cyprus fighting against Isaac Dukas, a breakaway provincial ruler.[61] Christians in the East, most notably Guy of Lusignan, had been besieging Acre for nearly two years when the French King arrived. Philip's arrival, however, boosted the Christian efforts. In the weeks leading up to Richard's arrival, the French King spent his time scouting the walls of the city to 'see what part might be the easiest to capture'.[62] He also ordered the construction of a number of siege engines in preparation for the eventual battle. According to a number of sources, the French King could have easily taken the city of Acre at this point.[63] The conditions of the mostly Muslim inhabitants were poor, and they were not equipped to put up much of a fight. However, it is significant that Philip felt compelled to await the arrival of Richard before attacking. Eventually the English King arrived, and the siege began in earnest. Despite the illness of both kings, the city ended up surrendering after only a few days. It was French miners who eventually brought down the walls, paving the way for the city's surrender on 12 July. The French King played a crucial role not only in bringing about the recapture of Acre, but also in his willingness to wait for Richard before commencing the attack. Nonetheless, his departure from Acre in a matter of weeks has coloured subsequent opinions of his role in the siege.

Modern scholars have tended to focus on Philip's early departure from the Third Crusade, finding evidence in the Anglo-Norman sources for an extreme sense of displeasure on the part of those crusaders who remained in the East.[64] The author of the *Itinerarium*, for example, which is related to Ambroise's *Estoire*, praised Philip's role in the siege of Acre, but noted that his army was outraged by his decision to return to France: 'A rumour spread among the army that the French King ... wished to return to France. The French [crusading host] would have renounced their obligations to Philip's authority and lordship if they could have.'[65] Roger of Howden recorded in his chronicle a letter composed by Richard in which he said Philip as having 'dishonourably abandoned the purpose of his pilgrimage, and broken his vow, against God's will to the perpetual disgrace of himself and of his kingdom'.[66] Why, one ought to ask, are the Anglo-Normans so intent on denigrating Philip's contribution? If, as they suggest, his departure from the expedition proved his cowardice, then why go to such lengths to highlight his behaviour several years afterwards?

Indeed, it is highly significant that virtually all of the sources that lambast Philip's return to France are Anglo-Norman and were written after Richard failed to recapture Jerusalem himself. They perhaps were looking to shift the blame. Other sources, however, such as the Muslim account of Saladin's life by Baha al-Din, are not aware of Philip's departure, noting simply that Philip contracted a disease during the siege of Acre and died a short time afterwards.[67] Baha al-Din was a generally well informed source, and his dismissive account of Philip's behaviour indicates that the King's departure was less important at the time of the siege of Acre than it was to the Anglo-Norman authors, most of whom wrote several years afterwards. Not only have scholars tended to follow the Anglo-Norman line concerning Philip's behaviour because, in a sense, it's most of what survives, but they have also internalized its distortions without due regard to Philip as a sort of corrective, thus belying the significance of the crusade in shaping Philip's overall vision of monarchy.

Philip's return to France was motivated less by his spite for Richard and more by the shift in political balance that had been caused by the death of several of his most fierce opponents in the East. Count Theobald of Blois, Henry of Troyes, and Stephen of Sancerre were all killed during the siege of Acre, as was Count Philip of Flanders. The French King, as John Baldwin remarked, 'had left the major barons of his father's generation buried in the Syrian sands'.[68] The death of Philip of Flanders, in particular, may have motivated Philip's return to France. As Cartellieri argued, French kings had always worried about Flanders, and Philip needed to be back in France to protect his interest in the Flemish succession.[69] Indeed, Count Philip had died on 1 June, which means that news of his death was nearly two months old by the time the King departed from the Holy Land. This provided plenty of time for King Philip's rivals to have moved against his claims. Ultimately, from a political perspective, Philip's return to France to defend his interests in the Flemish succession proved a smart move; the French King ended up gaining Artois, the Amiénois, and Vermandois as well as much of Beauvais as a consequence of his return. From the royal perspective, being a crusader was important, but so was having a strong France, which would protect the Church in the long run.

Philip suffered surprisingly little negative publicity from his return to France in 1191. There is some evidence that the French King stopped in Rome, where he met with Pope Celestine III in order to brief the new Pope on the status of the Third Crusade and to be absolved of his vow. Of course, it is possible that the Pope would have acceded to these wishes on political grounds, but a majority of sources indicate no ill feeling toward

Philip among his peers. In fact, there is reason to conclude that the French crusaders who remained in the East actually worried about preserving the French King's reputation. The author of the *Continuation de Guillaume de Tyr* recalled the Duke of Burgundy's concern about Richard's decision to besiege Jerusalem.

> This [decision] set the Duke thinking, and when he had considered the matter he sent for the leading men from France and told them what was on his mind. 'Sirs, you all know well that Philip has departed, but the whole contingent of his army remains. By comparison the King of England has only a few men. If we go to Jerusalem and take it, it will not be said that the French have taken it. Rather it will be said that the King of England has done so. Great shame it will be to the King of France and great reproach to the whole kingdom, and all will say that the King of France had fled and the King of England won back Jerusalem, and never again will France be without reproach.'[70]

This passage is significant because it reveals a deep concern among French crusaders for the reputation of their kings. The Duke of Burgundy was no close friend of King Philip's; we have already seen the punishments meted out by Philip to the Duke as a consequence of his treatment of local churches. Duke Hugh, it seems, was less concerned about the man, Philip of France, and more troubled about the potential damage to the reputation of the French royal dynasty. If this is true, it offers a glimpse into the way the nobility understood the connection between the crusade and rulership. The recapture of Jerusalem could have bolstered Richard's reputation, thus making him a more potent enemy of the French King. With Philip back in France, it was essential that the French crusaders do nothing to undercut the crusading image of the Capetians. Indeed, this point neatly sums up King Philip's relationship with crusading in the early part of his reign. He was supportive of crusading, as his ancestors had been, but he also understood the Capetian legacy of broader service to the Church, a point that he always had to balance against actual participation in an expedition. Indeed, this would define Philip's relationship with crusading for the remainder of his life.

At the time, Philip did not suffer any ill effect for his early departure from the Third Crusade, and it seems likely that the death of several leading French barons on the expedition placed the French King in a stronger position to assert royal prerogatives that he had been contemplating since he was a young child. Gerald of Wales recalls a story that Louis VII took (then Prince) Philip to meet Henry II at the castle of Gisors. Despite the splendour of the palace, Philip complained that Gisors was not even stronger and richer, since 'the more valuable the materials of the castle, the more pleasure I will have in holding it when it falls into my hands'.[71] The King was forced to tread carefully in his attempt to do this in the years leading up to the Third Crusade. Henry II and his sons dominated most of his time, though the King could ill afford to confront the counts of Champagne and Flanders. However, with many of these powerful nobles being left in the deserts of Syria, Philip was free in the years immediately after the Third Crusade to begin constructing the French monarchy in a new way.[72] Of particular note is a change in the structure of the royal council. Up to this point, the Capetians had relied on the leading magnates from northern France – men like Philip of Flanders and his mother's cousin, Theobald of Blois.[73] Both men had died on crusade, however, and Philip did not replace them with advisors of similar rank. Instead, the French King increasingly surrounded himself with members of the lower nobility who posed less threat and who owed their new-found status to the King. The cumulative effect of this was to restrict the direct participation of the leading French magnates in the royal court. In addition, it was in the years directly after the Third Crusade that Philip began asserting France's division as a feudal hierarchy; once imagined by Suger as an ideal toward which to work, over the course of the 1190s Philip worked to make feudal suzerainty a reality.[74] Any participation in future crusading endeavours would have to be balanced against political circumstances at home.

## Post Third Crusade

Philip did not participate in any more crusades, and thus the sources from the latter part of his reign are more difficult to interpret from a crusading perspective. Nevertheless, there is evidence that the King remained committed to the movement, and that the crusades continued to shape Philip's vision of kingship. The dominant feature of the early thirteenth century was the papacy of Innocent III, who from the very beginning of his tenure in January 1198 signalled his strong support for the crusading movement.[75] It is no exaggeration to claim that Innocent was the pope most obsessed with crusading in the Middle Ages. While the Third Crusade had solidified the image of Richard I as the ideal Christian knight, it had only made modest territorial gains by securing a small strip of coastal territory that could provide a beachhead for future expeditions. So long as Jerusalem and the True Cross remained in Muslim hands, western Christians had an obligation to fight for their return.[76] Innocent was determined to oversee the return of Christ's patrimony, and set about erecting the necessary framework to bring that about. In the late summer of 1198, scarcely seven months after ascending the throne of St Peter, Innocent III proclaimed a new expedition to recover Jerusalem – what would become the Fourth Crusade. While the Fourth Crusade is one of the better-known episodes of medieval history, attention has been largely focused on the crusaders' sack of Constantinople in 1204.[77] The period of recruitment and planning, in contrast, has received far less attention, which is in part, as Vince Ryan noted, 'the product of a school of thought in Fourth Crusade scholarship that maintains that Innocent was against royal participation in this campaign'.[78] It is true, of course, that no kings participated in the Fourth Crusade, but this result does not necessarily equate with design or disinterest. Many scholars have emphasized Innocent's objection to any sort of royal involvement in the crusade.[79] In fact, Innocent made a concerted effort to convince kings, particularly Richard I and Philip II, to join the Fourth Crusade. And, both kings showed a willingness to consider his request. In the case of Richard, of course, it was his untimely death in the spring of 1199 that took him out of the running. For Philip, once again political circumstances at home militated against joining a crusade. This does not mean he was uninterested.

The crusading bull *Post miserabile* was issued on 13 August 1198.[80] In the text of this document Innocent laid out his vision for the new crusade, highlighting the privileges and protections to be enjoyed by those who took the cross. He also expressed his displeasure at Richard and Philip's behaviour in the years after Philip's return from the Third Crusade and Richard's release from captivity. Innocent argued that Muslim leaders grew bolder as a consequence of infighting between Christian kings. 'Our enemies insult us by saying … as for your kings and princes who we drove out of the lands of the East, in order that they would conceal their terror by putting on a show of bravery, after returning … they prefer to attack each other.'[81] Vince Ryan, who has considered *Post miserable* from the perspective of Richard I, has convincingly demonstrated that 'the mocking tone that Innocent employed – under the pretext of describing the purported jeers of the infidel – had a very specific purpose: that of shaming in order to provoke a desired response'.[82] Against this backdrop, Innocent asked Christendom 'how then, brothers and sons, are we to rebut the scorn of these insulters …?'.[83] He went on to urge the knights of Christendom to take up the charge, but in contrast to scholars who have argued that Innocent imagined a king-free crusade, he also signalled

RESPONSE

his desire to end the conflict between Richard and Philip, presumably with an eye toward their joining the new expedition.

> Wherefore, in the meantime, we have sent the noted Peter [of Capuano], cardinal deacon and titular of Santa Maria in Via Lata, to our most dearly beloved sons in Christ, the most illustrious kings Philip, king of the Franks, and Richard, king of the English, in order to effect a reconciliation between them, or at least obtain a truce to last for at least five years.[84]

The consistent specific references in a crusading bull to the ongoing conflict between Richard and Philip are highly suggestive of the Pope's desire to secure royal participation, albeit with papal direction.

Achieving peace between the two kings was the critical first step in this plan, and to this end, Innocent threatened both monarchs that he would place the two kingdoms under interdict if they did not come to a consensus.[85] Nevertheless, when the legate Peter Capuano travelled to France to meet the two kings in January 1199, he had his work cut out.[86] The two kings had been fighting since February 1194, when Richard was released from captivity and returned home to find that Philip had taken possession of much of his territorial holdings in northern France and allied against him with Richard's brother, John.[87] Richard's return to England in the early spring of 1194 led to the collapse of John's rebellion, and the weak brother attempted to make amends by fighting for Richard in his conflict with Philip Augustus. The ensuing war was characterized by bitter fighting on both sides, and restoring peace between the two kings was not going to be an easy task for Peter Capuano.[88]

Peter was able ultimately to convince both kings to accept a peace treaty.[89] Innocent was pleased with the news, since it would allow his new expedition to move forward. He shared this feeling with Philip Augustus in a letter from late March 1199.[90] Only a matter of weeks later, King Richard died, throwing Innocent's (and perhaps Philip's) carefully laid plans into disarray. In particular, Philip was anxious about Innocent's increasingly powerful claims of papal authority over the European monarchs. Indeed, the Fourth Crusade is a good example of Innocent's attempt to centralize control in the hands of the papacy. Jonathan Riley-Smith has argued that with the failure and disunity of the Third Crusade still a fresh memory at the papal curia, Innocent's seemingly passive methods of courting royal support for the Fourth Crusade were driven by his insistence on having more papal control over the expedition.[91] The idea of Innocent wanting to control the progress of the Fourth Crusade certainly fits with what we know about his behaviour at several key

130

moments during the expedition. He wrote a number of letters to the leaders of the expedition in an attempt to direct the crusade back on track, sometimes threatening ecclesiastical sanction if his wishes were not followed.[92] The fact is that while King Philip had generally positive relations with the papacy, he was not willing to support the fully centralizing policies of Innocent, particularly now that Richard was dead. As evidence of this point, it was at the time of the Fourth Crusade that Pope Innocent attempted to enact much more stringent regulations governing French crusaders. Philip was supportive of the actual regulations, but contested the Pope's right to enact such legislation without his permission.[93]

Not only was Philip unsupportive of Innocent's desire to control the crusade, but the death of Richard I had opened up several possibilities to advance Capetian territorial claims in France at the expense of the Angevins. Richard's successor, John, was less capable than his brother, and Philip was in a position to take advantage of his comparatively weak position. It was unlikely that the French King would sign on to support a crusade to the East so long as the possibility existed of territorial aggrandizement at home, particularly if it came with the added bonus of being at the expense of the Angevins. The first several years of John's reign were difficult ones for the English King. He was not nearly as popular as Richard, and in addition to dealing with this public relations issue he also had to contend with the French King's continued attempts to undermine his position by supporting Richard's nephew, Arthur, as the legitimate heir to the English throne.[94] By the autumn of 1203, with John's position still tenuous, Philip was in a position to launch a military attack on Normandy. John remained in England as the French King swarmed into Plantagenet holdings across the duchy. By 1204, the French King had added Normandy to his territory. In terms of the present chapter it is important that the events in Normandy paralleled the Fourth Crusade. Had Philip joined that expedition, he would have missed the valuable opportunity to consolidate his power at home. We must remember that in 1204 the future of France was still being secured; the crusading reputation of the French kings, as we have seen, was a key mechanism by which the kings secured their image and power, but it was generally not allowed to compete with actual military conquest. Thus, in the same way that Louis VII remained a 'crusader in image' during the later part of his life, Philip Augustus continued to portray himself and be portrayed by others as having the virtues of a crusader, even if he was not able to participate in any further expeditions to the East.

The later part of Philip's reign bears out a central and unique point concerning the French kings' relationship to the crusades: that it had to function alongside and not in the place of a broader political programme. This peculiar point to royal crusading is essential to contextualizing the place of kings in the movement, a point illustrated by a new expedition called by Innocent III against the Cathar heretics in southern France, the Albigensian Crusade. King Philip never participated in the expedition, a fact that has been used by some historians to support an image of a king antagonistic to the institution of crusading. While the sources are limited, enough evidence survives to suggest that the King was indeed supportive of Innocent's quest against the southern French heretics, but was unable to participate because of political circumstances at home.

Alleged Cathar heretics had been a problem in southern France for quite some time, which probably stemmed from the Bogomil dualist heresy prevalent in Byzantium since the tenth century.[95] While local solutions had been tried to rein in the heresy since the mid-twelfth century, upon taking office, Innocent undertook a broader approach to confront the Cathars. On several occasions (1198, 1200–01, and 1203–04), the Pope sent a number of legates to investigate the extent of the heresy and the steps being taken by local bishops to confront it. Over the series of missions, Innocent became increasingly alarmed at what he perceived to be ineffective bishops, and thus in 1204 he appointed several new legates, among them Peter of Castelnau and Arnaud Aimery, charging them with rooting out the heresy. The legates were especially troubled by the perceived indifference of local lords, particularly Count Raymond VI of Toulouse, who, while not guilty of being a Cathar himself, they believed had failed to act against the heretics in his community. As the Pope grew more concerned, he also moved closer to a military solution to the problem. In 1204 he issued Holy Land indulgences to knights who fought against the heretics.

On two occasions, in 1205 and again in 1207, the Pope wrote to King Philip requesting his help rooting out the heretics. In a letter sent to the King in November 1207, the Pope offered the King a Holy Land indulgence if he participated, and hinted that any lands he purified could be conquered for the French Crown. The French King was probably tempted by such an offer. Since returning from the Third Crusade he had demonstrated a keen interest in expanding the boarders of royal territory, and southern France was a powerful economic centre. Unfortunately, as noted above, Philip was not in a political position to leave Paris. In addition to having to defend himself against King John, Philip was growing increasingly wary about the German Emperor Otto IV, whose opponent the French King had backed in a contentious election and who was increasingly involving himself in

Philip's feud with the King John. The French King thus demurred, though it is worth noting that he did not refuse the Pope's offer outright.

The murder of Peter of Castelnau in January 1207 accelerated the move toward a military response to the heretics. Count Raymond VI, described by one author as 'changeable, crafty, slippery, and inconsistent', was widely suspected by the papal curia of inciting the assassins, and Innocent soon turned the crusade against him.[96] The Cistercian chronicler of the expedition, Peter of Vaux-de-Cernay, criticized Philip for not showing enough support for the fight against the heretics, but this is unfair and has been a position too often adopted by modern scholars.[97] It is true that Philip did not participate himself, and that he did not allow his son, Prince Louis (the future Louis VIII) to travel to the south despite his having taken a crusading vow in 1213. However, Bradbury has argued that the royal French involvement with the Albigensian Crusade was approached by the King in a wider context. The French King faced several obstacles to his participation in the expedition. In the first place, since Count Raymond of Toulouse was a vassal of the French King, Philip refused to condemn him unless the Church officially declared him a heretic (which he was not). There were other concerns as well. Once the crusade was underway, the Pope again wrote to Philip, whom he described as 'a most Christian prince', requesting that he travel south to lead the crusading forces or else send 'a strong, wise, and faithful man' in his stead. Innocent III's simultaneous release of a general call to crusade suggests that he did not seriously expect Philip to participate, though he may have had Prince Louis in mind when he asked for a suitable replacement. The King did not allow his son to join the expedition, however, but he did allow some of his more important nobles and barons to join the papal army in southern France, which must not be underestimated. In his reply to Innocent, King Philip reminded the Pope that he was still locked in conflict with the English King and German Emperor (whom the Pope supported). Thus, his willingness to allow several key barons to abandon the defence of northern France in favour of fighting the heretics in the south offers a glimpse into the King's difficult position. Philip was in a strong position by 1209, and had he wished to, he could have refused Innocent outright, perhaps chastising the Pope for his support of the German Emperor. However, while he and his son were required to stay near Paris to confront the twin Anglo-German threat, his willingness to release several key barons from their service indicates a genuine desire to support the crusading endeavour.

Prince Louis had taken the cross in 1213, though Philip did not allow him to fulfil his vow at that time, citing the same Anglo-German threat.

King John and Emperor Otto were defeated respectively at the battles of La Roche-aux-Moines and Bouvines. By the end of the summer of 1214, therefore, the main threats to French royal safety were dispatched. While Philip did not now express a willingness to join the crusade, it is worth considering that he was nearly fifty years old. Moreover, he did allow Prince Louis finally to fulfil his vow, which he did in the spring of 1215, leading a group of high-ranking French nobles to southern France. While this royal contingent achieved little of value for the crusade (one recent scholar described them 'more as sightseers than soldiers'), nevertheless the Capetians had demonstrated a willingness to support the crusade to the best of their ability within the current political climate. Prince Louis again went on crusade in 1219, though he returned home quickly having achieved little. By 1223 it looked as if the Albigensian Crusade was over and the papal forced defeated. Raymond VII of Toulouse, son of Raymond VI, had retaken most of his father's land. In part, the papacy had lost interest in southern France in favour of the other major crusading campaign launched during Philip's lifetime, the Fifth Crusade. While Philip did not participate, he did agree to attend a council of French clerics in 1223, called together to plan a suitable response. Philip died before the meeting took place.[98]

Four major crusading expeditions were launched during the reign of Philip Augustus, and he only participated in one of them. While he left the Third Crusade early, he did not return home to much criticism, and indeed used the years after the Third Crusade to consolidate his rule in France. Moreover, while Philip never went on crusade again, like his father, he continued to be an active supporter of the institution so far as political circumstances allowed. More crucial, however, is the fact that the crusading image of the French King survived intact. By the time Philip died in the summer of 1223, French kings had assimilated crusading ideology into their own imagery and ideology, and thus they espoused crusading ideals even when they were not actually fighting in the East.

Although the Albigensian Crusade appeared to be over in 1223, with Raymond VII regaining most of his father's land and the papal forces thus defeated, Louis VIII (king since his father's death in 1223) was prepared to venture once again to the region. The French had recently (1225) lost hold of Gascony, and the new King was concerned about the Capetian presence in the south. With the support of a new pope, Honorius III, the French King took the cross for the third time in the winter of 1226, leading a small royal force to the south of France in early June of that year. The region had suffered more than two decades of war by this point, and few were willing to put up defences against the royal army. Despite a prolonged siege at Avignon, the King passed through southern France easily and quickly. He died in early November as he travelled back to Paris, leaving behind his twelve-year-old son to rule as King Louis IX. The Treaty of Paris was signed in April 1229, ending the Albigensian Crusade and vastly expanding French royal territory in the south. Louis IX was brought up in a world in which the crusade was identified with French kingship and the Capetian dynasty. It was this that forged his crusading piety, which would lead him to the East on two occasions and which led him to believe that the French King was, by his nature, a crusading king.

## Notes

1 Alexander Cartellieri, *Philipp II. August, König von Frankreich*, 4 vols (Leipzig, 1899–1922), Vol. I, pp. 1–10.
2 Lewis, *Royal Succession*, pp. 64–77.
3 See *Recueil des actes de Philippe Auguste*, ed. H.-F. Delaborde, Ch. Petit-Detaillis, J. Boussard, and M. Nortier, 4 vols (Paris, 1916–79), Vol. I, pp. 2–3.
4 Rigord, *Histoire de Philippe Auguste*, ed. and trans. Elisabeth Carpentier, Georges Pon, and Yves Chauvin (Paris, 2006), pp. 122–4; Roger of Howden, *Chronica magistri Rogeri de Hovedene*, ed. William Stubbs, RS 51, 4 vols (London, 1868–71), Vol. II, pp. 193–4; Gislebert of Mons, *La chronique de Gislebert de Mons*, ed. Léon Vanderkindere (Brussels, 1904), p. 127; 'Historia regum Francorum', *RHGF*, Vol. XII, pp. 217–21 (p. 221). Discussed in Cartellieri, *Philipp II.*, Vol. I, pp. 29–48.
5 For what follows in this paragraph see Baldwin, *The Government of Philip Augustus*, pp. 374–5. Also see Marcel David, 'Le Serment du sacre du IXe au XVe siècle: Contribution à l'étude des limites juridiques de la souveraineté', *Revue du moyen âge latin* 6 (1950), 5–272; Elizabeth A. R. Brown, '"Franks, Burgundians, and Aquitanians" and the Royal Coronation Ceremony in France', *Transactions of the American Philosophical Society* 82 (1992), 54–68.
6 See Schneidmüller, 'Constructing Identities of Medieval France', pp. 15–42.
7 One measure of this is royal territory, which was scattered widely around the Ile-de-France. William Newman, *Le domaine royal sous les premiers Capétiens (987–1180)* (Paris, 1937), pp. 161–201.
8 Baldwin, *The Government of Philip Augustus*, pp. 355–93.
9 Rigord, *Histoire de Philippe Auguste*, pp. 121–2.
10 Baldwin, *The Government of Philip Augustus*, pp. 77–80 and 101–75.
11 For example see the sources cited by John Gillingham, *Richard I* (New Haven, 1999), p. 87 n. 36.
12 Ambroise, *The History of Holy War: Ambroise's Estoire de la Guerre Sainte*, ed. and trans. Marianne Ailes and Malcolm Barber, 2 vols (Woodbridge, 2003), Vol. I, p. 137.

RESPONSE

13 Sidney Painter, 'The Third Crusade: Richard the Lionhearted and Philip Augustus', in *A History of the Crusades: The Later Crusades, 1189-1131*, ed. Kenneth M. Setton (Madison, WI, 1969), pp. 44-85 (p. 48); Gillingham, *Richard I*.

14 Rigord, *Histoire de Philippe Auguste*, pp. 178-80. The Master of the Temple was also part of the original embassy, but died en route to Paris.

15 *Ibid.*, p. 180; Paul, *To Follow in Their Footsteps*, pp. 194-9. For discussion of the significance of keys see above, pp. 103-4.

16 Rigord, *Histoire de Philippe Auguste*, p. 182.

17 Howden, *Chronica*, Vol. II, pp. 299-302. For comment see Fred A. Cazel, 'The Tax of 1185 in Aid of the Holy Land', *Speculum* 30 (1955), 385-92.

18 There has been an active debate about the tax implemented to raise the funds, which is well summarized in W. E. Lunt, 'The Text of the Ordinance of 1184 Concerning an Aid for the Holy Land', *EHR* 146 (1922), 235-42. Also see the lively debate contained in Achille Luchaire and Alexander Cartellieri, 'Correspondance', *Revue historique* 72 (1900), 334-7; 73 (1900), 61-4; 76 (1901), 329-30; Cartellieri, *Philipp II.*, Vol. I, p. 171 and Vol. II, pp. 16-25.

19 Suger, *De glorioso*, pp. 158-60.

20 Rigord, *Histoire de Philippe Auguste*, p. 184.

21 *Ibid.*, pp. 184-6.

22 *Ibid.*, p. 190.

23 Baldwin, *The Government of Philip Augustus*, pp. 3-24; Jim Bradbury, *Philip Augustus: King of France 1180-1223* (London, 1998), pp. 40-51 and 54-68.

24 Roger of Howden, *Gesta regis Henrici secondi Benedicti abbatis*, ed. William Stubbs, RS 49, 2 vols (London, 1867), Vol. I, p. 34.

25 Baldwin, *The Government of Philip Augustus*, p. 15.

26 Cartellieri, *Philipp II.*, Vol. I, pp. 37-41.

27 Eljas Oksanen, *Flanders and the Anglo-Norman World, 1066-1216* (Cambridge, 2012), pp. 42 and 89. Roger of Howden, *Chronica*, Vol. II, p. 192.

28 Malcolm Lyons and D. E. P. Jackson, *Saladin: The Politics of Holy War* (Cambridge, 1982), pp. 81-95.

29 Bernard Hamilton, *The Leper King and His Heirs: Baldwin IV and the Crusader Kingdom of Jerusalem* (Cambridge, 2005), pp. 198-210; Peter W. Edbury, 'Propaganda and Faction in the Kingdom of Jerusalem: The Background to Hattin', in *Crusaders and Muslims in Twelfth-Century Syria*, ed. M. Shatzmiller (Leiden, 1993), pp. 173-89.

30 *La continuation de Guillaume de Tyr (1184-1197)*, ed. Margaret R. Morgan (Paris, 1982), p. 36.

31 Tyerman, *God's War*, p. 368.

32 Benjamin K. Kedar, 'The Battle of Hattin Revisited', in *The Horns of Hattin: Proceedings of the Second Conference of the Society for the Study of the Crusades and the Latin East* (Jerusalem, 1992), pp. 190-207; C. P. Melville and Malcolm Lyons, 'Saladin's Hattin Letter', in *The Horns of Hattin*, pp. 208-12; Lyons and Jackson, *Saladin*, pp. 258-564.

33 *La continuation de Guillaume de Tyr*, p. 82.

34 *Ibid.*, pp. 82–3; Roger of Howden, *Gesta regis Henrici secondi Benedicti abbatis*, Vol. II, p. 15.
35 Roger of Howden, *Chronica*, Vol. II, p. 322.
36 *La continuation de Guillaume de Tyr*, p. 84.
37 Hans Mayer, 'Henry II of England and the Holy Land', *EHR* 97 (1982), 721–39; Tyerman, *England and the Crusades*, pp. 36–56; Alan Forey, 'Henry II's Crusading Penances for Becket's Murder', *Crusades* 7 (2008), 153–64.
38 Tyerman, *God's War*, pp. 382–9.
39 Although France is the focus of this study, it is worth considering that the Pope sought support from courts across Europe. See Alan Macquarrie, *Scotland and the Crusades, 1095–1560* (Edinburgh, 1985), pp. 27–32.
40 Roger of Howden, *Chronica*, Vol. II, p. 325; William of Newburgh, *Historia rerum Anglicarum*, ed. Richard Howlett, in *Chronicles of the Reigns of Stephen, Henry II, and Richard I*, RS 82 (London, 1884–89), Vol. I, p. 271; Gerald of Wales, *Opera*, ed. J. S. Brewer, RS 21, 8 vols (London, 1861–91), Vol. VIII, pp. 239–40. For commentary see Gillingham, *Richard I*, p. 87.
41 *Quellen zur Geschichte des Kreuzzuges Kaiser Friedrichs I*, ed. Anton Chroust, *MGH SS rerum Germanicarum*, n.s. 5, pp. 6–10 (p. 8). See also Christoph Maier, 'Crisis, Liturgy and the Crusade in the Twelfth and Thirteenth Centuries', *Journal of Ecclesiastical History* 48 (1997), 628–57.
42 *Quellen zur Geschichte des Kreuzzuges Kaiser Friedrichs I*, p. 8.
43 *Ibid.*; Roger of Howden, *Chronica*, Vol. II, pp. 322–3.
44 Ambroise, *The History of Holy War*, p. 2; Roger of Howden, *Gesta regis Henrici secondi Benedicti abbatis*, Vol. II, pp. 29–30; *Itinerarium peregrinorum et gesta regis Ricardi*, ed. William Stubbs, *The Chronicles and Memorials of the Reign of Richard I*, RS 38 (London, 1864), pp. 33–40 and 140–1; William of Newburgh, *Historia rerum Anglicarum* I, p. 272.
45 Rigord, *Histoire de Philippe Auguste*, p. 245.
46 See Jean Richard, 'National Feeling and the Legacy of the Crusades', in *Palgrave Advances in the Crusades*, ed. Helen Nicholson (Houndmills, 2005), pp. 204–22.
47 Roger of Howden, *Chronica*, Vol. II, p. 185. Coloured crosses had also been adopted by participants on the Wendish expedition of the Second Crusade, though they were more ideological and political in nature.
48 Bradbury, *Philip Augustus*, p. 78.
49 Cartellieri, *Phillip II.*, Vol. I, pp. 100–4.
50 Rigord, *Histoire de Philippe Auguste*, p. 276.
51 *Ibid.*, pp. 276–84.
52 Baldwin, *The Government of Philip Augustus*, pp. 101–2.
53 Bradbury, *Philip Augustus*, pp. 79–80.
54 Rigord, *Histoire de Philippe Auguste*, p. 273.
55 *Ibid.*
56 See above, pp. 65–6.
57 Rigord, *Histoire de Philippe Auguste*, p. 274.
58 *Itinerarium peregrinorum et gesta regis Ricardi*, pp. 152–3. As Helen Nicholson points out, the chronicler Ambroise gives a different version of this incident, noting

that the kings crossed the bridge together. Nicholson demonstrates, however, that the author of the *Itinerarium* was the one source to give an accurate account of the crusaders' journey across Europe, making it highly likely that he was a crusader himself. *The Chronicle of the Third Crusade: The 'Itinerarium peregrinorum et gesta regis Ricardi'*, trans. Helen J. Nicholson (Aldershot, 1997), p. 153 n. 36.

59 See Painter, 'The Third Crusade'.

60 Ambroise, *The History of Holy War*, Vol. II, pp. 1–3. For Ambroise's treatment of French versus English crusaders see Brian Levy, 'Pèlerins rivaux de la 3e croisade: Les personnages des rois d'Angleterre et de France d'après les chroniques d'Ambroise et d'"Ernoul" et le récit Anglo-Normand de la *Croisade et mort Richard Coeur de Lion*', in *La Croisade: Réalités et fictions. Actes du colloque d'Amiens, 1987* (Göppingen, 1989), pp. 143–55; Marianne J. Ailes, 'Heroes of War: Ambroise's Heroes of the Third Crusade', in *Writing War: Medieval Literary Responses to Warfare*, ed. Corinne Saunders and Françoise Le Saux (Woodbridge, 2004), pp. 29–48.

61 *La continuation de Guillaume de Tyr*, p. 109. For Richard's time on Cyprus see *Itinerarium peregrinorum et gesta regis Ricardi*, pp. 177–209.

62 *La continuation de Guillaume de Tyr*, p. 109.

63 *Ibid.*, p. 111.

64 See John Gillingham, 'Roger of Howden on Crusade', in *Richard Coeur de Lion: Kingship, Chivalry and War in the Twelfth Century* (London and Rio Grande, 1994), pp. 141–53; Gillingham, *Richard I*; Tyerman, *God's War*, pp. 402–43; Painter, 'The Third Crusade'.

65 *Itinerarium peregrinorum et gesta regis Ricardi*, pp. 236–7.

66 Roger of Howden, *Chronica*, Vol. III, pp. 129–30.

67 Baha al-Din, *The Rare and Excellent History of Saladin*, trans. D. S. Richards (Aldershot, 2002), p. 183.

68 Baldwin, *The Government of Philip Augustus*, p. 80.

69 Cartellieri, *Philipp II.*, Vol. II, pp. 240–4.

70 *La continuation de Guillaume de Tyr*, p. 132.

71 Cited in Gabrielle. M. Spiegel, *Romancing the Past: The Rise of Vernacular Prose Historiography in Thirteenth-Century France* (Berkeley, 1993), p. 16 n. 23. See also Robert-Henri Bautier, 'Philippe Auguste: La personnalité du roi', in *La France de Philippe Auguste: Le temps des mutations. Actes du colloque international organisé par le CNRS, Paris, 29 septembre–4 octobre 1980* (Paris, 1982), pp. 33–57 (p. 35).

72 Spiegel, *Romancing the Past*, pp. 14–54.

73 Baldwin, *The Government of Philip Augustus*, p. 260.

74 Spiegel, *Romancing the Past*, pp. 16–18; Bournazel, *Le gouvernement capétien*, Chapters 3 and 4.

75 See for example a letter Innocent sent to the Patriarch of Jerualem in which he assured him that he would focus his attention on supporting the Holy Land; *Die Register Innocenz' III*, ed. Othmar Hageneder and Anton Haidacher, 5 vols (Graz and Cologne, 1964), Vol. I, pp. 18–20.

76 Such was the main theme of the sermons delivered by James of Vitry in the early thirteenth century; Tyerman, *God's War*, p. 477.

77 Thomas F. Madden, 'Outside and inside the Fourth Crusade', *International History Review* 17 (1995), 726-43.
78 Ryan, 'Richard I and the Early Evolution of the Fourth Crusade', p. 3.
79 See Steven Runciman, *A History of the Crusades*, 3 vols (Cambridge, 1955), Vol. III, p. 91; Hans Mayer, *The Crusades*, 2nd edn, trans. John Gillingham (Oxford, 1988), p. 197; John Godfrey, *1204: The Unholy Crusade* (Oxford, 1980), p. 45; Michael Angold, *The Fourth Crusade: Event and Context* (Harlow, 2003), p. 78.
80 Several versions of *Post miserabile* exist. Although there are minor differences, the basic framework is the same. The crusading bull has been extensively studied and discussed by Penny J. Cole, *The Preaching of the Crusades to the Holy Land, 1095-1270* (Cambridge, MA, 1991), pp. 81-3.
81 *Die Register Innocenz' III*, Vol. I, p. 500.
82 Ryan, 'Richard I and the Early Evolution of the Fourth Crusade', p. 9; Brenda Bolton, '"Serpent in the Dust: Sparrow on the Housetop": Attitudes to Jerusalem and the Holy Land in the Circle of Pope Innocent III', *Studies in Church History* 36 (2000), 154-80, esp. p. 159.
83 *Die Register Innocenz' III*, Vol. I, p. 501.
84 *Ibid.*
85 *Ibid.*, pp. 530-2.
86 Roger of Howden, *Chronica*, Vol. IV, p. 80.
87 Bradbury, *Philip Augustus*, pp. 109-13. For references to Richard's captivity see Roger of Howden, *Chronica*, Vol. III, p. 203; Roger of Howden, *Gesta regis Henrici secundi Benedicti abbatis*, Vol. II, p. 286.
88 Bradbury, *Philip Augustus*, pp. 117-29; P. N. Lewis, 'The Wars of Richard I in the West', M.Phil. dissertation, University of London, 1977, p. 207. For reference to the war see Roger of Wendover, *Flowers of History*, ed. and trans. J. A. Giles, 2 vols (London, 1899), Vol. II, p. 145; William the Breton, *Philippide*, in *Oeuvres de Rigord et de Guillaume le Breton*, pp. 125-34 and 193.
89 While we do not know all the details of the negotiations it is worth pointing out that Peter Capuano was not above following Pope Innocent's lead and also using the threat of interdict in his attempts to mediate between the kings. Several decades later Roger of Wendover would write that the treaty was beneficial to the kings since it allowed them to discharge their crusading vows, which remained unfulfilled after the Third Crusade. Ryan, 'Richard I and the Early Evolution of the Fourth Crusade', p. 11 n. 48. It is difficult to reconcile this claim with the fact that Philip would not ultimately join the Fourth Crusade; nor, as we have seen, did he appear to suffer any negative publicity for his early departure from the Third Crusade.
90 *Die Register Innocenz' III*, Vol. II, pp. 33-4, 32-3, and 35. See Ryan, 'Richard I and the Early Evolution of the Fourth Crusade', p. 11.
91 Jonathan Riley-Smith, *The Crusades: A Short History* (New Haven, 1987), p. 113.
92 See Donald E. Queller and Thomas F. Madden, *The Fourth Crusade: The Conquest of Constantinople* (Philadelphia, 1997), pp. 65-6 and 88-90.
93 *Layettes du Trésor des Chartes*, ed. Alexandre Teulet, Henri-François Delaborde, and Elie Berger, 5 vols (Paris, 1863-1909), Vol. I, nos. 768, 292. Discussed in Cartellieri, *Philipp II.*, Vol. IV, pp. 77-8.

94 Bradbury, *Philip Augustus*, pp. 130-9; Ralph Turner, *King John* (Harlow, 1994), pp. 48-52; Jacques Boussard, 'Philippe Auguste et les Plantagenêts', in *La France de Philippe Auguste, le temps des mutations: Actes du Colloque International organisé par le Centre National de la Recherche Scientifique*, ed. Robert-Henri Bautier (Paris, 1982), pp. 263-89.
95 Tyerman, *God's War*, pp. 573-82.
96 For the expedition see Mark Gregory Pegg, *A Most Holy War: The Albigensian Crusade and the Battle for Christendom* (Oxford, 2008); Jonathan Sumption, *The Albigensian Crusade* (London, 1978); Tyerman, *God's War*, pp. 563-605.
97 Peter of Vaux-de-Cernay, *Hystoria Albigensis*, ed. P. Guégin and E. Lyon, 2 vols (Paris, 1930), Vol. II, pp. 109-10, 134-5, 243-6.
98 Cartellieri, *Philipp II.*, pp. 556-65.

# BIBLIOGRAPHY

### Primary sources

*Manuscripts*

Chantilly, Musée Condé, MS 869.
Paris, Bibliothèque Mazarine, 2013.
Paris, Bibliothèque nationale de France, MS Lat. 4628A.
Paris, Bibliothèque nationale de France, MS Lat. 5543.
Rome, Bibliotheca Apostolica Vaticana, Reg. Lat. 550.
Rome, Bibliotheca Apostolica Vaticana, Reg. Lat. 624.

*Printed*

Abelard, *Historia calamitatum*, ed. Jacques Monfrin (Paris, 1959).
*Acta sanctorum*, ed. Jean Bolland, Jean Carnedet, *et al.*, 70 vols (Paris, 1863, repr. Brussels, 1965).
Adalbero of Laon, *Poème au roi Robert*, ed. Claude Carozzi (Paris, 1970).
Albert of Aachen, *Historia Ierosolimitana: History of the Journey to Jerusalem*, ed. and trans. Susan B. Edgington (Oxford, 2007).
Ambroise, *The History of Holy War: Ambroise's Estoire de la Guerre Sainte*, ed. and trans. Marianne Ailes and Malcolm Barber, 2 vols (Woodbridge, 2003).
Anna Comnena, *The Alexiad*, trans. E. R. A. Sewter (Baltimore, 1969).
'Annales Aquicinctini', *MGH SS* 16, pp. 503–6.
'Annales Laureshamenses', *MGH SS* 1, pp. 22–39.
*Annales regni Francorum*, ed. F. Kurze, *MGH SS rerum Germanicarum* 6 (Hanover, 1895), pp. 1–178.
'Annales S. Benigni Divionensis', *MGH SS* 7, pp. 37–50.
*Archives d'Anjou: Recueil de documents et mémoires inédits sur cette province*, ed. Paul A. Marchegay, 3 vols (Angers, 1843–54).
Baha al-Din, *The Rare and Excellent History of Saladin*, trans. D. S. Richards (Aldershot, 2002).
Bernard of Clairvaux, *Sancti Bernardi opera*, ed. Jean Leclercq and Henri Rochais, 8 vols (Rome, 1955–77).
'Breve Chronicon ecclesiae Sancti Dionysii ad cyclos paschales', *RHGF*, Vol. XII, pp. 215–17.
*Die Briefe Heinrichs IV*, ed. Carl Erdman, *MGH Deutsches Mittelalter* (Leipzig, 1937).

## BIBLIOGRAPHY

*Cartulaire de l'abbaye de Saint-Corneille de Compiègne*, ed. Emile Morel and Louis Carolus Barré, 3 vols (Montdidier, 1904-77).
*Cartulaires de l'abbaye de Molesme*, ed. Jacques Laurent, 2 vols (Paris, 1907-11).
*La chanson d'Antioch*, ed. Susanne Duparc-Quioc (Paris, 1976).
*Chanson de Roland*, ed. Gerard J. Brault, *The Song of Roland: An Analytical Edition* (University Park, 1978).
*La chronique de Morigny 1095-1152*, ed. Léon Mirot, 2nd edn (Paris, 1912).
*La chronique de Saint-Maixent*, ed. and trans. Jean Verdon (Paris, 1979).
*La continuation de Guillaume de Tyr (1184-1197)*, ed. Margaret R. Morgan (Paris, 1982).
*The Correspondence of Thomas Becket*, ed. Anne Duggan, 2 vols (Oxford, 2000).
'De laude dominici sepulchri', ed. Giles Constable, in *'Petri Venerabilis sermones tres'*, *Revue Bénédictine* 64 (1954), 234-54.
Dufour, M. Jean, *Recueil des actes de Louis VI, roi de France (1108-1137)*, 4 vols (Paris, 1992-94).
Fulcher of Chartres, *Historia Hierosolymitana: Mit Erläuterungen und einem Anhange*, ed. Hans Hagenmeyer (Heidelberg, 1913).
*Gallia Christiana in provincias ecclesiasticas distributa*, ed. Scévole de Sainte-Marthe and Louis de Sainte-Marthe, 16 vols (Farnborough, 1970).
*Genealogiae comitum Flandriae*, ed. L. C. Bethmann, *MGH SS* 9, pp. 302-36.
Gerald of Wales, *Opera*, ed. J. S. Brewer, RS 21, 8 vols (London, 1861-91).
'"Gesta abbatum sancti Bertini Sithiensium": Continuation', *MGH SS* 13, pp. 635-63.
'Gesta Dagoberti I regis Francorum', ed. Bruno Krusch, *MGH SS rerum Merovingicarum* 2, pp. 396-425.
'Gesta Eugenii III papae', *RHGF*, Vol. XV, pp. 423-83.
*Gesta triumphalia Pisanorum in captione Hierosolymae*, *RHC Oc.*, Vol. V, pp. 368-9.
Gislebert of Mons, *La chronique de Gislebert de Mons*, ed. Léon Vanderkindere (Brussels, 1904).
Helgaud of Fleury, *Vie de Robert le Pieux*, ed. Robert Henri Bautier and Gillette Labory (Paris, 1965).
Henry of Huntingdon, *Historia Anglorum: The History of the English People*, ed. and trans. Diana Greenway (Oxford, 1996).
Herbert of Bosham, 'Vita sancti Thomae', in *Materials for the History of Thomas Becket*, ed. James C. Robertson, RS 67 (London, 1875-85), Vol. III, pp. 155-534.
Hincmar of Reims, *Vita sanctii Remigii*, *PL* 125, cols 1129-88.
'Historia belli sacri', *RHC Oc. 3*, pp. 165-229.
'Historia regum Francorum', *RHGF*, Vol. XII, pp. 217-21.
'Historia regum Francorum monasterii sancti Dionysii', *MGH SS* 9, pp. 395-406.
Hugh of Fleury, *Liber qui modernorum regum Francorum continet actus*, ed. Georg Waitz, *MGH SS* 9, pp. 376-95.
Ibn al-Qalanisi, *The Damascus Chronicles of the Crusades*, ed. and trans. Hamilton A. R. Gibb (London, 1932).
*Itinerarium peregrinorum et gesta regis Ricardi*, ed. William Stubbs, *The Chronicles and Memorials of the Reign of Richard I*, RS 38 (London, 1864). Translated as *The Chronicle of the Third Crusade: The 'Itinerarium peregrinorum et gesta regis Ricardi'*, trans. Helen J. Nicholson (Aldershot, 1997).

*Die Kreuzzugsbriefe aus den Jahren 1088–1100*, ed. Hans Hagenmeyer (Innsbruck, 1901).
Lambert of Wattrelos, 'Annales Cameracenses', *MGH SS* 16, pp. 509–54.
*Layettes du trésor des Chartes*, ed. Alexandre Teulet, Henri-François Delaborde, and Elie Berger, 5 vols (Paris, 1863–1909).
Matthew of Paris, *Chronica majora*, ed. Henry Luard, 7 vols (London, 1872).
'Narratio quomodo reliquiae martyris Georgii ad nos Aquicinenses pervenerunt', *RHC Oc.*, Vol. V, pp. 248–52.
Nerses Snorhali, 'Lament on Edessa', in *East and West in the Crusader States II: Contest, Contacts, Confrontations*, ed. Krijna N. Ciggaar and Herman G. B. Teule, trans. Theo Van Lint (Leuven, 1999), p. 75.
Norman Anonymous, *Tractates*, ed. Heinrich Böhmer, in *MGH Libelli de lite* 3, pp. 642–87.
Odo of Deuil, *De Profectione Ludovici VII in orientem: The Journey of Louis VII to the East*, ed. and trans. Virginia G. Berry (New York, 1947).
Orderic Vitalis, *Historia ecclesiastica*, ed. and trans. Marjorie Chibnall, 6 vols. (Oxford, 1969–80).
*Oeuvres de Rigord et de Guillaume le Breton*, ed. Henri François Delabode, 2 vols (Paris, 1892).
*Ordines coronationis Franciae: Texts and Ordines for the Coronation of Frankish and French Kings and Queens in the Middle Ages*, ed. Richard A. Jackson, 2 vols (Philadelphia, 1995).
Otto of Freising, *Gesta Friderici seu rectius Chronica*, ed. Georg Waitz and Bernhard Simson (Berlin, 1965).
Peter of Vaux-de-Cernay, *Hystoria Albigensis*, ed. P. Guégin and E. Lyon, 2 vols (Paris, 1930).
Peter the Venerable, *The Letters of Peter the Venerable*, ed. Giles Constable, 2 vols (Cambridge, MA, 1967).
*Quellen zur Geschichte des Kreuzzuges Kaiser Friedrichs I*, ed. Anton Chroust, *MGH SS rerum Germanicarum*, n.s. 5, pp. 6–10.
Ralph Niger, *Chronica universalis*, *MGH SS* 27, pp. 327–43.
Ralph of Caen, 'Gesta Tancredi', *RHC Oc.* 3, pp. 587–716.
*Recueil des actes de Philippe Ier, roi de France (1059–1108)*, ed. Maurice Prou (Paris, 1908).
*Recueil des actes de Philippe Auguste*, ed. H.-F. Delaborde, Ch. Petit-Detaillis, J. Boussard, and M. Nortier, 4 vols (Paris, 1916–79).
*Recueil des chartes de Saint-Benôit-sur-Loire*, ed. Maurice Prou and Alexandre Vidier (Paris, 1900).
*Die Register Innocenz' III*, ed. Othmar Hageneder and Anton Haidacher, 5 vols (Graz and Cologne, 1964).
Richer of Saint-Rémi, *Histories*, ed. and trans. Justin Lake, 2 vols (Cambridge, MA, 2011).
Rigord, *Histoire de Philippe Auguste*, ed. and trans. Elisabeth Carpentier, Georges Pon, and Yves Chauvin (Paris, 2006).
Robert the Monk, *Robert the Monk's History of the First Crusade: 'Historia Iherosolimitana'*, trans. Carol Sweetenham (Aldershot, 2005).

Roger of Howden, *Chronica magistri Rogeri de Hovedene*, ed. William Stubbs, RS 51, 4 vols (London, 1868–71).

Roger of Howden, *Gesta regis Henrici secondi Benedicti abbatis*, ed. William Stubbs, RS 49, 2 vols (London, 1867).

Roger of Wendover, *Flowers of History*, ed. and trans. J. A. Giles, 2 vols (London, 1899).

*Sacrorum conciliorum nova, et amplissima collectio*, ed. J. D. Mansi, 55 vols (Paris, 1901–27).

Sigebert of Gembloux, 'Continuatio Praemonstratensis', *MGH SS* 6, pp. 447–56.

Suger, *The Deeds of Louis the Fat*, trans. Richard C. Cusimano and John Moorhead (Washington, DC, 1992).

Suger, *Vie de Louis le Gros par Suger suivie de l'Histoire du roi Louis VII*, ed. Auguste Molinier (Paris, 1887).

'Vita prima S. Bernardi', *PL* 185, cols 225–426.

William of Malmesbury, *Gesta regum anglorum: The History of the English Kings*, ed. and trans. R. A. B. Mynors, completed by Rodney M. Thomson and Michael Winterbottom, 2 vols (Oxford, 1998).

William of Newburgh, *Historia rerum Anglicarum*, ed. Richard Howlett, in *Chronicles of the Reigns of Stephen, Henry II, and Richard II*, RS 82 (London, 1884–89).

William of Tyre, *Chronicon*, ed. R. B. C. Huygens, 2 vols, *CCCM* 63 and 63A (Turnhout, 1986).

## Secondary sources

Ailes, Marianne J., 'Heroes of War: Ambroise's Heroes of the Third Crusade', in *Writing War: Medieval Literary Responses to Warfare*, ed. Corinne Saunders and Françoise Le Saux (Woodbridge, 2004), pp. 29–48.

Aird, William M., *Robert Curthose, Duke of Normandy (1054–1134)* (Woodbridge, 2008).

Angold, Michael, *The Fourth Crusade: Event and Context* (Harlow, 2003).

Ashley, Kathleen, 'Introduction: The Moving Subjects of Processional Performance', in *Moving Subjects: Processional Performance in the Middle Ages and the Renaissance*, ed. Kathleen Ashley and Wim Hüsken (Amsterdam, 2001), pp. 7–34.

Baldwin, John, *The Government of Philip Augustus: Foundations of French Royal Power in the Middle Ages* (Berkeley, 1986).

Barlow, Frank, 'The King's Evil', *EHR* 95 (1980), 3–27.

Barroux, Robert, 'L'anniversaire de la mort de Dagobert à Saint-Denis au XIIe siècle: Charte inédite de l'abbé Adam', *Bulletin philologique et historique de comité des travaux historiques et scientifiques* (1942–43), 131–51.

Barthélemy, Dominique, *La mutation de l'an mil a-t-elle eu lieu? Servage et chevalerie dans la France des Xe et XIe siècles* (Paris, 1997).

Barthélemy, Dominique, *L'ordre seigneurial: XIe–XIIe siècle* (Paris, 1990).

Barton, Richard E., 'Aristocratic Culture: Kingship, Chivalry, and Court Culture', in *A Companion to the Medieval World*, ed. Carol Lansing and Edward English (Malden, MA, 2009), pp. 500–24.

Bautier, Robert-Henri, 'Philippe Auguste: La personalité du roi', in *La France de Philippe Auguste: Le temps des mutations. Actes du colloque international organisé par la CNRS, Paris, 29 septembre–4 octobre 1980* (Paris, 1982), pp. 33–57.

Bautier, Robert-Henri, 'La place de l'abbaye de Fleury-sur-Loire dans l'historiographie française du IXe au XIIe siècle', in *Etudes ligériennes d'histoire et d'archéologie médiévales*, ed. René Louis (Auxerre, 1975), pp. 23–33.

Bautier, Robert-Henri, 'Sacres et couronnements sous les Carolingiens et les premiers Capétiens', in *Recherches sur l'histoire de la France medieval: Des Mérovingiens aux premiers Capétiens* (London, 1991), pp. 7–56.

Beaune, Collette, *The Birth of an Ideology: Myths and Symbols of Nation in Late-Medieval France*, trans. Susan R. Huston, ed. Fredric L. Cheyette (Berkeley, 1991).

Becker, Alfons, *Papst Urban II. (1088–1099)*, 2 vols (Stuttgart, 1964–88).

Berry, Virginia, 'Peter the Venerable and the Crusades', in *Petrus Venerabilis 1156–1956: Studies and Texts Commemorating the Eighth Centenary of His Death*, ed. Giles Constable and James Kritzeck (Rome, 1956), pp. 152–5.

Bisson, Thomas N., *The Crisis of the Twelfth Century: Power, Lordship, and the Origins of European Government* (Princeton, 2009).

Bisson, Thomas N., 'The "Feudal Revolution",' *Past and Present* 142 (1994), 6–42.

Bloch, Herbert, 'A New Fascination with Ancient Rome', in *Renaissance and Renewal in the Twelfth Century*, ed, Robert L. Benson and Giles Constable (Cambridge, MA, 1982), pp. 615–36.

Bloch, Marc, *Feudal Society*, trans. L. A. Manyon, 2 vols (Chicago, 1961).

Bloch, Marc, *The Royal Touch: Sacred Monarchy and Scrofula in England and France*, trans. J. E. Anderson (London, 1973).

Bolton, Brenda, '"Serpent in the Dust: Sparrow on the Housetop": Attitudes to Jerusalem and the Holy Land in the Circle of Pope Innocent III', *Studies in Church History* 36 (2000), 154–80.

Bournazel, Eric, *Le gouvernement capétien au XIIe siècle 1108–1180: Structures sociales et mutations institutionelles* (Paris, 1975).

Bournazel, Eric, 'Suger and the Capetians', in *Abbot Suger and Saint-Denis: A Symposium*, ed. Paula Gerson (New York, 1987), pp. 55–72.

Boussard, Jacques, 'Philippe Auguste et les Plantagenêts', in *La France de Philippe Auguste, le temps des mutations: Actes du Colloque International organisé par le Centre National de la Recherche Scientifique*, ed. Robert-Henri Bautier (Paris, 1982), pp. 263–89.

Bradbury, Jim, *Philip Augustus: King of France 1180–1223* (London, 1998).

Brandt, William J. *The Shape of Medieval History: Studies in Modes of Perception* (New Haven, 1966).

Brown, Elizabeth A. R., '"Franks, Burgundians, and Aquitanians" and the Royal Coronation Ceremony in France', *Transactions of the American Philosophical Society* 82 (1992), 54–68.

Brown, Elizabeth A. R. and Michael W. Cothren, 'The Twelfth-Century Crusading Window of the Abbey of Saint-Denis: *Praeteritorum enim recordatio futurorum est exhibitio*', *Journal of the Warburg and Courtauld Institutes* 49 (1986), 1–40.

Bruguière, Marie-Bernadette, 'Canon Law and Royal Weddings, Theory and Practice: The French Example, 987–1215', in *Proceedings of the Eighth International Congress of Medieval Canon Law*, ed. Stanley Chodorow (Vatican, 1992), pp. 473–96.

Brundage, James, 'The Army of the First Crusade and the Crusade Vow: Some Reflections on a Recent Book', *Medieval Studies* 33 (1971), 334–44.

Brundage, James, 'An Errant Crusader: Stephen of Blois', *Traditio* 16 (1960), 380–95.

Buc, Philippe, *The Dangers of Ritual: Between Early Medieval Texts and Social Scientific Theory* (Princeton, 2001).

Buc, Philippe, 'The Monastery and the Critics: A Ritual Reply', *Early Medieval Europe* 15 (2007), 441–54.

Bull, Marcus, 'The Capetian Monarchy and the Early Crusade Movement: Hugh of Vermandois and Louis VII', *NMS* 40 (1996), 25–46.

Bull, Marcus, ed., *France in the Central Middle Ages* (Oxford, 2002).

Bull, Marcus, *Knightly Piety and the Lay Response to the First Crusade: The Limousin and Gascony, c. 970–1130* (Oxford, 1993).

Bull, Marcus, 'Overlapping and Competing Identities in the Frankish First Crusade', in *Concile de Clermont de 1095 et l'appel à Croisade: Actes du Colloque Universitaire International de Clermont-Ferrand (23–25 juin 1995) organisé et publié avec le concours du Conseil Régional d'Auvergne* (Rome, 1997), pp. 195–211.

Bur, Michel, 'Reims, ville des sacres', in *Le sacre des rois: Actes du colloque international d'histoire sur les sacres et couronnements royaux* (Reims, 1985), pp. 39–48.

Bur, Michel, *Suger, abbé de Saint-Denis, régent de France* (Paris, 1991).

Canteaut, Oliver, 'Quantifier l'entourage politique des derniers Capétiens', in *Les entourages princiers à la fin du Moyen Âge: Une approche quantative*, ed. Alexandra Beauchamp (Madrid, 2013), pp. 77–92.

Carozzi, Claude, 'Du baptême au sacre de Clovis selon les traditions rémoises', in *Clovis: Histoire et mémoire, le baptême de Clovis, son echo à travers l'histoire*, ed. Michel Rouche, 2 vols (Paris, 1997), Vol. II, pp. 29–44.

Carozzi, Claude, 'La vie du roi Robert par Helgaud de Fleury: Historiographie et hagiographie', *Annales de Bretagne et des pays de l'Ouest* 37 (1980), 219–35.

Cartellieri, Alexander, *Philipp II. August, König von Frankreich*, 4 vols (Leipzig, 1899–1922).

Cazel, Fred A., 'The Tax of 1185 in Aid of the Holy Land', *Speculum* 30 (1955), 385–92.

Clastres, Pierre, *Society against the State*, trans. Robert Hurley (New York, 1989).

Claussen, Peter C., '*Renovatio Romae*: Erneuerungsphasen römischer Architektur im 11. und 12. Jahrhundert', in *Rom im hohen Mittelalter: Studien zu den Romvorstellungen und zur Rompolitik vom 10. bis zum 12. Jahrhundert. Reinhard Elze zur Vollendung seines siebzigsten Lebensjahres gewidmet*, ed. Bernhard Schimmelpfennig and Ludwig Schmugge (Sigmaringen, 1992), pp. 87–125.

Cole, Penny J., *The Preaching of the Crusades to the Holy Land, 1095–1270* (Cambridge, MA, 1991).

Collins, Roger, *Charlemagne* (Toronto, 1998).

Constable, Giles, 'The Crusade Project of 1150', in *Montjoie: Studies in Crusade History in Honour of Hans Eberhard Mayer*, ed. Benjamin Kedar *et al.* (Aldershot, 1997), pp. 67–75.

Cothren, Michael, 'The Twelfth-Century Infancy of Christ Window at Saint-Denis: A Re-evaluation of Its Design and Iconography', *Arts Bulletin* 68 (1986), 398–420.

Cowdrey, H. E. J., 'The Anglo-Norman *Laudes regiae*', *Viator* 12 (1981), 39–78.

Cowdrey, H. E. J., 'The Genesis of the Crusades: The Springs of Western Ideas of Holy War', in *The Holy War*, ed. T. P. Murphy (Columbus, OH, 1976), pp. 9–32.

Cowdrey, H. E. J., 'Martyrdom and the First Crusade', in *Crusade and Settlement: Papers Read at the First Conference of the Society for the Study of the Crusades and the Latin East and Presented to R. C. Smail, ed. Peter Edbury* (Cardiff, 1985), pp. 46–56.

Crosby, Sumner McKnight, *The Royal Abbey of Saint-Denis from Its Beginning to the Death of Suger, 475–1151*, ed. Pamela Blum (New Haven, 1987).

Crosby, Sumner McKnight and Pamela Z. Blum, 'Le portail central de la façade occidentale de Saint-Denis', *Bulletin monumental* 131 (1973), 209–66.

Crouch, David, *The Birth of Nobility: Constructing Aristocracy in England and France, c. 900–c. 1300* (London, 2005).

David, Marcel, 'Le serment du sacre du IXe au XVe siècle: Contribution à l'étude des limites juridiques de la souveraineté', *Revue du moyen âge latin* 6 (1950), 5–272.

Delisle, Léopold, 'Notes sur quelques manuscrits du Musée britannique', *Mémoires de la Société de l'Histoire de Paris et de l'Ile-de-France* 4 (1878), 183–238.

Demouy, Patrick, *Genèse d'une cathédrale: Les archevêques de Reims et leur église aux IXe et XIIe siècles* (Langres, 2005),

Depreux, Philippe, 'Saint Remi et la royauté carolingienne', *Revue historique* 578 (1991), 235–60.

Dhondt, Jan, 'Sept femmes et un trio de rois', *Contributions à l'histoire économique et sociale* 3 (1964–65), 37–70.

Duby, Georges, *The Chivalrous Society*, trans. Cynthia Postan (Berkeley, 1977).

Duby, Georges, *Medieval Marriage: Two Models from Twelfth-Century France*, trans. Elborg Forster (Baltimore, 1978).

Duby, Georges, *Les trois ordres; ou, L'imaginaire du féodalisme* (Paris, 1978).

Dunbabin, Jean, *France in the Making, 843–1180*, 2nd edn (Oxford, 1985).

Duparc-Quioc, Susanne, *Le cycle de la croisade* (Paris, 1955).

Edbury, Peter W., 'Propaganda and Faction in the Kingdom of Jerusalem: The Background to Hattin', in *Crusaders and Muslims in Twelfth-Century Syria*, ed. M. Shatzmiller (Leiden, 1993), pp. 173–89.

Edgington, Susan, 'The First Crusade: Reviewing the Evidence', in *The First Crusade: Origins and Impact*, ed. Jonathan Phillips (Manchester, 1997), pp. 57–77.

Eley, Geoff, 'Is All the World a Text? From Social History to the History of Society Two Decades Later', in *Practicing History: New Directions in Historical Writing after the Linguistic Turn*, ed. Gabrielle M. Spiegel (New York, 2005), pp. 33–61.

Erdmann, Carl, *The Origin of the Idea of Crusade*, trans. Walter Goffart and Marshall W. Baldwin (Princeton, 1977).

Erlande-Brandenburg, Alain, *Le roi est mort: Etude sur les funérailles, les sépultures et les tombeaux des rois de France jusqu'à la fin du XIIIe siècle* (Geneva, 1975).

Fawtier, Robert, *The Capetian Kings of France: Monarchy and Nation, 987-1328*, trans. Lionel Butler and R. J. Adam (London, 1960).
Field, Sean L. and M. Cecilia Gaposchkin, 'Questioning the Capetians, 1180-1328', *History Compass* 12/7 (2014), 567-85.
France, John, 'The Anonymous *Gesta Francorum* and the *Historia Francorum qui ceperunt Iherusalem* of Raymond of Aguilers and the *Historia de Hierosolymitano itinere* of Peter Tudebode: An Analysis of the Textual Relationship between the Primary Sources for the First Crusade', in *The Crusades and Their Sources: Essays Presented to Bernard Hamilton*, ed. John France and William Zazaj (Aldershot, 1998), pp. 39-70.
France, John, 'Use of the Anonymous *Gesta Francorum* in the Early Twelfth Century: Sources for the First Crusade', in *From Clermont to Jerusalem: The Crusades and Crusader Societies, 1095-1500*, ed. Alan V. Murray (Turnhout, 1998), pp. 29-42.
Fliche, Augustin, *Le règne de Philippe 1er, roi de France (1060-1108)* (Paris, 1912).
Fliche, Augustin, 'Urbain II et la croisade', *Revue d'histoire de l'Eglise de France* 13 (1927), 289-306.
Flori, Jean, *Bohémond d'Antioche: Chevalier d'aventure* (Paris, 2007).
Flori, Jean, *Chroniqueurs et propagandistes: Introduction critique aux sources de la première croisade* (Geneva, 2010).
Forey, Alan, 'Henry II's Crusading Penances for Becket's Murder', *Crusades* 7 (2008), 153-64.
Formigé, Jules, *L'Abbaye Royale de Saint-Denis: Recherches novelles* (Paris, 1960).
Friedman, Yvonne, 'Miracle, Meaning, and Narrative in the Latin East', *Studies in Church History* 41 (2005), 123-34.
Gabriele, Matthew, *An Empire of Memory: The Legend of Charlemagne, the Franks, and Jerusalem before the First Crusade* (Oxford, 2011).
Gabriele, Matthew, 'The Provenance of the *Descriptio qualiter Karolus Magnus*: Remembering the Carolingians in the Entourage of King Philip I (1060-1108) before the First Crusade', *Viator* 39 (2008), 93-117.
Gaposchkin, M. Cecilia, 'Louis IX, Crusade and the Promise of Joshua', *JMH* 33 (2008), 245-74.
Gaposchkin, M. Cecilia, *The Making of Saint Louis: Kingship, Sanctity, and Crusade in the Later Middle Ages* (Ithaca, NY, 2008).
Gaposchkin, M. Cecilia, 'Role of the Crusades in the Sanctification of Louis IX', in *Crusades: Medieval Worlds in Conflict*, ed. Thomas F. Madden, James Naus, and Vince Ryan (Aldershot, 2010), pp. 195-209.
Gardner, Christopher K., 'The Capetian Presence in Berry as a Consequence of the First Crusade', in *Autour de la Première Croisade: Actes du colloque de la Society for the Study of the Crusades and the Latin East (Clermont-Ferrand, 22-25 juin 1995)*, ed. Michel Balard (Paris, 1996), pp. 71-81.
Gardner, Stephen, 'The Influence of Castle Building on Ecclesiastical Architecture in the Paris Region, 1130-1150', in *The Medieval Castle: Romance and Reality*, ed. Kathryn Reyerson and Faye Power (Dubuque, IA, 1984), pp. 97-123.
Garipzanov, Ildar, 'The Carolingian Abbreviation of Bede's World Chronicle and Carolingian Imperial "Genealogy"', *Hortus artium medievalium* 11 (2005), 291-8.

Gasparri, Françoise, *L'écriture des actes de Louis VI, Louis VII et Philippe Auguste* (Geneva, 1973).

Geertz, Clifford, 'Centers, Kings, and Charisma: Reflections on the Symbolics of Power', in *Local Knowledge: Further Essays in Interpretive Anthropology* (New York, 1983), 121–46.

Gerson, Paula, 'Suger as Iconographer: The Central Portal of the West Façade of Saint-Denis', in *Abbot Suger and Saint-Denis: A Symposium*, ed. Paula Gerson (New York, 1987), pp. 183–98.

Gerson, Paula, 'The West Façade of St Denis: An Iconographic Study', Ph.D. dissertation, Columbia University, 1970.

Gillingham, John, *Richard I* (New Haven, 1999).

Gillingham, John, 'Roger of Howden on Crusade', in *Richard Coeur de Lion: Kingship, Chivalry and War in the Twelfth Century* (London and Rio Grande, 1994), pp. 141–53.

Glaser, Hubert, 'Wilhelm von Saint Denis: Ein Humanist aus der Umgebung des Abtes Suger und die Krise seiner Abtei von 1151 bis 1152', *Historisches Jahrbuch* 85 (1965), 257–323.

Godfrey, John, *1204: The Unholy Crusade* (Oxford, 1980).

Graboïs, Aryeh, 'Charlemagne, Rome and Jerusalem', *Revue belge de philologie et d'histoire* 59 (1981), 782–809.

Graboïs, Aryeh, 'The Crusade of Louis VII, King of France: A Reconsideration', in *Crusade and Settlement: Papers Read at the First Conference of the Society for the Study of the Crusades and the Latin East and Presented to R. C. Smail*, ed. Peter Edbury (Cardiff, 1985), pp. 95–104.

Graboïs, Aryeh, 'Louis VII pèlerin', *Revue d'histoire de l'Eglise de France* 74 (1988), 5–22.

Grant, Lindy, *Abbot Suger of St-Denis: Church and State in Early Twelfth-Century France* (London, 1998).

Grant, Lindy, 'Suger and the Anglo-Norman World', *Anglo-Norman Studies* 19 (1997), 51–68.

Grierson, Philip, 'The Coronation of Charlemagne and the Coinage of Pope Leo III', *Revue belge de philologie et d'histoire* 30 (1952), 825–33.

Grodecki, Louis, *Les vitraux de Saint-Denis: Etude sur le vitrail au XIIe siècle* (Paris, 1976).

Grosse, Rolf, 'Reliques du Christ et foires de Saint-Denis au XIe siècle: A propos de la Descriptio clavi et corone Domini', *Revue d'histoire de l'Eglise de France* 87 (2001), 357–75.

Grosse, Rolf, *Saint-Denis zwischen Adel und König: Die Zeit vor Suger (1053–1122)* (Stuttgart, 2002).

Grosse, Rolf, 'Überlegungen zum Kreuzzugsaufruf Eugens III. von 1145/46. Mit einer Neuedition von JL 8876', *Francia* 18 (1991), 85–92.

Grousset, René, *Histoire des croisades et du royaume franc de Jérusalem* (Paris, 1934–36).

Guenée, Bernard, 'Chanceries and Monasteries', in *Rethinking France: Les lieux de mémoire*, ed. Pierre Nora, trans. Deke Dusinberre, 4 vols (Chicago, 2014), Vol. IV: *Histories and memories*, pp. 1–26.

Guenée, Bernard, 'Les généalogies entre l'histoire et la politique: La fierté d'être Capétien, en France, au Moyen Âge', *Annales* 33 (1978), 450–77.

Guenée, Bernard, 'Les grandes chroniques de France, le "Roman aux roys" (1274–1518)', in *Les lieux de mémoire*, ed. Pierre Nora, 2 vols (Paris, 1986), Vol. II, pp. 189–214.

Hallam, Elizabeth, 'Royal Burial and the Cult of Kingship in France and England 1060–1330)', *JMH* 8 (1982), 210–14.

Hallam, Elizabeth M. and Judith Everard, *Capetian France, 987–1328*, 2nd edn (Harlow, 2001).

Hamilton, Bernard, *The Leper King and His Heirs: Baldwin IV and the Crusader Kingdom of Jerusalem* (Cambridge, 2005).

Hamilton, Sarah, 'A New Model for Royal Penance? Helgaud of Fleury's Life of Robert the Pious', *Early Medieval Europe* 6 (1997), 189–200.

Harari, Yuval Noah, 'Eyewitnessing in Accounts of the First Crusade: The *Gesta Francorum* and Other Contemporary Narratives', *Crusades* 3 (2004), 77–99.

Hayward, Jane, *Radiance and Reflection: Medieval Art from the Raymond Pitcairn Collection* (New York, 1982).

Head, Thomas, *Hagiography and the Cult of Saints: The Diocese of Orléans, 800–1200* (Cambridge, 1990).

Hélary, Xavier, *L'armée du roi de France: La guerre de Saint Louis à Philippe le Bel* (Paris, 2012).

Isaïa, Marie-Céline, *Remi de Reims: Mémoire d'un saint, histoire d'une église* (Paris, 2010).

Jordan, William Chester, *Louis IX and the Challenge of the Crusade: A Study in Rulership* (Princeton, 1979).

Kantorowicz, Ernst, 'The King's Advent and the Enigmatic Panels in the Doors of Santa Sabina', *Art Bulletin* 26 (1944), 207–31.

Kantorowicz, Ernst, *The King's Two Bodies: A Study in Medieval Political Theology* (Princeton, 1981).

Kantorowicz, Ernst, *Laudes regiae: A Study in Liturgical Acclamations and Medieval Ruler Worship* (Berkeley, 1946).

Kedar, Benjamin K., 'The Battle of Hattin Revisited', in *The Horns of Hattin: Proceedings of the Second Conference of the Society for the Study of the Crusades and the Latin East* (Jerusalem, 1992), pp. 190–207.

Kemp, Wolfgang, *The Narratives of Gothic Stained Glass*, trans. Caroline D. Saltzwedel (Cambridge, 1997).

Kempf, Damien, 'Towards a Textual Archaeology of the First Crusade', in *Writing the Early Crusades: Text, Transmission and Memory*, ed. Damien Kempf and Marcus Bull (Woodbridge, 2014), pp. 116–26.

Kierkegaard, Søren, *Papers and Journals: A Selection*, trans. Alastair Hannay (London, 1996).

Kirshenblatt-Gimblett, Barbara and Brooks McNamara, 'Processional Performance: An Introduction', *The Drama Review* 29 (1985), 2–5.

Knoch, Peter, 'Kreuzzug und Siedlung: Studien zum Aufruf der Magdeburger Kirche von 1108', *Jahrbuch für die Geschichte Mittel und Ostdeutschlands* 23 (1974), 1–33.

Koziol, Geoffrey, *Begging Pardon and Favor: Ritual and Political Order in Early Medieval France* (Ithaca, NY, 1992).

Koziol, Geoffrey, 'Charles the Simple, Robert of Neustria and the *Vexilla* of Saint-Denis', *Early Medieval Europe* 14 (2006), 371–90.

Koziol, Geoffrey, 'The Dangers of Polemic: Is Ritual Still an Interesting Topic of Historical Study?', *Early Medieval Europe* 11 (2002), 267–88.

Koziol, Geoffrey, 'England, France, and the Problem of Sacrality in Twelfth-Century Ritual', in *Cultures of Power: Lordship, Status, and Process in Twelfth-Century Europe*, ed. Thomas N. Bisson (Philadelphia, 1995), pp. 124–48.

Koziol, Geoffrey, 'Is Robert I in Hell? The Diploma for Saint-Denis and the Mind of a Usurper, January 25, 923', *Early Medieval Europe* 14 (2006), 233–67.

Koziol, Geoffrey, *The Politics of Memory and Identity in Carolingian Royal Diplomas: The West Frankish Kingdom (840–987)* (Turnhout, 2012).

Kraft, Friedrich, *Heinrich Steinhöwels Verdeutschung der 'Historia Hierosolymitana' des Robertus Monachus: Eine literarhistorische Untersuchung* (Strasbourg, 1905).

Lair, Jules, 'Fragment inédit de la Vie de Louis VII préparé par Suger', *Bibliothèque de l'Ecole des Chartes* 34 (1873), 583–96.

Lair, Jules, 'Mémoire sur deux chroniques latines composées au XIIe siècle à l'abbaye de Saint-Denis', *Bibliothèque de l'Ecole des Chartes* 35 (1874), 543–80.

LaMonte, John L., 'The Lords of le Puiset on Crusade', *Speculum* 17 (1942), 100–18.

Lapierre, Jean-William, *Essai sur le fondement du pouvoir politique* (Aix-en-Provence, 1968).

Lapina, Elizabeth, '"Nec signis nec testibus creditor:" The Problem of Eyewitnesses in the Chronicles of the First Crusade', *Viator* 38 (2007), 117–39.

Lapina, Elizabeth, 'La représentation de la bataille d'Antioche (1098) sur les peintures murales de Poncé-sur-le-Loir', *Cahiers de civilisation médiévale* 52 (2009), 137–57.

Laureau, Jean, 'Les seigneurs du Puiset à la Croisade', *Bulletin de la Société archéologique d'Eure-et-Loire* 62 (1999), 23–35.

Le Goff, Jacques, 'Reims, City of Coronation', in *Realms of Memory: The Construction of the French Past*, ed. Pierre Nora and Lawrence D. Kritzman, trans. Arthur Goldhammer, 3 vols (New York, 1996), Vol. III, pp. 193–251.

Le Goff, Jacques, *Saint Louis*, trans. Gareth E. Gollrad (South Bend, IN, 2009).

Le Jan, Régine, 'La sacralité de la royauté mérovingienne', *Annales: Histoire, Sciences Sociales* 58 (2003), 1217–41.

Lemarignier, Jean-François, 'Autour de la date du sacre d'Hugues Capet (1er juin ou 3 juillet 987?)', in *Miscellanea mediaevalia in memoriam Jan Frederik Niermeyer*, ed. Dirk Peter Blok (Gronigen, 1967), pp. 125–35.

Lemarignier, Jean-François, *Le gouvernement royal aux premiers temps capétiens (987–1108)* (Paris, 1965).

Lemarignier, Jean-François, 'Le monachisme et l'encadrement religieux des campagnes du royaume de France situées au nord de la Loire, de la fin du X à la fin du XIe siècle', in *Le instituzioni ecclesiastiche della 'Societas Christiana' dei secoli XI–XII: Diocesi, pievi e parrocchie* (Milan, 1977), pp. 357–99.

Levillain, Léon, 'Essai sur les origines du Lendit', *Revue historique* 155 (1927), 241–76.

Levy, Brian, 'Pèlerins rivaux de la 3e croisade: Les personnages des rois d'Angleterre et de France d'après les chroniques d'Ambroise et d'"Ernoul" et le récit Anglo-Normand de la *Croisade et mort Richard Coeur de Lion*', in *La Croisade: Réalités et fictions. Actes du colloque d'Amiens, 1987* (Göppingen, 1989), pp. 143–55.

Lewis, Andrew W., 'Anticipatory Association of the Heir in Early Capetian France', *American Historical Review* 83 (1978), 906–27.

Lewis, Andrew W., 'Dynastic Structures and Capetian Throne Right: The View of Giles of Paris', *Traditio* 33 (1977), 225–52.

Lewis, Andrew W., *Royal Succession in Capetian France: Studies on Familial Order and the State* (Cambridge, MA, 1981).

Lewis, P. N., 'The Wars of Richard I in the West', M.Phil. dissertation, University of London, 1977.

Leyser, Karl, *Rule and Conflict in Early Medieval Society: Ottonian Saxony* (Bloomington, 1979).

Loomis, Laura Hibbard, 'The Oriflamme of France and the War-Cry "Monjoie" in the Twelfth Century', in *Studies in Art and Literature for Belle da Costa Greene*, ed. Dorothy Miner (Princeton, 1954), pp. 67–82.

Lower, Michael, 'Conversion and Saint Louis's Last Crusade', *Journal of Ecclesiastical History* 58 (2007), 211–31.

Luchaire, Achille, *Etudes sur les actes de Louis VII* (Brussels, 1964).

Luchaire, Achille, *Histoire des institututions monarchiques de la France sous les premiers Capétiens (987–1180)* (Brussels, 1964).

Luchaire, Achille, *Louis VI le gros: Annales de sa vie et de son règne (1081–1137)* (Paris, 1890).

Luchaire, Achille and Alexander Cartellieri, 'Correspondance', *Revue historique* 72 (1900), 334–7; 73 (1900), 61–4; 76 (1901), 329–30.

Lunt, W. E., 'The Text of the Ordinance of 1184 Concerning an Aid for the Holy Land', *EHR* 146 (1922), 325–42.

Lyons, Malcolm and D. E. P. Jackson, *Saladin: The Politics of Holy War* (Cambridge, 1982).

McCormack, Michael, *Eternal Victory: Triumphal Rulership in Late Antiquity, Byzantium and the Early Medieval West* (Cambridge, 1990).

MacCormack, Sabine, *Art and Ceremony in Late Antiquity* (Berkeley, 1981).

Macquarrie, Alan, *Scotland and the Crusades, 1095–1560* (Edinburgh, 1985).

Madden, Thomas F. 'Outside and inside the Fourth Crusade', *International History Review* 17 (1995), 726–43.

Maier, Christoph, 'Crisis, Liturgy and the Crusade in the Twelfth and Thirteenth Centuries', *Journal of Ecclesiastical History* 48 (1997), 628–57.

Marcombe, David, *Leper Knights: The Order of St Lazarus of Jerusalem in England, 1150–1544* (Woodbridge, 2003).

Marquardt, Georg, *Die 'Historia Hierosolymitana' des Robertus Monachus: Ein quellenkritischer Beitrag zur Geschichte des ersten Kreuzzugs* (Königsberg, 1892).
Mayer, Hans, *The Crusades*, 2nd edn, trans. John Gillingham (Oxford, 1988).
Mayer, Hans, 'Henry II of England and the Holy Land', *EHR* 97 (1982), 721–39.
Mayr-Harting, Henry, 'Odo of Deuil, the Second Crusade and the Monastery of Saint-Denis', in *The Culture of Christendom: Essays in Medieval History in Commemoration of Denis L. T. Bethell*, ed. Marc Anthony Meyer (London, 1993), pp. 225–41.
Melville, C. P. and Malcolm Lyons, 'Saladin's Hattin Letter', in *The Horns of Hattin: Proceedings of the Second Conference of the Society for the Study of the Crusades and the Latin East* (Jerusalem, 1992), pp. 208–12.
Moore, Michael E., *A Sacred Kingdom: Bishops and the Rise of Frankish Kingdoms, 300–850* (Washington, DC, 2001).
Morris, Colin, 'The *Gesta Francorum* as Narrative History', *Reading Medieval Studies* 19 (1993), 55–71.
Naus, James, 'The French Royal Court and the Memory of the First Crusade', *NMS* 55 (2011), 49–78.
Naus, James, 'The *Historia Iherosolimitana* of Robert the Monk and the Coronation of Louis VI,' in *Writing the Early Crusades: Text, Transmission and Memory*, ed. Damien Kempf and Marcus Bull (Woodbridge, 2014), pp. 105–15.
Nebbiai-Dalla Guarda, Donatella, *La Bibliothèque de l'abbaye de Saint-Denis en France du IXe au XVIIIe* (Paris, 1984).
Nelson, Janet T., 'Charlemagne and Empire', in *The Long Morning of Medieval Europe: New Directions in Early Medieval Studies*, ed. Jennifer R. Davis and Michael McCormick (Burlington, VT, 2008), pp. 223–34.
Newman, William, *Le domaine royal sous les premiers Capétiens (987–1180)* (Paris, 1937).
Nierenberg, David, *Communities of Violence: Persecution of Minorities in the Middle Ages* (Princeton, 1998).
Oksanen, Eljas, *Flanders and the Anglo-Norman World, 1066–1216* (Cambridge, 2012).
Pacaut, Marcel, 'Louis VI et Alexandre III', *Revue d'histoire de l'Eglise de France* 39 (1953), 5–45.
Painter, Sidney, 'The Third Crusade: Richard the Lionhearted and Philip Augustus', in *A History of the Crusades: The Later Crusades, 1189–1131*, ed. Kenneth M. Setton (Madison, WI, 1969), pp. 44–85.
Paul, Nicholas L., 'The Chronicle of Fulk Réchin: A Reassessment', *Haskins Society Journal* 18 (2007), 19–35.
Paul, Nicholas L., 'Crusade, Memory, and Regional Politics in Twelfth-Century Amboise', *JMH* 31 (2005), 127–41.
Paul, Nicholas L., *To Follow in Their Footsteps: The Crusades and Family Memory in the High Middle Ages* (Ithaca, NY, 2012).
Paul, Nicholas L., 'A Warlord's Wisdom: Literacy and Propaganda at the Time of the First Crusade', *Speculum* 85 (2010), 534–66.

Paxton, Frederick S., '*Abbas* and *rex*: Power and authority in the literature of Fleury, 987–1044', in *The Experience of Power in Medieval Europe, 950–1350*, ed. Robert F. Berkhoffer, Alan Cooper, and Adam J. Kosto (Aldershot, 2005), pp. 197–212.

Pegg, Mark Gregory, *A Most Holy War: The Albigensian Crusade and the Battle for Christendom* (Oxford, 2008).

Phillips, Jonathan, *Defenders of the Holy Land: Relations between the Latin East and the West, 1119–1187* (Oxford, 1996).

Phillips, Jonathan, 'Odo of Deuil's *De profectione Ludovici VII in orientem* as a Source for the Second Crusade', in *The Experience of Crusading*, ed. Marcus Bull, Norman Housley, Jonathan Phillips, and Peter Edbury, 2 vols (Cambridge, 2003), Vol. I, pp. 80–95.

Phillips, Jonathan, *The Second Crusade: Extending the Frontiers of Christendom* (New Haven, 2010).

Poly, Jean-Pierre and Eric Bournazel, *The Feudal Transformation: 900–1200*, trans. Caroline Higgitt (New York, 1991).

Poncelet, Albert, 'Boémond et S. Léonard', *Analecta Bollandiana* 31 (1912), 24–44.

Prawer, Joshua, *Crusader Institututions* (Oxford, 1980).

Pryor, John H. 'The Oath of the Leaders of the First Crusade to the Emperor Alexius Comnenus: Fealty, Homage', *Parergon* 2 (1984), 111–41.

Queller, Donald E. and Thomas F. Madden, *The Fourth Crusade: The Conquest of Constantinople* (Philadelphia, 1997).

Reuter, Timothy, 'The Non-Crusade of 1150', in *The Second Crusade: Scope and Consequence*, ed. Jonathan Phillips and Martin Hoch (Manchester, 2001), pp. 150–63.

Richard, Jean, 'National Feeling and the Legacy of the Crusades', in *Palgrave Advances in the Crusades*, ed. Helen Nicholson (Houndmills, 2005), pp. 204–22.

Richard, Jean, 'La politique orientale de saint Louis: La croisade de 1248', in *Septième centenaire de la mort de saint Louis: Actes de colloques de Royaumont et de Paris (21–27 mai 1970)* (Paris, 1976), pp. 197–207.

Riley-Smith, Jonathan, *The Crusades: A Short History* (New Haven, 1987).

Riley-Smith, Jonathan, 'Crusading as an Act of Love', *History* 65 (1980), 177–92.

Riley-Smith, Jonathan, *The First Crusade and the Idea of Crusading* (Philadelphia, 1986).

Riley-Smith, Jonathan, *The First Crusaders, 1095–1131* (Cambridge, 1997).

Robinson, Ian S., 'Gregory VII and the Soldiers of Christ', *History* 58 (1973), 169–92.

Robinson, Ian S., *Henry IV of Germany, 1056–1106* (Cambridge, 1999).

Rosenwein, Barbara H., Thomas Head, and Sharon Farmer, 'Monks and Their Enemies: A Comparative Approach', *Speculum* 66 (1991), 764–96.

Rowe, John G., 'Bohemond of Antioch, Paschal II, and the Byzantine Empire', *Bulletin of the John Rylands Library* 49 (1966–67), 165–202.

Rubenstein, Jay, *Armies of Heaven: The First Crusade and the Quest for Apocalypse* (New York, 2011).

Rubenstein, Jay, *Guibert of Nogent: Portrait of a Medieval Mind* (New York, 2002).

Rubenstein, Jay, 'Putting History to Use: Three Crusade Chronicles in Context', *Viator* 35 (2004), 131–68.

Rubenstein, Jay, 'What Is the *Gesta Francorum*, and Who Is Peter Tudebode?', *Revue Mabillon* 16 (2005), 179–204.
Runciman, Steven, *A History of the Crusades*, 3 vols (Cambridge, 1955).
Russo, Luigi, 'Ricerche sull'"Historia Iherosolimitana" di Roberto di Reims', *Studi medievali* 43 (2002), 651–91.
Russo, Luigi, 'Il viaggio di Boemundo d'Altavilla in Francia', *Archivio storico Italiano* 603 (2005), 3–42.
Ryan, Vincent, 'Richard I and the Early Evolution of the Fourth Crusade', in *The Fourth Crusade: Events, Aftermath, and Perceptions*, ed. Thomas F. Madden (Aldershot, 2008), pp. 3–14.
Salin, Edouard, *Les tombes gallo-romaines et mérovingiennes de la basilique de Saint-Denis (fouilles de janvier–février, 1957)* (Paris, 1958).
Sassier, Yves, *Louis VII* (Paris, 1991).
Sassier, Yves, '*Rex Francorum, dux Francorum*: Le gouvernement royal au dernier demi-siècle carolingien', in *Le monde carolingien: Bilan, perspectives, champs de recherches. Actes du colloque international de Poitiers, Centre d'Etudes Supérieures de Civilisation médiévale, 18–20 novembre 2004*, ed. Wojciech Falkowski and Yves Sassier (Turnhout, 2010), pp. 357–75.
Schein, Sylvia, *Gateway to the Heavenly City: Crusader Jerusalem and the Catholic West (1099–1187)* (Aldershot, 2005).
Schneidmüller, Bernd, 'Constructing Identities of Medieval France', in *France in the Central Middle Ages*, ed. Marcus Bull (Oxford, 2002), pp. 15–42.
Shepard, Jonathan, 'When Greek Meets Greek: Alexius Comnenus and Bohemond in 1097–8', *Byzantine and Modern Greek Studies* 12 (1988), 185–277.
Siberry, Elizabeth, *Criticism of Crusading, 1095–1274* (Oxford, 1985).
Simson, Otto G. von, *The Gothic Cathedral: Origins of Gothic Architecture and the Medieval Concept of Order* (Princeton, 1988).
Sommerville, Robert, 'The French Councils of Pope Urban II: Some Basic Considerations', *Annuarium historiae conciliorum* 2 (1970), 98–114.
Southern, Richard W., *The Making of the Middle Ages* (New Haven, 1953).
Spiegel, Gabrielle M., *The Chronicle Tradition of Saint-Denis: A Survey* (Brookline, MA, 1978).
Spiegel, Gabrielle M., *The Past as Text: The Theory and Practice of Medieval Historiography* (Baltimore, 1997).
Spiegel, Gabrielle M., *Romancing the Past: The Rise of Vernacular Prose Historiography in Thirteenth-Century France* (Berekeley, 1993).
Strayer, Joseph R., *On the Medieval Origins of the Modern State* (Princeton, 1970).
Sumption, Jonathan, *The Albigensian Crusade* (London, 1978).
Thorau, Peter, 'Der Kreuzzug Ludwigs des Heiligen: Planung – Organisation – Durchführung', in *Stauferzeit: Zeit der Kreuzzüge*, ed. Karl-Heinz Ruess (Göppingen, 2011), pp. 124–43.
Töpfer, Bernhard, 'Tendenzen zur Entsakralisierung der Herrscherwürde in der Zeit des Investiturstreites', *Jahrbuch für Geschichte des Feudalismus* 6 (1982), 164–71.
Turner, Ralph, *King John* (Harlow, 1994).

Turner, Victor, *Dramas, Fields, and Metaphors: Symbolic Action in Human Society* (Ithaca, NY, 1974).
Turner, Victor, 'Process, System and Symbol', *Daedalus* 106 (1977), 61-80.
Twyman, Susan, *Papal Ceremonial at Rome in the Twelfth Century* (London, 2002).
Tyerman, Christopher, *England and the Crusades, 1096-1588* (Chicago, 1988).
Tyerman, Christopher, *God's War: A New History of the Crusades* (Cambridge, MA, 2006).
Waitz, Georg, 'Ueber die Gesta und Historia regis Ludovici VII', *Neues Archiv der Gesellschaft für ältere deutsche Geschichtskunde* 6 (1881), 119-28.
Wallace-Hadrill, J. M., 'History in the Mind of Archbishop Hincmar', in *The Writing of History in the Middle Ages: Essays Presented to R. W. Southern*, ed. R. H. C. Davis and J. M. Wallace-Hadrill (Oxford, 1981), pp. 43-79.
Werner, Karl-Ferdinand, 'Das hochmittelalterliche Imperium im politischen Bewusstsein Frankreichs (10.-12. Jahrhundert)', *Historische Zeitschrift* 200 (1965), 1-60.
Werner, Karl-Ferdinand, 'Die Legitimität der Kapetinger und die Entstehung des *Reditus regni Francorum ad stirpem Karoli*', *Die Welt als Geschichte* 12 (1952), 203-25.
Whalen, Brett E., 'God's Will or Not? Bohemond's Campaign against the Byzantine Empire (1105-1108)', in *Crusades: Medieval Worlds in Conflict*, ed. Thomas Madden, James Naus, and Vince Ryan (Aldershot, 2010), pp. 111-25.
Wolf, Kenneth B., 'Crusade and Narrative: Bohemond and the *Gesta Francorum*', *JMH* 17 (1991), 207-16.
Yewdale, Ralph B., *Bohemond I, Prince of Antioch* (Princeton, 1924).

# INDEX

*Note*: 'n' after a page reference indicates the number of a note on that page.

page numbers in *italic* refer to illustrations.

Abbey of Anchin 36
Abbey of Morigny 35
Abbo (Abbot) 20
Abelard 24
Acre 114, 119, 124–6
Adalbero of Reims (Archbishop) 15, 19
Adalia 90
Adam 59
Adam (Abbot) 23, 62, 65
Adela (of Blois) 44
Adela (of Champagne) 118, 123–4
Adela (of Vermandois) 43
Adhémar of Le Puy 32
*adventus* and *triumphus* 37–40, 76, 93
  *see also* ceremony
Aimo (of Fleury) 20
Albigensian Crusade 2, 8, 11n10, 113, 132–5
Aleppo 87, 102
Alexander the Great 7
Alexius I 29, 43, 67, 68–9
Ambroise 124–5
Amiénois 126
Anjou 117
Anna of Kiev 34
Antalya *see* Adalia
Antioch 28–9, 34, 40, 43, 46, 67, 68, 73, 87, 89–90
Aquitaine 96, 117
Arch of Constantine 75
Arnaud Aimery 132
Arnegonde (Queen) 22
Arnulf (Archbishop) 22
Arthur (nephew of Richard I) 131
Artois 126
Ascalon (Battle of) 78
Aubré (brother of William of Grandmesnil) 46
*Audita tremendi* 121
Avignon 135

Baldric of Bourgueil 32, 69
  influence on Suger's historical writing 70–4
Baldwin III (of Jerusalem) 118
Baldwin IV (a.k.a. the Leper King) 119
Baldwin of Boulogne 78
Baldwin of Hainault 43
Balkans 89
Bede 59
Beirut 119
Benjamin 97–8
Bernard of Clairvaux 23, 75, 89, 94–5
  and Crusade of 1150 99–102
  and reaction to failure of the Second Crusade 97–8
Bertha 41–2
Bertrade of Montfort 41–2
Blanche of Castile 1
Bogomils 132
Bohemond 33–4, 37, 44, 46, 87
  1105 trip to France 28–30, 33–5, 68–9
  appearance in *Gesta Ludovici Grossi* 67–9
  *see also* Suger
  homecoming celebrations 28–9, 37
  treatment by northern French monastic crusade chroniclers 47–8
Bohemond III 99
Boniface VIII 1
Bosphorus 89
Bourges 88, 100, 121
  *see also* Second Crusade; Louis VII
Bouvines 134
Bruno of Segni 68
Burgundy 18, 124
Byzantium 29, 33, 68, 132

Cairo 119
Calixtus II 72, 81n29
Cambridge 91

157

# INDEX

Canterbury 106, 118
Cathars 132
Cecile (of France) 35
Celestine III 126
ceremony
  coronation of Philip II Augustus at Reims 112–13
  first crusaders and prestige 35–9
  repurposing of *adventus* and *triumphus* celebrations by First Crusaders 37–9
  *see also* Guy the Red; Robert of Flanders; Robert of Normandy; Rotrou of Mortagne; Thomas of Marle
Châlons 72
Charlemagne 62, 117
  appearance in Crusading Window of Saint-Denis 77–8
  comparison to early twelfth-century French kings 37–9
  connection of early French notions of kingship 17–18, 31–2
  influence on Suger's vision of kingship 71–3, 86–7
  legend 31–2
  pilgrimage to the East 104–5
  reception of keys to Jerusalem 104
Charles IV 15, 16
Charles the Bald 17–18, 21, 23
Charles the Fat 59
Charles of Lorraine 15
Charles Martel 104
Charles the Simple 59
Chartres 38, 100
  marriage of Bohemond and Constance 28–9
Chinon 122
Christian kingship *see* sacral kingship
Clairvaux 95
Clerkenwell 116
Clermont 32, 39, 42, 56n119, 69, 78, 104
Clothar I 22
Clovis 21, 22
Compiègne 22, 31, 61, 94, 101
Conon (papal legate) 65, 81n29
Conrad II 34
Conrad III 98
  Second Crusade 89–90
Constance (of France) 48–9, 67
  marriage to Bohemond 28–9, 34, 68
Constantine (Emperor) 37, 77
Constantinople 43, 48, 68, 78, 89–90, 104–5, 129
coronation
  connection to Reims 20–1
  of Philip II 112–13
Council of Clermont *see* Clermont
Council of Nîmes 42
Council of Poitiers 29
Crusade of 1150
  background and appeals from the East 99–100
  failure to materialize 100–2
  crusading window (of Saint-Denis) 62, *63*, 76–8, 93, 105
  *see also* Suger
Cyprus 125

Dagobert 23, 62
Damascus 90, 96–7, 102, 119
Damietta 2
David (King) 18, 20, 76
*De consideration see* Bernard of Claivaux
*De glorioso rege Ludovico see* Suger
Demaratus 98
*De profectione Ludovici VII in orientem see* Odo of Deuil
*Descriptio qualiter Karolus Magnus* 78
Divine Easter Fire 91
Dorylaeum 36, 73, 89
Dyrrachium 49

Ebles of Roucy 22
economy of status 9, 30, 39, 65, 70, 86
Edessa 87–8, 90, 121
Egypt 97, 102–3, 118–19
Einhard 67
Eleanor of Aquitaine 90, 96, 102, 117
Elizabeth (daughter of Guy Trousseau) 44
*Estoire de la guerre sainte see* Ambroise
Etampes 72
Eugenius III 64, 85, 88, 91, 97, 99–101, 105
Everard III (of Le Puiset) 32
Exodus 73

Fifth Crusade 2, 113, 134
First Crusade 3, 106, 114

158

## INDEX

failed record of the French kings, 32–3
   *see also* Hugh of Vermandois
   impact on European power structure 33–4
   influence on the the Second Crusade 91–2
   *see also Quantum praedecessores*
   influence on *Gesta Ludovici Grossi* 66–7
   prestige of the castellans 34–9
   response of European rulers 40–5
   Watershed nature of and transformative impact on Western culture 7–8, 30, 33
First Lateran Council 75
Fleury *see* Saint-Benôit-sur-Loire
Fourth Crusade 113, 129–31
Frederick Barbarossa 96, 103
Frederick of Tyre (Archbishop) 103–5
Fulk of Anjou (Count) 7, 41–2
Fulrad (Abbot) 23

Ganelon 30
Gascony 134
Geoffrey (son of Henry II), 112
Gervais (Archbishop) 22
*Gesta Francorum*
   and influence on French monks 43–9, 69
*Gesta Philippi Augusti see* Rigord
Ghumushtgin 29
Gilbert Payen (of Garlande) 42
Gisors 122, 127–8
Godfrey of Bouillon 30, 40, 47–8, 78, 87
*Grandes chroniques de France* 5, 95
Gregory VIII 120–2
Guibert of Nogent 69
   discussion of virtues of French kingship 39
   influence on Suger's historical writing 70–4
   and special status of the Franks 32
   treatment of Capetian participation on First Crusade 48–9
   use of Old Testament 8
Guy II (a.k.a. Guy the Red, Count of Rochefort) 35, 37, 38, 42, 44
Guy of La Roche-Guyon 66
Guy of Lusignan 119, 125
Guy Trousseau 44, 46–7

Hattin 119, 121
Hebrews 97–8
Helgaud (of Fleury) 20–1, 61

Henry (the Young King) 112
Henry I (of England) 28, 34, 40, 72
Henry I (of France) 18, 22–3, 34, 59
Henry II (of England), 112, 117–18, 127–8
   background to Third Crusade 120–2
   crusade appeals made to 102–4
   death 122
   pilgrimage to Paris (Saint-Denis) 105
   *see also* keys
Henry IV (Emperor) 40
Henry V (Emperor) 65, 123
   invasion of France and the *Gesta Ludovici Grossi* 72–3
Henry of Reims (Archbishop) 103
Henry of Troyes 126
Heraclius (Emperor) 104
Heraclius (Patriarch of Jerusalem) 115
Hilduin (Abbot) 23
Hincmar (of Reims) 21, 46
*Historia Iherosolimitana see* Robert the Monk
Holy Land 40, 61, 88, 101–5, 115–17, 120–1, 126, 132
Holy Sepulchre 68, 70, 91, 115
Honorius III 134
Hugh (son of Robert II) 22
Hugh of Burgundy (Duke) 116–17, 127
Hugh Capet 23, 39, 59
   fragility of his accession 15–19
Hugh of Cluny 40
Hugh of Die 41
Hugh of Fleury 39, 62
Hugh of Le Puiset 32, 71–2
Hugh of Troyes (Count of Champagne) 34
Hugh of Vermandois 40, 59
   abandonment of the First Crusade 32–3
   background to and preparations for the First Crusade 42–5
   Robert the Monk's rehabilitation of his image 47–8

Infancy of Christ Window (at Saint-Denis) 77
Innocent III 128–34, 139n89
   Albigensian Crusade 131–4
   Fourth Crusade 128–31
   *see also* Philip II
Innocent IV 1

159

# INDEX

Investiture Contest 38
Isaac Dukas 125
Ivo of Chartres 46, 71

Jacob's Ford 115, 121
Jerusalem 1, 7, 8, 16, 29, 35, 37, 39–40, 44, 60, 68–9, 74, 87, 91, 93, 95–6, 103–4, 106, 115–18
   Innocent III's plant to recover 129
   *see also* Fourth Crusade
   and the Third Crusade 118–28
John (papal legate) 41
John Lackland 130–2
Joscius of Tyre (Archbishop) 120, 122
Joshua 91
Justinian 59

Kerboga 28–9, 40, 73
   and appearance in Robert the Monk 47–8
keys
   to the gates of Jerusalem and Henry II 116
   to the gates of Jerusalem and Louis VII 103–4
   to the gates of Jerusalem and Philip II 115
Kilij Arslan 89
Kingdom of Jerusalem 90, 99, 103–4, 116, 118

Lambert the Poor 46
Laon 72, 100
Lendit Fair 74, 85, 123
Louis V 15
Louis VI 6, 9, 18, 28–9, 31–2, 35, 38–9, 42–3, 46, 49, 62, 85–7, 92, 123
   recasting as crusading hero in *Gesta Ludovici Grossi* 70–4
   *see also* Suger
Louis VII 3, 5, 10, 11n10, 64, 78–9, 112–13, 115, 117–18, 121, 123–4, 127, 131
   criticism for failed Second Crusade 98
   Crusade of 1150 100–2
   departure ceremony for the Second Crusade 85–7, 93
   impact of Second Crusade on shaping reputation 92–7
   planned crusade with Henry II 102–6
   on the Second Crusade 87–91
   Suger's planned biography of 94–7
   *see also* Suger
Louis VIII 2, 11n10, 121

   on the Albigensian Crusade 133–5
Louis IX 10, 95, 107, 135
   and connection between crusade and kingship 1–3
Louis the German 17
Louis the Pious 23, 39, 59, 104
Lucienne (daughter of Guy II) 44
Lyon-sur-Rhône 124

Manuel I Comnenus 89–90
marriage
   and impact of First Crusade on 34–5, 44–5, 69
   *see also* royal legitimacy
Matilda (of Germany) 34
Melisende 118
Monte Cassino 20
Montlhéry family
   and marriage to Capetians 35–6
   *see also* Guy the Red
Moses 73, 76, 91, 96–7
Mosul 87

Nicaea 78, 89
Nogent-sous-Coucy 36
Normandy 40, 80n9, 117–18, 131
Nur-al-Din 90, 99, 102–3, 118

Odo of Deuil 64, 85
   career at Saint-Denis 93–4
   and *De profectione Ludovici VII in orientem* 94–6
   potential authorship of the Crusading Window 78–9
Odo of Paris 59
Old Testament
   link to early French royal power 17–20
   *see also* Robert the Monk; Guibert of Nogent
Order of St Lazarus 86
*oriflamme* 85–6, 93, 105, 123
Orléans 20, 46, 72
Otto IV 132–4

Paris 33, 35, 42, 72, 88, 91, 103, 105, 113, 115–17, 132–3, 135
*Pèlerinage de Charlemagne* 104
   *see also* Charlemagne
Peter of Capuano 130, 139n89

## INDEX

Peter of Castelnau 132-3
Peter Roux (Bishop of Clermont) 72
Peter the Venerable (Abbot of Cluny) 91, 98
   and the Crusade of 1150 99-102
Philip (brother of Louis VII) 88
Philip (Count of Mantes) 44
Philip I (King of France) 6, 21-3, 28-9, 33-4, 38, 40, 68, 79, 87
   burial at Fleury 59-62
   response to First Crusade 41-5
   *see also* marriage
Philip I (Count of Flanders, a.k.a. Philip of Alsace) 118, 126, 128
Philip II (a.k.a. Augustus) 5, 6, 10, 11n10, 15, 18, 32, 86, 106-7
   and Albigensian Crusade 132-4
   background to Third Crusade 118-22
   coronation 112-13
   departure from Acre 125-8
   and Fifth Crusade 134
   and Fourth Crusade 128-31
   preparations for Third Crusade 122-4
   support for crusades early in his reign 115-18
Pippin (the short) 23
Pippin (son of Charlemagne) 38
Pippin of Herstal 59
Plateae 98
*Post miserabilei* 129
Pseudo-Dionysius the Areopagite 65

*Quantum praedecessores* 88, 91, 121
   and reissuance for Crusade of 1150 101

Ralph the Green 56n109
Ralph of Vermandois 73
Raymond IV (of St Gilles) 68
Raymond V of Toulouse (Count) 122
Raymond VI of Toulouse (Count) 132-4
Raymond VII of Toulouse (Count) 134
Raymond of Antioch 90, 99
Raynold of Châtillon 119
Red Sea 73
Regensburg 89
Reims 46, 48, 72, 112
   and coronation 21-2
*renovatio Romae* 75-6
   *see also* Suger
Rhône River 124

Richard I (a.k.a. the Lionhearted) 112, 114
   Third Crusade 120-8
   potential involvement in Fourth Crusade 129-30
Richard of the Principality 68
Rigord 66, 113, 115, 121
Robert I 59
Robert II 18, 20-11, 23, 59, 67
Robert Curthouse 40
Robert of Flanders 36, 42
Robert the Frisian 41
Robert the Monk (a.k.a Robert of Reims) 69
   connection between the First Crusade and Charlemagne 31-2, 38, 70, 78, 104
   influence on Suger's historical writing 70-4
   treatment of Capetian participation in the First Crusade 45-8
   use of Old Testament 7, 73-4
Robert of Normandy 36, 42
Roland 30
Rome 23, 75-6, 120, 126
Rotrou of Mortagne 36
Rouen 40
royal legitimacy
   challenge of the First Crusade 31-4
   early Capetian claims 19
   and Fleury 20
   marriage patterns after the First Crusade 34-5, 44-5, 69
   *see also* sacral kingship
royal touch 86
Rudolf 59

sacred kingship
   coronation and anointing 18, 21
   French kings' claim to be most Christian 3-4, 86
   in relation to the power of the castellans 16-17
   link to crusading 6-7, 37-9, 123-8
   origins 17-24
   *see also* royal legitimacy
Saint-Arnoul (in Crépy) 43
Saint-Arnoult-en-Yvelines 35, 37
Saint-Aubert (in Cambrai) 103
Saint-Benôit-sur-Loire (a.k.a Fleury) 20-1, 59-61
   and competition with Saint-Denis for royal burial 61-3

INDEX

Saint-Corneille 64, 101
Saint-Denis 18, 19, 116
   departure of Louis VII for crusade 85-7
      see also Suger
   departure of Philip II Augustus for crusade 123-4
   early influence on French royal image 4, 22-4
   function as royal necropolis 22-3, 61-4
   and Louis VII's time in the East 92-8
   and Philip II's interest in crusade before 1189 115-18
   twelfth-century renovation of the abbey see Suger
Saint-Léonard-de-Noblat 29
Saint-Remi 61
   and special relationship with the Capetians 46-8
   see also Reims
Sainte-Sévère 66
Saladin 115-16
   and background to Third Crusade 118-21
*Salles des croisades* 10n7
Santa Maria in Via Lata 130
Saul 18
Second Crusade 3, 10, 11n10, 77, 86, 106, 118, 120, 123-4
   connection to the First Crusade and Old Testament 90-2
   departure of Louis VII 85-7
   historical background 87-90
   perception of failure 96-8
   see also Suger; Louis VII
Seneca 98
Senlis 20
Shroud of Christ 61
Sidon 119
Solomon (King) 76
*Song of Roland* 29-30, 31, 73
St Bartolomeo at Benevento (church) 75
St Clement (in Rome)
St Dionysius 64-5, 72, 76, 77, 85, 94, 105, 123
Stephen of Blois 32, 42-3, 49, 99
Stephen of Sancerre 126
St George 36
St John the Baptist (Feast of) 123
St Louis see Louis IX
St Nicholas in Bari 28, 75
St Peter 129
St Peter (church of) 75

St Remigius 21-2
   see also Reims
Suetonius 67
Suger (Abbot of Saint-Denis) 6, 9, 18-19, 24, 32, 42, 44, 46, 60, 62, 114-15, 128
   and Bohemond 34
   concern for the status of Saint-Denis 60-2
   Crusade of 1150 99-102
   crusading window 62, 76-9, 93, 105
   departure ceremony of Louis VII for the East 85-6, 93
   influence of the crusades on renovation of Saint-Denis 62, 74-6
   involvement with the Second Crusade 92-3
   partial biography of Louis VII 94-7
   and Rome 75-6
   sculptural program at Saint-Denis 76
   structural link between crusade and *Gesta Ludovici Grossi* 9
   crusading texts as model 64-71
   heroic prose 71-4
   see also Saint-Denis

Tancred 35, 44, 46
Templars 99, 101, 102
Theobald V of Blois (Count) 126
Theobald of Chartres (and Champagne from 1125) 70-1, 73, 88
Third Crusade 5-6, 11n10, 96, 113, 128, 129-30, 132, 134
   background and expedition 117-25
Thomas Becket 102, 105-6, 118, 120
Thomas of Marle
   appearance in *Gesta Ludovici Grossi* 71-2
   crusading reputation 36
Tiberias 119
Tigris River 119
Tours 118
Transjordan 119
Treaty of Paris 8, 135
Treaty of Verdun 17
triumphal arch 75-6
True Cross (relic)
   and Third Crusade 119-21, 128
Tyre 119

Urban II 8, 22, 31, 38, 41, 43, 69, 78, 104, 120
Urban III 120

## INDEX

Vaudreuil 116
Vermandois 126
*vexillum beati Petri* 43
Vexin 72
Vézelay 88, 124
　*see also* Louis VII; Second Crusade
*via Sacra* 76
*Vita Ludovici Grossi see* Suger
Vitry 87

Wallo II (of Chamont-en-Vexin) 42
western façade of Saint-Denis *see*
　　Suger
William (brother-in-law of Guy of La
　　Roche-Guyon) 66
William (of Saint-Denis) 78, 92, 98, 99

William (of the White hands, Archbishop
　　of Reims) 112
William I (of England) 80n9
William II (King of Sicily) 120
William IV (Count of the Auvergne) 72
William of Grandmesnil 46
William of Poitiers 67
William of Reims (Archbishop) 123-4
William Rufus 42

Xerxes 98

Yaroslav I (Grand Duke of Kiev) 34

Zachary (Pope) 23
Zengi 87, 90, 118